THE
SBS
IN WORLD WAR II

OSPREY
PUBLISHING

THE
SBS
IN WORLD WAR II

Gavin Mortimer

First published in Great Britain in 2013 by
Osprey Publishing,
Midland House, West Way, Botley, Oxford,
OX2 0PH, UK
43-01 21st Street, Suite 219, Long Island City,
NY 11101, USA
E-mail: info@ospreypublishing.com

OSPREY PUBLISHING IS PART OF THE OSPREY
GROUP
© 2013 Gavin Mortimer

A CIP catalogue record for this book is
available from the British Library

ISBN: 978 1 78200 189 8
E-pub ISBN: 978 1 4728 0481 5
PDF ISBN: 978 1 4728 0480 8

Index by Alan Thatcher
Typeset in Bembo
Originated by PDQ Digital Media Solutions,
UK
Printed in China through Worldprint Ltd.

13 14 15 16 17 18   10 9 8 7 6 5 4 3 2 1

Osprey Publishing is supporting the Woodland
Trust, the UK's leading woodland conservation
charity, by funding the dedication of trees.

www.ospreypublishing.com

FRONT COVER IMAGE: Squadron patrol the
streets of Greece in a clearly staged photo
(Courtesy of Ian Layzell)
BACK COVER IMAGE: Members of the Greek
Sacred Squadron, who served alongside the
SBS on Simi in July 1944. (Courtesy of Angie
English)
PAGE 2: SBS patrols in the Bay of Salamis prior
to the advance into Athens in October 1944.
(Courtesy of Ian Layzell)
THIS PAGE: The SBS act the tourists in Greece
with a visit to the acropolis. (Courtesy of the
SBS Archives)

CONTENTS

Dedication 6

Acknowledgements 7

Introduction 9

CHAPTER 1   Birth of the Boat Service   15

CHAPTER 2   From Service to Squadron   27

CHAPTER 3   Sick in Sardinia   43

CHAPTER 4   A Close Call in Crete   55

CHAPTER 5   Armistice and Uncertainty   73

CHAPTER 6   The Germans Fight Back   87

CHAPTER 7   Defeat in the Dodecanese   97

CHAPTER 8   New Recruits for a New Year   113

CHAPTER 9   Piracy on the High Seas   123

CHAPTER 10   Turkish Deceit for the SBS   133

CHAPTER 11   Caught, Questioned, Vanished   145

CHAPTER 12   Vengeance   157

CHAPTER 13   Germany on the Run   169

CHAPTER 14   Into the Balkans   177

CHAPTER 15   The Nazis' Greek Tragedy   187

CHAPTER 16   Adriatic Offensive   199

CHAPTER 17   Andy Lassen's Big War   211

CHAPTER 18   The End of the Odyssey   223

Glossary 234

Notes 236

Bibliography 247

Index 250

DEDICATION

For the men of the Alimnia Patrol, and for their mothers, who went to their graves without knowing the truth.

ACKNOWLEDGEMENTS

In researching a book such as this, the many hours that one spends in archives are made all the easier by the efficiency of the staff. In the case of this book I could not have wished for more amiable assistance. I am therefore indebted to all the staff at the National Archives in Kew; the London Metropolitan Archives; the Imperial War Museum; and the Wiener Library, a charming archive in Russell Square focusing on contemporary Jewish history. I am particularly grateful to all at the SAS Regimental Association who once again allowed me to rummage through their extensive archive.

Thank you to the Board of Deputies of British Jews for granting me permission to view the Report on British Servicemen captured in Greece in 1944 housed in the Metropolitan Archives, and I tip my hat once again to John Robertson, whose exhaustive research has resulted in the superb website www.specialforcesroh.com.

As ever Emily Holmes and all the team at Osprey have been accommodating and patient, indulging my whims and editing with precision. Thank you.

And thanks to the following publishers who gave me permission to quote from their titles: *Going to the Wars* by John Verney (Collins, 1955), *Anders Lassen's War* by Thomas Harder (Informations Forlag, 2010), *Anders Lassen* by Mike Langley (New English 1988), *The Filibusters* by John Lodwick (Metheun, 1947) and the Imperial War Museum Collections Department.

Although, regrettably, the number of veterans from World War II is a dwindling band, the relatives of combatants continue to honour the memory of those who served. In the writing of this book I received great help and support from Lynne Perrin (daughter of Duggie Pomford), Angie English and Raymond Duggan (daughter and son of John Duggan), Holly Kendrick (niece of George Evans), Paul Ogden (nephew of Tom Kitchingman), David Henry (grandson of Jack Emerton) and Ian Layzell (son of Albert Layzell).

Finally I would like to thank Dick Holmes and Reg Osborn for giving me so much of their time and delving so deep into their memory to relive events of so long ago. It was a privilege and I hope this book honours those who never returned.

INTRODUCTION

In September 1942 General McCreery, chief of staff to General Harold Alexander, Commander-in-Chief Middle East Command, wrote to his superior about a small special forces unit operating in North Africa.* It had been a 'conspicuous success in the past', wrote McCreery, 'and its morale is high'. He then added:

> The personality of the present commander, L Detachment SAS [Special Air Service] Brigade, is such that he could be given command of the whole force with appropriate rank. In view of this I make the following suggestion. That L Detachment SAS Brigade, 1 SS [Special Service] Regiment, Special Boat Section should all be amalgamated under L Detachment SAS Brigade and commanded by Major D. Stirling with the rank of lieutenant-colonel.[1]

Alexander accepted the recommendation and on 28 September 1942 General Headquarters Middle East Forces issued an order promoting the 26-year-old David Stirling and authorising him to expand his unit into a regiment.

Stirling envisaged the SAS regiment comprising five squadrons – A, B, C, D and HQ – and he set its war establishment at 29 officers and 572 other ranks. His most pressing challenge was to fill his nascent regiment with suitable soldiers, while assisting in the Eighth Army's imminent offensive against Axis forces at El Alamein. Stirling formed his most experienced men, the bulk of L Detachment, into A Squadron under the command of the formidable Blair 'Paddy' Mayne, and instructed them to attack targets along the coast between Tobruk and the rear of the enemy front line. While A Squadron headed into the desert to harass the Germans, Stirling returned to the SAS base at Kabrit,

OPPOSITE
David Stirling, the brilliant young officer who founded the SAS in the summer of 1941. (Author's Collection)

---

* For a detailed account of this unit read Gavin Mortimer, *The Illustrated History of the SAS in World War II* (Osprey, 2011).

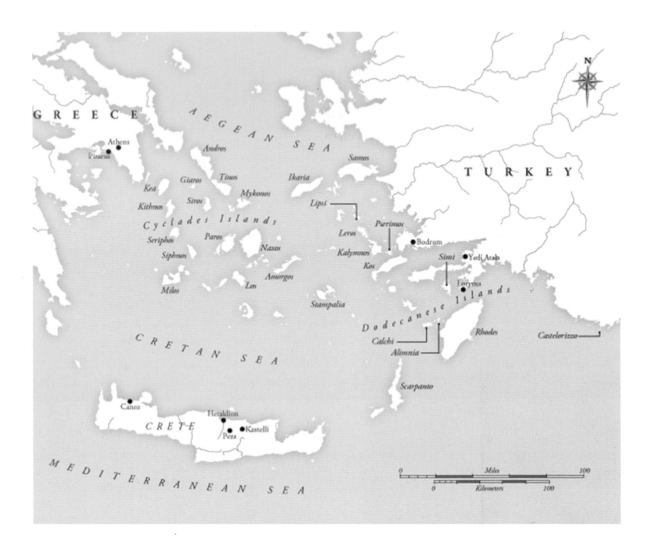

Map of the Aegean Sea. (© Osprey Publishing)

90 miles east of Cairo, to continue recruiting and to oversee the training of the new soldiers.

It was a confused period, both for the SAS then and for historians now, endeavouring to unravel the administrative knots that Stirling unintentionally tied through his abhorrence of paperwork. The only time Stirling committed anything to paper was shortly after the war when, in a brief typewritten history of the regiment now housed in the SAS archives, he listed the units under his command in January 1943, the month he was captured by the Germans:

a) **1st SAS Regiment**. L Detachment had become the 1st SAS Regiment in October 1942. Its establishment consisted of five squadrons – a total of about 50 officers and 450 OR [other ranks]. At the time of my capture the full strength had not yet been recruited. I had about 40 officers and 350 OR but was hoping to make the full strength from the Middle East Commando, which I had taken over and was sorting.

b) **The French SAS Squadron**. This unit had been considerably added [sic] and in January 1943 consisted of about 14 officers and 80 OR. I hoped that this unit would form the nucleus of a French SAS Regiment, which I reckoned would be able to carry out useful operations in France preceding and during the inevitable 2nd Front in Europe.

c) **The Greek Sacred Squadron**. I had taken over this unit towards the end of 1942 and had not finally completed their training at the time of my capture. My idea was to use the Greek Sacred Squadron for raiding operations in the Eastern Mediterranean, where their local knowledge would be of great value. The unit consisted of 14 officers and about 100 OR.

d) **Folboat Section [Special Boat Section]**. This unit had had a separate existence up until August 1942 and had carried out many brilliant operations. My intention was to absorb them into the 1st SAS Regiment as a squadron but I was in the

Some of the original members of L Detachment in autumn 1941. Note the colour of the berets – they were changed from white to sand-coloured not long after this photo. (Author's Collection)

meantime giving them the full SAS training, including a parachute course. They had about 15 officers and about 40 OR.

e) **Captain Buck's German Unit**. Due to casualties and difficulties of recruitment, this unit had unfortunately ceased to exist.

f) **Middle East Commando**. I took command of the Middle East Commando about November 1942. Although of good material, the unit had been given very little opportunity and in my view were badly commanded. When I took over it consisted of about 30 officers and 300 OR, which I intended to disband all bar 10 officers and 100 OR, which would bring the 1st SAS Regt up to strength.[2]

Paddy Mayne, a pre-war Ireland rugby international and a gifted guerrilla fighter. (Author's Collection)

Stirling was captured on 24 January 1943 in Tunisia as he attempted to link up with the advance elements of the First Army advancing east from Algeria. The news was confirmed in the SAS war diary on 14 February, the entry stating that Stirling was officially 'missing believed prisoner of war'.[3]

The news was a crushing blow to the young regiment. The SAS medical officer, Malcolm Pleydell, wrote to a friend in England: 'I arrived back at Kabrit yesterday to hear that David Stirling is missing, believed Prisoner of War. I suppose that doesn't convey much to you, but he is our commanding officer and there is no one with his flair and gift for projecting schemes. He ran the unit … so now the ship is without a rudder.'[4]

The 'ship' was without a rudder, or a leader, and for several weeks the SAS drifted. Stirling's nominal successor, Paddy Mayne, loathed bureaucracy even more than his superior and the burden of trying to make sense of what paperwork there was at Kabrit fell on the regiment's adjutant, Captain Bill Blyth, who sat 'glumly at his desk piled high with files'.[5]

But even if Stirling had not been captured the future role of the SAS was

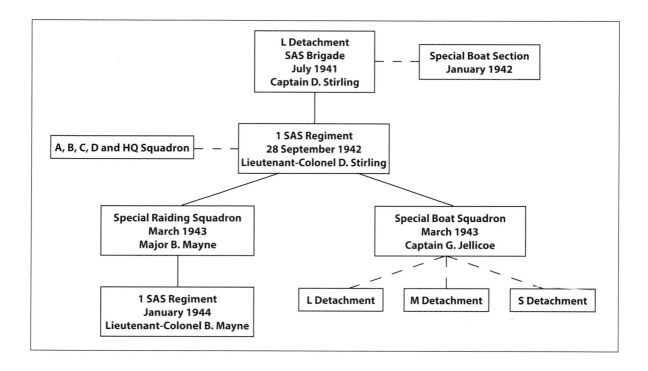

```
                    ┌─────────────────────┐
                    │    L Detachment     │        ┌────────────────────────┐
                    │     SAS Brigade     │─ ─ ─ ─ │  Special Boat Section  │
                    │      July 1941      │        │      January 1942      │
                    │  Captain D. Stirling│        └────────────────────────┘
                    └─────────────────────┘

┌────────────────────────┐     ┌──────────────────────────────┐
│ A, B, C, D and HQ Squadron │─ ─ ─ │       1 SAS Regiment         │
└────────────────────────┘     │      28 September 1942        │
                               │ Lieutenant-Colonel D. Stirling│
                               └──────────────────────────────┘

     ┌──────────────────────────┐              ┌──────────────────────────┐
     │  Special Raiding Squadron │              │   Special Boat Squadron  │
     │        March 1943         │              │        March 1943        │
     │      Major B. Mayne       │              │    Captain G. Jellicoe   │
     └──────────────────────────┘              └──────────────────────────┘

     ┌──────────────────────────┐     ┌──────────────┐ ┌──────────────┐ ┌──────────────┐
     │      1 SAS Regiment       │     │ L Detachment │ │ M Detachment │ │ S Detachment │
     │       January 1944        │     └──────────────┘ └──────────────┘ └──────────────┘
     │ Lieutenant-Colonel B. Mayne│
     └──────────────────────────┘
```

being discussed in Middle East Headquarters. The Desert War was nearly won and there was no longer a need for the sort of hit-and-run raids in which the SAS specialized. The Axis forces were on the retreat and would soon be pushed out of North Africa all together.

The question exercising the minds of Middle East HQ in the early spring of 1943 was how best to employ the unique skills of the Special Air Service. Eventually they decided to break up the regiment. The French Squadron returned to the UK where it was formed into two regiments; the Greek Sacred Squadron was sent into Palestine to begin preparations for operations in the Mediterranean, and four of the five squadrons of the SAS regiment were whittled down to form the Special Raiding Squadron. The fifth squadron, D Squadron, a mixture of new recruits and former members of what Stirling had referred to as the 'Folboat Section', was reconstituted as the Special Boat Squadron (SBS) under the command of Captain the Earl George Jellicoe.

Organizational diagram of the SAS and SBS. (© Osprey Publishing)

CHAPTER 1

BIRTH OF THE BOAT SERVICE

Not long after the war in Europe had ended Captain John Lodwick of the Special Boat Squadron wrote to Major David Sutherland requesting information about the unit's origins. Sutherland was the man in the know. The squadron's commander in May 1945, Sutherland had first seen action with the elite force in early 1942.

Lodwick, who was in the throes of researching a book about the SBS (*The Filibusters*, published in 1947 by Methuen), received a three-page potted history from Sutherland by way of response. Much of what Sutherland wrote was dry, factual and to the point, an enumeration of the squadron's activities from inception until expansion in 1943, at which time Lodwick had himself joined the unit. Sutherland's only digression from his concise narrative was to describe Roger Courtney, the officer who had first proposed the idea of a seaborne raiding force. Courtney, explained Sutherland to Lodwick, 'had pre-war canoeing experience on the Nile and elsewhere'. As for his character, he was 'a hard-drinking white hunter with a big line of bullshit and a persuasive tongue'.[1]

Courtney's plan was to use folding canoes – 'folboats' as they were also known – to launch daring raids on German-occupied Europe. After proving the efficacy of his idea with a successful mock attack on a Royal Navy ship, Courtney was granted permission to launch a Folboat Section in July 1940 by Admiral of the Fleet Lord Keyes, Director of Combined Operations.

Courtney took his section to the Middle East in February 1941 and in June that year they scored their first successful operation. Lieutenant 'Tug' Wilson and Marine Wally Hughes landed by canoe on the west coast of Italy and blew a goods train off the track before making good their escape. 'Wilson and Hughes were a magnificent team,' Sutherland told Lodwick in his SBS history, and consequently the 'folboat section enlarged with success and more jobs offered'. It was around this time, added Sutherland, that the 'Folboat Section [was] now called Special Boat Section'.[2] No sooner had this name change occurred, however, than Roger Courtney was obliged to return to the United Kingdom suffering from poor health. David Stirling, never a man to miss an opportunity, appropriated the Special Boat Section and attached them to L Detachment, which was aspiring to branch out into sabotaging shipping and not just aircraft.

Throughout the spring and summer of 1942 the men of the Special Boat Section used their amphibious skills to carry out a number of daring raids on enemy targets. In the most audacious of these, an 11-strong raiding party, commanded by Captain Allott, attacked targets on Rhodes, destroying more than a dozen aircraft and blowing up bomb stores and petrol dumps. In the aftermath all the SBS personnel were caught with the exception of Sutherland and Marine John Duggan. This intrepid pair evaded the hundreds of Italians on their tail and reached the rendezvous on the eastern coast of Rhodes at the arranged time. By now the two commandos were cold, exhausted and hungry, having eaten only a tin of sardines each in the preceding five days. Duggan flashed a recognition seaward at 2200 hours and, on receiving a reply, the pair dived into the surf and began to swim. It took them an hour to reach the submarine, which twice had to crash-dive to avoid prowling Italian Motor Transport Boats.

For sheer audacity Operation *Anglo*, as the attack on Rhodes was code-named, had been a stunning triumph but the cost in captured personnel drained the SBS of its finest operators.★

When Sutherland wrote to Lodwick in 1945 he described how in October 1942 the 'whole of the SBS … were swept into the SAS' when Stirling received permission to expand L Detachment into the SAS regiment.[3]

A rare shot of the Special Boat Section in late 1941, when it was still under the command of Roger Courtney. John Duggan is crouching far left on the front row. (Author's Collection)

★ The raid was made into a 1954 film with Dirk Bogarde as Sutherland and Denholm Elliott as Duggan.

All new recruits to the SBS had to learn to parachute at the British Parachute School at Ramat David in Palestine. (Courtesy of David Henry)

In January 1943 Stirling instructed Sutherland to take a detachment of 50 men to Beirut and school them in seamanship and guerrilla warfare tactics. Initially Sutherland protested. He wanted to join the SAS in driving the Germans out of North Africa. He later recalled Stirling's reaction: 'He turned on me, eyes flashing. "You are not going and I'll tell you why. You, George Jellicoe and Tom Langton have unique small boat operational experience. You will be needed soon to carry out raids on the soft underbelly of Europe. You are much too valuable to be wasted elsewhere."'[4]

Sutherland did as ordered, arriving in Beirut early in the morning of 20 January 1943.* The delights of the city soon made him forget all about the war in North Africa. 'The cloak of Lebanese intrigue surrounded the sun terrace of the St Georges hotel,' he recalled shortly after the war. 'Here at midday society reposed with martini and almonds peering forth with polarised gaze from beneath skilfully placed sun shades. Here one basked contentedly in the balmy Levantine atmosphere far removed from all reality.'[5] Four days later Stirling was captured and Sutherland was soon on his way back to Kabrit, to be met with confusion, uncertainty and Tommy Langton.

Tommy Langton was a special forces veteran, an officer in the Irish Guards who had joined 8 Commando before it was subsumed into Layforce, the short-lived Commando force that was sent to the Middle East in February 1941 and disbanded six months later. Subsequently he had volunteered for the Special Boat Section and proved his gallantry and fortitude on several occasions during the war in North Africa. A double rowing blue for Cambridge in the late 1930s, Langton was, recalled Sutherland, 'one of the most powerful swimmers I have ever seen'.[6]

* The British at this time referred to the Lebanon as Syria because the State of Greater Lebanon was one of six states incorporated into the French Mandate of Syria.

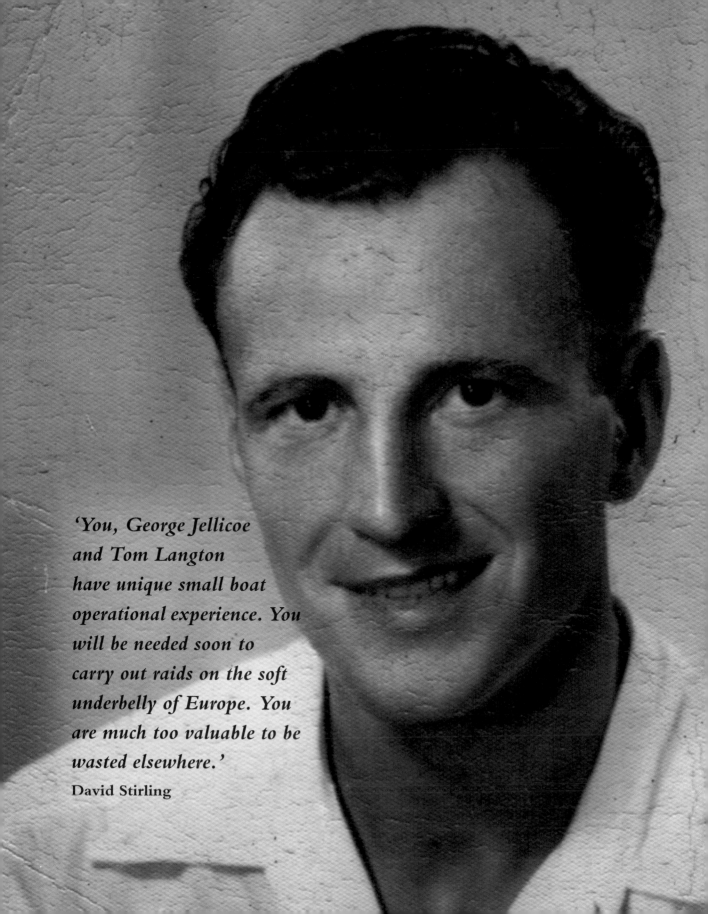

*'You, George Jellicoe
and Tom Langton
have unique small boat
operational experience. You
will be needed soon to
carry out raids on the soft
underbelly of Europe. You
are much too valuable to be
wasted elsewhere.'*
David Stirling

The sun terrace of the St Georges Hotel in Lebanon where Sutherland liked to wind down after a hard day's training in January 1943. (Courtesy of the SBS Archive)

PREVIOUS PAGE
John Duggan, along with David Sutherland, were the only two SBS men to escape from the raid on Rhodes in September 1942. (Author's Collection)

When the Special Boat Section was swept up into the SAS in October 1942, Langton made sure he brought to Kabrit his most experienced operators. Sergeant Cyril Feebery, a bull of a man from London, was one such soldier, as were Sean O'Reilly and Duggie Pomford, two of Langton's most trusted NCOs.

The 41-year-old O'Reilly was practically old enough to be Langton's father. A Southern Irishman who could work his fists well, he shared the same parent regiment as Langton and had proved his worth in the Special Boat Section. One of his comrades said he 'lived on women and beer'.[7] Pomford, a 22-year-old native of Liverpool, was an even better fighter than O'Reilly, having won Britain's amateur Golden Gloves middleweight title in 1938. Pomford was a self-confessed scallywag; as a boy he 'kept running away with the circus to join the boxing booths', just him and his dog whom he taught to do tricks. But boxing had imbued in Pomford an exceptional determination and self-discipline, enabling him 'to focus on an end objective and get there whatever the consequences'.[8]

Among the new recruits to D Squadron with no prior experience of special forces warfare were half a dozen strapping specimens from the 6th Battalion Grenadier Guards who had volunteered together in October 1942. One of the six was Corporal Sid Dowland, a veteran of Dunkirk who 'volunteered for the SAS because I was a bit fed up with normal soldiering'.[9] Dowland recalled that they were interviewed by Sergeant Dave Kershaw (one of the SAS originals from 1941) who asked if he was prepared to jump out of an aeroplane. Dowland replied that he was, and so did five of his comrades: Doug Wright, Bill Thomas, Chris 'Jumper' Workman, Jim Kosbab and Dick Holmes.

'The SAS liked Guards as recruits because they didn't argue about things,' said Dowland. 'But then some Guardsmen didn't know what to do when faced with SAS self-reliance. They'd been trained to do what they're told.'

It had first dawned on Dowland that he might not be cut out for the Guards two and a half years earlier as he waited to be evacuated from Dunkirk. 'We were

Lance-corporal Watson (standing) proved an invaluable help to Captain Milner-Barry during the evacuation of Cos. (Courtesy of Angie English)

(I) SOLDIER'S NAME and DESCRIPTION on ATTESTATION.

Army Number .... PLY/X 987

Surname (in capitals) .... JENKINS

Christian Names (in full) WILLIAM GEORGE

Date of Birth 6-3-1919

Place of Birth. { Parish / In or near the town of / In the county of .... DEVON

Trade on Enlistment .... SCHOLAR

Nationality of Father at birth .... BRITISH

Nationality of Mother at birth .... BRITISH

Religious Denomination .... C. of E.

Approved Society ....

Membership No. ....

Enlisted at .... R.M. BARRACKS, PLYMOUTH On 11-11-33

For the :—
* Regular Army.   * Supplementary Reserve.
* Territorial Army.   * Army Reserve Section D.
          * Strike out those inapplicable.

For .... years with the Colours and .... years in the Reserve.

Signature of Soldier .... WGJenkins

Date ....

DESCRIPTION ON ENLISTMENT.

Height .... 5 ..ft. ..11½.. ins.   Weight ... 180 ...lbs.

Maximum Chest ..42....ins.   Complexion. FRESH

Eyes ....BROWN....   Hair ..BROWN..

Distinctive Marks and Minor Defects ....

.... TATTOO RIGHT WRIST ....

CONDITION ON TRANSFER TO RESERVE.

Found fit for ....

Defects or History of past illness which should be enquired into if called up for Service ....

Date .... 19 ....

Initials of M.O. i/c ....

William George Jenkins was only 14 when he joined the Royal Marines in 1933, prior to joining the SBS later on in his career. By the time the photo was taken in the Yedi Atala in 1944, Sergeant Jenkins was known as the 'Soldier's Friend', such was his ability to find a solution to all problems. (Courtesy of Angie English)

on the beach and there were shells coming down and some bleedin' Coldstream [Guards] sergeant starts yelling, "form up in threes the Coldstream Guards". Immediately a Grenadier sergeant says the same thing. I said "fuck that for a game of soldiers!" And me and my mate "Shorty" grabbed a spade and began digging slit trenches.'

A particular pal of Dowland's was Jim Kosbab, a warrior in every sense of the word who could 'fight a town on his own' but who had been awarded a Military Medal in May 1940 for rescuing a wounded officer under heavy fire. Doug Wright and Dick Holmes were also the best of friends. Both were tall men, with Wright the slightly broader of the pair and Holmes the more fleet-footed. 'Not a lot of Guardsmen volunteered for the SAS,' recalled Wright. 'They all said we were mad.' His interview for the SAS lasted about 15 minutes during which time he was asked about his disciplinary record in the Guards. Wright had shifted on his chair. 'I'd had a few punishments, got a stripe and they had taken it away. But they didn't mind if you'd been in a bit of trouble, as long as you could think for yourself.'[10]

Holmes, Wright, Dowland and Kosbab shared a tent at Kabrit and the Guardsmen soon discovered the unorthodox way of life in their new unit. 'I went into one of [the] ablutions one day which was just a bloody trough,' recounted Holmes. 'I looked to my left and there was a German washing. Then the SAS corporal says "OK Jerry, finished?" And they walked out chatting to one another.'

'I'd had a few punishments, got a stripe and they had taken it away. But they didn't mind if you'd been in a bit of trouble, as long as you could think for yourself.'

Doug Wright

In charge of physical training at Kabrit was Sergeant-Major Gus Glaze, known as 'Nelly' to the former Grenadiers. Holmes remembered that he liked to pit the Guards against the line regiments, stoking up a good-natured rivalry in games of football, rugby and basketball.

Duggie Pomford was one of the first recruits to the SBS. (Courtesy of the SBS Archive)

Not long after he had arrived at Kabrit Holmes encountered Cyril Feebery, recently returned from operations 'up the Blue', as the SAS nicknamed the interior of the North African desert. The pair knew each other from their days in the Grenadier Guards. 'I'd recently completed my training when I ran into Feebery,' recalled Holmes. 'He suggested I join him in the SBS, so I did.'

Duggie Pomford joined the South Lancashire Fusiliers on the outbreak of war before volunteering for Special Boat Section and then the Special Air Service. (Courtesy of Lynne Perrin)

Members of L Squadron at Athlit in 1943. (Courtesy of David Henry)

Also recruited to the SBS at this time was Keith Killby, a man who could not have been more different in character to the pugnacious Guardsmen. Born in south London in 1916, Killby was a conscientious objector who refused to take up arms but had no hesitation in enlisting in the Royal Army Medical Corps (RAMC). In May 1942, during the ferocious battle of Gazala in Libya, Killby had been praised by his commanding officer for exhibiting 'courage and devotion to duty in assisting with the treatment of German wounded under shellfire'.[11]

Killby initially volunteered for the SAS because he believed the initials stood for the 'Special Ambulance Service'. An additional sixpence a day was on offer, and the chance to learn to parachute. Killby discovered the truth upon reaching Kabrit and was sure he would be wasting his time. 'But then I saw some officers playing a game of rugby and I recognized a school friend [from Lancing College in Sussex]. It was Tommy Langton and I said to him "You won't want one of me." He replied, "I don't know, I'll talk to Jellicoe." Jellicoe saw me and he said, "If you're willing to do the medical work you're OK."'[12]

Following Stirling's capture D Squadron were kept busy throughout February and early March as their fate was decided by well-dressed staff officers in Cairo. They went off in small batches to complete courses at the British Parachute School at Ramat David in Palestine; they practised canoeing and laying explosives and they embarked on several training exercises in the Cairo–Suez Road area. On one occasion they launched a mock attack against an Anglo-Egyptian oil refinery, but the men could sense these exercises were merely a case of officers finding work for idle hands.

David Stirling scoured Middle East training depots, such as this one, in his search for recruits to the SAS in the autumn of 1942. (Courtesy of the Evans family)

CHAPTER 2

FROM SERVICE TO SQUADRON

L egend has it that the official birthday of the Special Boat Squadron is 1 April 1943, a myth created – accidentally or otherwise – by David Sutherland in his missive to John Lodwick shortly after the end of the war. After all, didn't that encapsulate the rather impish nature of the unit, the fact that it sprang to life on April Fool's Day?

In fact, as the war diary notes, the Special Boat Squadron entered this world nearly a fortnight earlier, on the far more prosaic 19 March. That was the day the diarist recorded the following:

> Regiment reorganised into two parts. The Special Boat Section [It took a while for the new name to sink in; on 7 April the war diary referred to the 'SBS Squadron'] under Maj. Jellicoe and the Raiding Forces under Maj. Mayne. Various officers and men who the new establishment is unable to cater for, have been warned for other jobs or units.[1]

On 1 April there is but a one-word entry in the war diary – 'Training'.

The second historical inaccuracy regarding the birth of the SBS concerns the date they left Kabrit for their new base at Athlit, approximately 8 miles south of Haifa in Palestine. In Lodwick's book, *The Filibusters*, the move to Athlit and the

OPPOSITE
Corporals Napier and Martin Conby, Private Linder and (front) Sean O'Reilly looking unusually spick and span. (Courtesy of the SBS Archive)

27

Dick Holmes (far left) stands next to Jock Cree as they and some pals enjoy a rare day off from training in the early summer of 1943. (Courtesy of SAS Archive)

formation of the new unit dovetail on 1 April. But the war diary records that the SBS advance party arrived at Athlit on 23 March and welcomed the rest of the unit at 2200 hours on 30 March.

Jellicoe had chosen well in establishing the squadron's base at Athlit. In describing their new camp Sutherland recalled that it had 'a crescent-shaped beach about a mile across with a ruined Crusader castle at one end, the sea turning azure in the changing sunlight and the steep Carmel hills behind'.[2] The grass was carpeted with a myriad wild flowers, suffusing the air with an incongruous aroma considering the nature of the training upon which the squadron was about to embark. Sutherland pitched a tent with a westerly view of the sea and designated it his office.

In the days that followed the squadron's arrival at Athlit a steady stream of new recruits appeared, so that by 17 April Jellicoe had under his command 13 officers and 118 other ranks.

Among the former were two men who would feature prominently in the evolution of the SBS. The first was a 22-year-old Danish lieutenant called Anders Lassen, who arrived from 62 Commando. Tall, blond and rakishly handsome, Lassen arrived with a reputation as a natural born killer. He was skilled in the art of guerrilla fighting, able to move across ground swiftly and noiselessly. He was also possessed of exceptional endurance, not to mention tactical intelligence, and he had another priceless quality. 'He could anticipate the enemy's reaction to any given situation,' reflected Sutherland. 'We used to say that he knew how the enemy would react before they knew themselves.'[3]

But what really marked out Lassen from his peers was his love of the kill. Although he already had a Military Cross to his name when he joined the SBS (awarded for commando operations in the Channel Islands), Lassen was now among men of equal courage and fury. But soldiers such as Duggie Pomford, Cyril Feebery and George Jellicoe killed the enemy because it was their duty; Lassen did so because he enjoyed it. Dick Holmes soon discovered that Lassen had an 'ability to transform himself into a killing machine, to perform the task with a panache that earned him the reputation of a killer of Germans par excellence.'[4]

The other new arrival could not have been more different from Lassen. Walter Milner-Barry was a few weeks away from his 39th birthday when he joined the SBS. His breeding was impeccable, if a little eccentric, with one uncle knighted for his contribution to English literature while his aunt Annie, a Free Thought and Fabian lecturer, was responsible for organizing the 1888 London Matchgirls strike.

Milner-Barry's childhood was strict and austere. Charlie Chaplin films were off-limits because his parents considered them a 'moral danger' and instead he was rigorously schooled, a regime that resulted in his winning a place at Cambridge to read history. Throughout the 1930s Milner-Barry worked for Shell in the Middle East and it was in the bar of the King David Hotel in Jerusalem that he learned of the outbreak of war. 'Everybody instantly looking happy and cheered,' he reminisced.[5]

Initially Milner-Barry enlisted in the Transjordan Frontier Force, first seeing action in June 1941 when his unit engaged the Vichy French near Damascus. Having spent 1942 kicking his heels in Cairo, Milner-Barry joined the SBS for adventure.

Doug Wright (foreground) was a formidable soldier who at times appeared fearless. (Courtesy of the SBS Archive)

SBS Training Programme

```
COPY

Subject: - Training Programme
SBS Raiding Forces
Ref. SBS/10


To: - O.C.
R.F.H.Q


Training programme for week ending 25. April 1943.


1. 'S' Detachment. - Course at Jerusalem in Pistol & TSMG.
                     Boating in Syria & Athlit.
2. 'L' Detachment. - 2 Patrols Boating and Demolitions atAthlit.
                     2 Patrols Camouflage and Musketry at Athlit.
                     3 Days Leave - 23rd. to 25th. April
3. 'M' Detachment. - Map Reading, Boating, Hill Climbing, Musketry
                     at Athlit.
                     Parachute course, if vacancies obtainable.
4. Signals. -        Lecture by Signals Officer on new W/T set and
                     Procedure to Officers.
5. Demonstration. -  It is hoped to arrange a demonstration by
                     Capt. Schott, during week, in judging MG
                     Fire.


 (Sgd) J. Verney for
 Capt. Major.
 O.C. SBS Raiding Forces
 GWW
```

(Reproduced courtesy of the National Archives, WO218/97)

FIELD RETURN

As seen in the right-hand column of this SBS 'Field Return' the unit was still understrength a month after its formation.

Army Form W3009

<u>TO BE MADE UP TO AND FOR SATURDAY IN EACH WEEK</u>

<u>FIELD RETURN OF OTHER RANKS</u>

Special Boat Squadron (Unit). 17th April 1943 (Date).

(To be furnished by all Units of Cavalry, Royal Armoured Corps, Infantry, Royal Army Vetinary Corps, Royal Army Pay Corps, Army Educational Corps, Corps of Military Police, and all Headquarters units).

Part A. Strength, Surplus or Reinforcements Required

1 Detail	2 Posted strength counting against authorized establishment (excluding attached)	3 Surplus to Establishment	4 Reinforcements Required (i.e. deficits on establishment)
W.Os Class I			
W.Os Class II	1		
W.Os Class III			
Squadron or Company Quartermaster-Sergeants OR Colour Sergeants	1		
Staff Sergeants			
Sergeants	14		11
Buglers, Trumpeters, etc			
Corporals	18		15
Troopers, Privates, Guardsmen, Fusiliers, etc	84		30
TOTALS	118		56

These totals should agree with the details shown in Part D on page 2 of Army Form W.3009

(Reproduced courtesy of the National Archives, WO218/97)

On arriving at Athlit he was informed he would be David Sutherland's second-in-command. Milner-Barry was satisfied with the arrangement, as he was with his new home. 'The camp is certainly on a most beautiful site,' he wrote in his diary. 'Very near the sea and with a lovely view of Athlit castle. Also at present covered with wild flowers of every kind.'[6]

Sutherland was likewise happy with the posting. 'He was an important foil to our simpler, even naïve, impatience,' he wrote of Milner-Barry. 'Among his grey hairs there was much wisdom about the strategic and political aspects of SBS operations.'[7]

Jellicoe reconstituted his squadron into three squadrons: L, M and S, the initials denoting the surnames of the three commanders: Tommy Langton, Fitzroy Maclean and David Sutherland. Each squadron was divided into four 'patrols' (later increased to five) of ten men with at least one signaller assigned to each of the 12 patrols.

'On our type of operation the man who could make you laugh was more worth while having than the bore who could shoot straight.'

John Verney

From the start the training was punishing as Jellicoe sought to weed out the weak and unsuitable. Each day began at 0630 hours with 30 minutes of physical jerks led by Sergeant Henderson, a fine figure of a man not averse to a spot of nude sunbathing. Henderson's initials were B.B., and the men were soon calling him 'Brown Body'.

As well as the remorseless physical training there was instruction in all types of seamanship courses in navigation and detecting a sniper's movement, judging distance tests, training in close combat techniques and explosives demonstrations. Soon the men were going off on schemes into the surrounding countryside. On 8 April Milner-Barry led his patrol into the hills. He wrote in his diary:

We carried blankets and rations in Italian haversacks. First 2 hours v. heavy going over plough making use of whatever cover there was which wasn't much. Crossed the road by going under a culvert. Stopped to cook lunch and then did a long hill climb … finally rendezvousing at 10pm up a valley at a crossroads … attitude of various members of the patrol interesting … corporal Lewis rather non cooperative and blasé but they did the actual work alright.[8]

On the return to camp, however, Lewis strayed into a Jewish village in the hope of finding a beer. The normally equitable Milner-Barry was livid 'and told David he must go!' Sutherland agreed, so did Jellicoe, but when Lewis was informed he was being Returned to Unit (RTU'd) 'there were awkward scenes with the man and as a result 3 other members resigned or rather asked to be RTU'd'. If the trio had been hoping to call Jellicoe's bluff they had underestimated their commanding officer. The quartet were soon on their way back to Egypt. 'The whole affair was rather unpleasant and upset me a good deal,' Milner-Barry confided to his diary.[9] Jellicoe would have been less perturbed; better to find out the flaws in a man's character on an exercise than on an operation.

Other than that one incident the atmosphere at Athlit was agreeable. Dick Holmes recalled that he and his comrades in S Squadron 'spent many happy hours' swimming or playing other sports.[10] They built a basketball court on the beach, while there were also regular games of rugby against the Special Raiding Squadron (SRS), based a few miles north at Azzib. The SBS always came off second best, but then the SRS was commanded by Paddy Mayne, who had won several caps for Ireland and the British Lions before the war.

For the first two weeks at Athlit the Special Boat Squadron had been a squadron light, but on 13 April Fitzoy Maclean arrived from Persia with four officers and 100 men. M Squadron was here and immediately, observed Milner-Barry, the atmosphere changed. 'Fitzroy's ideas of discipline differed from the rather free and easy methods of George [Jellicoe] and David [Sutherland],' he wrote in his diary, adding that M Squadron 'created some mirth by marching into the sea for their early morning swim, whereas the rest of us bathed as we felt like it, after the inevitable PT and games, merely stripping off our shorts at the water's edge. The atmosphere in the officers Mess also became somewhat stilted.'[11]

It is not hard to imagine Maclean intimidating most of the Mess. He was

older, wiser and far more travelled than his fellow SBS officers and his status as a sitting Member of Parliament (MP) was another reason to hold him in awe. Jellicoe's approach to leadership was different. Described by a fellow officer as having a gift for irony, Jellicoe was remembered by Dick Holmes as being 'laid back and brave, and a very good commander'. He also had the priceless ability, in the eyes of his men, 'of being able to get whatever he wanted from depots, whether it was jeeps for operations or pork chops for supper'.

One of the most inexperienced officers in the officers' mess was 23-year-old Lieutenant Kenneth Lamonby. Commissioned into the Suffolk Regiment in December 1940, Lamonby was untested in battle but had been accepted into the SBS on account of his seafaring skills. Lamonby was an expert sailor, and so he was put in charge of instructing S Squadron in sea training.

On 16 April the war diary noted that 'the boating of the SBS is gradually improving since the rough seas have subsided and more settled weather has come'.[12] Six days later the sea was being used for another purpose, as Milner-Barry noted in his diary on 22 April: 'In the morning did some Tommy gun shooting at our bathing beach using petrol tins filled with sand and firing seawards.'[13]

For pistol training the SBS were sent in small groups to attend a course in Jerusalem run by the legendary Leonard Hector Grant-Taylor. There are so many stories swirling round Grant-Taylor that it is hard to separate the real from the

The temple of Bacchus, considered by David Sutherland to be the 'most impressive relics in the Levant' when he visited them in 1943. (Courtesy of the SBS Archive)

apocryphal. Was it the visit of the Buffalo Bill Wild West Show to Scotland in 1903 that started his schoolboy obsession with pistols? Did he really learn to shoot on a Montana ranch? And how much truth was there in the rumour that he was loaned by the British government to the Chicago Police Department in the 1920s to help fight Al Capone's gangsters? Even his wartime activities are shrouded in mystery. There are claims that he led an assassination team to Norway in 1940 to despatch several collaborators, although no evidence exists to substantiate the claim; and would the British government really have sent on such a dangerous mission a 49-year-old overweight man, one who during the Great War had been deemed a better instructor than a front-line soldier?

What is not in doubt is that Grant-Taylor – with the rank of lieutenant – schooled commandos in close-quarter shooting in late 1940. David Sutherland came under his tutelage at this time and recalled that he 'taught us to nail a playing card at 20 paces'.[14] This was because Grant-Taylor insisted that all his pupils must concentrate their shots on a target zone the size of a playing card. Grant-Taylor also instructed Special Operations Executives (SOE) before they were sent into occupied Europe, and by 1943 he was based in Jerusalem.* The first batch of SBS personnel, two officers and seven other ranks, were sent there on 11 April 'for a course of Instruction in the pistol'.[15]

Grant-Taylor was in the habit of welcoming his pupils with a brief introduction about his school and its techniques: 'This is a school for murder, murder is my business. Not the vague shooting of people in combat, but the personal, individual killing of a man in cold blood. It's an art which you have to study, practise and perfect.' Once the practical instruction started Grant-Taylor taught the SBS how to adopt a battle crouch, 'an offensive stance [showing] the gunman means business'. Then they must raise the pistol on a centre line, through the target, before firing with 'the forearm parallel to the ground, bent, at navel height'.[16] Dick Holmes remembered that the first impression of Grant-Taylor was misleading. 'He was a little tubby fellow, but he was good. There was no pissing about with him and he taught us well.'

Once the SBS had received instruction from Grant-Taylor they returned to Athlit and put into practice all they had learned using .38 Smith & Wessons and Colt 45s. By early May a typical week for the SBS included foreign weapon training, pistol shooting, demolitions and a 'paddle to Haifa'.[17]

Officers and men alike had to be proficient in all aspects of training, one of the characteristics of the SBS that appealed to Captain John Verney, erstwhile of the

---

* After the war Grant-Taylor became an instructor to the Palestine Police and published a shooting manual entitled *Close Quarter Battle*.

North Somerset Yeomanry and the son of a baronet. 'I found peace,' he wrote in comparing the two, 'in a unit where officers and men shared their hardships on a more nearly equal basis.'[18] However, added Verney, there was far more required to be a successful SBS operator than just accurate marksmanship:

> We pretty soon came to know one another's physical and mental capacities, and with them our own. Strength and skill were respected, and a fair degree of both were essential, but everyone recognised that there were other qualities, such as a cool head, or a good temper, that might well prove more valuable. On our type of operation the man who could make you laugh was more worth while having than the bore who could shoot straight.[19]

On 2 May Azzib staged the Palestine sports programme. The men of the Special Boat Squadron and the Special Raiding Squadron didn't yet know it but training was about to intensify in preparation for the first operations at the end of the month. A day of sport and beer was Jellicoe and Paddy Mayne's way of having one final blowout before the hard work began in earnest.

To give the day more of an edge, invitations were extended to an Officer Cadets Training Unit (OCTU) and an unnamed New Zealand regiment stationed in Palestine. 'The meeting was a great success,' explained the SBS diary. 'The New Zealanders provided plenty of beer and the tote made a profit of £17, out of which a shield is being made for the winning team.'[20]

The Crusader castle ruins at Athlit. (Courtesy of the SBS Archive)

It was the war diarist's sad duty to record that OCTU won overall, with the SBS second ahead of the SRS. At any rate OCTU triumphed on the sports field; where the consumption of beer was concerned the SBS and SRS showed the opposition a clean pair of heels. Dick Holmes was limbering up to compete in the shot putt when one of his former commando comrades now in the SRS – Harold 'Ginger' Brook – invited him and another soldier into his tent. 'Waiting was a crate of beer,' recalled Holmes, who proceeded to chug back a couple of bottles before being called upon to

RELAXING AT ATHLIT

The men slept under canvas at Athlit but opportunities to relax, as this SBS soldier is doing, were rare as the training intensified in the summer of 1943. (Courtesy of Angie English)

Waiting for lunchtime at Athlit. (Courtesy of the SBS Archive)

Lunchtime's arrived! (Courtesy of the SBS Archive)

compete. 'I made my first three putts still wearing my bush jacket and my brothel creeper shoes. But I made a good enough shot to qualify for the final.'

Holmes scurried back to the tent and got stuck into more beer. 'The final took place in the mid-afternoon and by this time I was well pissed,' he recounted. Not only was Holmes three sheets to the wind but he was also facing a formidable opponent in Lieutenant Oscar Heidenstam of OCTU. The 32-year-old Heidenstam was a pioneer of body-building, or what was known in the 1930s as 'physical excellence'. In 1937 he was crowned Mr Britain and two years later he travelled to France and triumphed in the Grand Prix event organized by the Federation Française de Culture, the forerunner to Mr Europe. In short, Heidenstam fancied his chances in the Palestine sports programme. 'Heidenstam came out of a tent wearing a natty blue singlet and looking very pleased with himself,' recalled Holmes. 'Then he struck a pose, flexing his muscles. We all found it hilarious and thereafter it was adopted by the squadron as our gesture of strength!'

Going into the final round of putts, Heidenstam was in first place with an effort of 29 feet and Holmes was in second, 6 inches shy of that mark. 'For my last effort my two mates insisted that I remove my beret and my bush jacket,' said Holmes. 'They then made a great show of massaging my arms urging me on. Quite a crowd had gathered as I stepped up for my last putt, the last of the contest.' With a herculean effort Holmes threw the putt 29 feet and 3 inches, beating Heidenstam and his rippling muscles into second place. 'The crowd went wild and through my drunken haze I accepted the congratulations of the big man, Paddy Mayne.'

Heidenstam salvaged his honour in the high jump, beating James Baker of the SRS into second place, while Aylmer Sparrow gave the special forces more reasons to cheer with a rousing run in the mile, even if, according to Holmes, 'he was probably as drunk as I was'.★

There were hangovers aplenty the following day, Monday 3 May, when training recommenced. Four members of the Special Raiding Squadron were admitted to hospital; whether for sore heads or otherwise was not recorded by the war diarist. The Special Boat Squadron training programme for the week described Monday afternoon's activities as 'General toughening up in swimming, marching and load carrying.'[21] Another clue that their weeks of relative inactivity would soon be over was the departure of a group of SBS personnel to Beirut to test the new Davis submarine escape equipment, a breathing and buoyancy bag used by submariners and frogmen.

★ Both Baker and Sparrow were killed on subsequent operations.

On 4 May Tommy Langton's L Squadron marched out of Athlit and headed east towards Lake Tiberias, a distance of 45 miles over rough and difficult country. Sid Dowland described the exercise as 'horrible' because: 'The more we marched inland the hotter it became. There was no cooling sea breeze just a baking hot sun. It was a good lesson in water discipline. The likes of me, Kosbab and Doug [Wright] had learned about water discipline the hard way but others really struggled on that march.'[22]

While L Squadron were toiling under a cruel sun, S Squadron were preparing for Operation *Bronx*, a training exercise designed with the impending invasion of Sicily in mind. On 5 May Captain Milner-Barry attended a conference at the Parachute Brigade HQ where he was informed that a company of paratroopers would attack objectives on the Cyprus coast eight days hence. 'The role of the SBS,' wrote Milner-Barry, 'was to get signallers of the Brigade to the dropping zone and protect them while they were guiding in the aircraft by means of the REBECCA wireless set.'[23]

Meanwhile another S Squadron patrol consisting of ten soldiers, two signallers and a medical orderly would 'test the local defences' around the Syrian coastal town of Latakia on the night of 14 May. Each raider was issued with a list of clothing and equipment to draw from the quartermaster's stores, including: 'Desert boots or any

The coastline close to Athlit where the SBS trained in the early summer of 1943. (Courtesy of the SBS Archive)

strong marching boot … Arab headdress … web belt and holster pouches, 6 per man, German depending on availability … Italian rucksack … knife … string and rope … dovers cream [a mosquito repellent].'[24] In addition three pairs of binoculars were issued to each patrol as well as a similar number of sniper's nets and two pairs of wire cutters.

Milner-Barry's patrol sailed towards Cyprus in a 100-ton schooner called *Apostolos* and, having anchored off the east coast near the old battlements of Famagusta, the SBS raiders paddled ashore unobserved. Or so they thought. The men had just finished camouflaging their folboats when a searchlight picked up the *Apostolos* and held the boat in its beam. Milner-Barry described what happened next in his report of the incident:

> The signaller I had left onboard promptly got working with a flashlight, but this did not prevent a shot being fired over the ship. I was not unduly disturbed by this … it is customary to fire a shot across a ship's bow to bring her to. In this case the ship had been anchored for three quarters of an hour, but it was a dark night. When a second shot was fired, however, closer than the first, it was obvious that some misunderstanding had occurred, and I sent in one of my party, a gunner, to the fort just above the landing place to telephone the Battery Commander to stop shooting as we were merely taking part in an exercise.[25]

Though the shooting ceased, the gunner did not return [he had been arrested by the Cypriot commander] and after a brief wait Milner-Barry decided to press inland. He had not got far, however, when they were surrounded by military policemen and taken into custody. The following day Milner-Barry attended a court of enquiry where he learned 'that the [wireless] signal which I supposed had been sent from SBS had never been received'.[26]

A couple of hundred miles east of Famagusta, the SBS raid on Latakia was also not going to plan. The patrol had split into two, with No.1 party comprising four experienced soldiers in Sergeant Jack Nicholson, a veteran of Layforce who had been involved in the evacuation of Crete two years earlier, Sergeant Robinson, and privates Dick Morris and George Miller. The latter was a 22-year-old from Camberwell, south London, who had joined the SBS from the 3rd County of London Yeomanry (Sharpshooters), an armoured regiment that had seen much action in North Africa the previous year.

The quartet paddled ashore without problem and soon spied two French guards patrolling the beach. Miller ambushed the pair and with an unloaded pistol 'covered the sentries from a distance of 2 yards'.[27] Though they had been forewarned of the exercise the Frenchmen were piqued at being outmanoeuvred and refused to enter into the spirit of the occasion, 'threaten[ing] the party with their rifles'.[28] These weapons were loaded, but nonetheless the sentries were overpowered and disarmed by the SBS raiders. To teach the unsporting sentries a lesson, the commandos held them prisoner for an hour and then released them to the accompaniment of much Gallic profanity. The Frenchmen soon returned with reinforcements and Robinson and Morris 'decided to surrender and explain matters to the umpire'.[29]

Nearby No.2 party, including Corporal Sydney Greaves and privates Ray Jones and Leo Rice, the latter an Australian, had landed unobserved further up the coast. They moved inland and after a few hundred yards encountered a military camp. Challenged by an alert sentry, the SBS went to ground among the sand dunes as a shot ran out. Greaves and Jones were captured by a patrol despatched from the camp, while Rice evaded his pursuers and set off towards Latakia. Just after daylight he too was caught and after spending two hours in French hands – during which time his cigarettes were confiscated much to his annoyance – Rice was released by the umpire.

Although at first glance the exercise appeared a failure, as a lesson in seaborne raiding techniques it had proved invaluable experience. In his report of the mock attack, Dick Morris commented:

Ken Lamonby (left) is guided back to the SBS base by a young boy at the end of a hard day's march. The backpack he has on is an Italian one with which the SBS experimented. (Courtesy of SAS Archive)

> Points brought out were, the time taken to bury the canoes, the necessity for each man to wear rubber soled boots and the virtual impossibility of hiding up in cultivated land without being discovered by natives … the wireless sets carried did not maintain communication and after receiving one message they broke down. The signallers and the medical orderly who had not worked with the patrol before proved to be fit and efficient men.[30]

There was much food for thought for George Jellicoe and his squadron commanders, but not much time to digest it. The Allied invasion of Sicily was drawing ever nearer and the Special Boat Squadron would have a small but significant part to play. The next time the SBS landed on a stretch of coast at night would be for real.

CHAPTER 3

SICK IN SARDINIA

O n Friday 28 May the men of L Squadron were given a break from training. They spent the afternoon in Haifa at the cinema watching Nova Pilbeam and Jack Hawkins in *The Next of Kin*. The next day they drew kits in preparation for their departure from Athlit and on the morning of 30 May L Squadron 'proceeded to an unknown destination'.[1] Tommy Langton was too ill to lead them so Captain John Verney took over command.

Two weeks later the six officers and 50 men reached their destination in Philippeville (now called Skikda), north-eastern Algeria, 'tired and dirty from hastening three thousand miles across North Africa in summer dust and heat'.[2] Verney knew nothing of the reason behind the move, 'beyond the common knowledge that a combined force was assembling in Algiers and Tunis to invade – where? Greece, Italy, Sicily, the South of France even?'[3]

The men embarked upon a new phase in their training in the warm waters of the Mediterranean Sea. They practised launching inflatable boats from submarines, in the day and at night. The next task was to exit the submarine in the dark 2 or 3 miles offshore and then paddle towards a stretch of beach on a compass bearing provided by the Royal Navy: in theory not too difficult a task but in practice a challenge, given the current and wind.

OPPOSITE
The SBS trained on caiques, traditional Greek fishing boats that proved ideal for clandestine warfare. (Courtesy of the SBS Archive)

Passing the Source d'antillias on return from one week's exercise in the hills in May 1943 are Duggie Pomford, Grainger Laverick and Marine Watson. (Courtesy of the SBS Archive)

The SBS shared Philippeville with Bill Stirling's 2 SAS, among whom was Lieutenant Jimmy Hughes. He described how the camp appeared to be an idyll. 'It lay on a long sandy bay a few miles to the east of the town where the high rolling hills curved round, hugging its little cluster of tents and dipping down straight into the sea immediately beyond. Great foamy breakers rolled in over the sandy beach … [and] the surrounding hills were thickly forested with cork trees.'[4]

But the picture postcard image concealed a mortal danger – malaria, a disease that was rife in this region of Algeria. On 22 June L Squadron left Philippeville and travelled 250 miles west to Algiers where they were billeted in a submarine depot ship in the harbour. The soldiers soon began reporting sick with Jumper Workman and Jim Kosbab among the first to be confined to their bunks. 'We attributed their headaches, difficulty in breathing and lack of appetite to their conditions of living,' wrote John Verney, a claim disputed by Keith Killby, the medical orderly. 'We were never allowed to call it malaria,' he recalled. 'We had a lot of cases and I started giving Mepacrine to the men every day but some of the men were complacent about taking it unfortunately.'[5] Mepacrine was an anti-malerial drug that tasted bitter and turned the skin yellow; it wasn't popular with the men who, despite the best efforts of Killby, were complacent about taking the pills believing that they were only suffering from the fetid conditions of the depot ship.

At Algiers details of Operation *Hawthorn* were revealed by George Jellicoe to the officers. The Allied invasion of Sicily would begin in the early hours of 10 June and it was feared that German aircraft would inflict heavy losses to the invasion fleet from their bases in Sardinia. The task of L Squadron, in conjunction with ongoing raids by the RAF, was to launch a series of sabotage attacks on six Sardinian airfields. John Verney recalled Jellicoe's words at the briefing:

> There are roughly two hundred German bombers dispersed over the half-dozen airfields we hope to attack. Each bomber is potentially capable of sinking a troop carrier, that is of putting perhaps 2,000 men out of action before the Sicily landing. If, between us, we succeed in destroying only one German bomber, then the operation will have been worth attempting. And, of course, I believe we shall destroy many more than that.[6]

Jellicoe then went into detail about the attacks, explaining that a submarine would land small parties of raiders on the west coast of Sardinia on three consecutive nights – 30 June, 1 July and 2 July. Each of the three parties would comprise two

Jack Nicholson and his two best friends. (Courtesy of the SBS Archive)

The boiling sun made all training exercises in the Transjordan a real challenge for the men. (Courtesy of the SBS Archive)

officers and 12 men and would sub-divide once ashore, giving six raiding parties in total, each of one officer and six men.

Meanwhile a second submarine would deposit a fourth party on the east coast who would establish a rendezvous point from which a submarine would return on 24 July.

It was audacious, ambitious and, in the men's eyes, wildly optimistic to expect that they could evade capture for more than three weeks on an island swarming with enemy troops. 'In a way the craziness of the project was its attraction,' reflected Verney. 'Whatever each of us may have felt privately about the chances of success, we agreed with them now that it was well worth attempting.'[7]

Sid Dowland's patrol consisted of Sergeant-Major Cyril Feebery, Leonard Thomas and Frank Noriega, with Lieutenant Allan Duggin in command. Jim Kosbab and Jumper Workman should have gone but they were bed-ridden. They were not the only ones. 'At the time I was taking a lot to the sick bay,' remembered Killby, who by now had also gone down with malaria. Nonetheless he requested – and was granted – permission to go on the operation to attend to the inevitable sick.

One soldier who was refused permission to take part in Operation *Hawthorn* was Randolph Churchill, the Prime Minister's son and a thorough nuisance to the

SBS. David Stirling had invited him into the SAS the previous year and subsequently admitted it had been a mistake. Churchill was fat, unfit and lazy. 'Randolph wasn't really interested in joining the SAS to fight the Germans,' recalled Stirling. 'He wanted the insignia. He would wear whatever badge and rank seemed the most appropriate at the time for getting the best out of a situation.'[8]

Stirling's capture curtailed Churchill's days in the SAS so he next invited himself into the SBS and joined L Squadron in Philippeville. 'He was most unpopular,' said Killby. 'I remember one incident very clearly. All officers had to go off on a run and he set off with them but dropped back after ten minutes and came back to camp.'

Churchill was adamant that he was going on Operation *Hawthorn*. Jellicoe had seen at first hand in 1942 how unsuited Churchill was to special forces soldiering; he appeared, however, to acquiesce to Churchill's demands, designating him one of the six patrol leaders. But behind the scenes Jellicoe cabled Middle East HQ and an order soon arrived instructing Churchill that he was not to go on the mission – the risk of his being captured was too great. Everyone's face had been saved.

Shortly before the raiding party left Algiers an American soldier of Italian extraction called Louis Tempanyro was attached to Captain Ian Brinkworth's patrol. Tempanyro knew Sardinia and could speak Italian, and was to act as *Hawthorn's* guide. 'It was stupid, he hadn't even really volunteered,' reflected Killby of the decision to employ Tempanyro. 'Normally the SBS vetted people very thoroughly. Within an hour of meeting him I disliked him.'

Lamonby (centre) was a skilled sailor who instructed the SBS in basic seamanship in the spring of 1943. (Courtesy of the SBS Archive)

Brinkworth's party sailed from Algiers aboard a submarine on 27 June and arrived at their destination four days later without mishap. First they destroyed their rubber boats and Mae Wests and then struck off in the darkness towards their target airfield. 'We marched on our bearing for about three hours,' wrote Sergeant Pat Scully in his report of the mission. 'On reaching a very steep wadi we made our way down. On arriving at the bottom we checked up on personnel and found the American guide Louis Tempanyro missing. We searched all over for him but could not find him.'[9]

It was now daylight. They had lost their guide and Wilson, the signaller, and another soldier were feverish with malaria. Brinkworth ordered them to lie up in the wadi and wait until dusk. For five days and nights the party made painstakingly slow progress towards their target until eventually Brinkworth split up the party. Scully was detailed to remain with the sick men and their heavy kit while the rest of them proceeded to the airfield laden with bombs.

Lieutenant John Cochran's party reached the east coast of Sardinia at daybreak on 2 July and at nightfall, remembered Killby, the submarine surfaced. 'We got into the rubber boats and by this time I was useless [with malaria]. The other two men had to paddle and then practically drag me up the beach. I lay delirious for two days and the only thing I remember saying is to the officer "Go and leave me beside the road, they'll pick me up". Of course he said that they couldn't do that because it would give the game away.'

The SBS also used the caiques to mess about on the sea, when the opportunity arose. (Courtesy of the SBS Archive)

It was Cochran's job to establish a base camp and wait for the arrival of the sabotage parties once they had accomplished their missions. The stretch of coastline on which they had landed was isolated and in the first five days they spotted just one lone figure in the distance. By now Killby's fever had broken but James Murray, one of the men who had dragged him up the landing beach, had succumbed to malaria.

Duggin's patrol, along with Captain John Thomson's, had come ashore on the south-west coast near Capo Pecora on 30 June minus Doug Wright. 'I was as sick as a dog with malaria,' Wright said. 'Keith Killby had done a great job looking after me in Algiers but I spent the whole voyage in a raging fever. In the end they decided I was too sick to leave the sub.'[10]

The party grew smaller still shortly after landing. Sid Dowland and Leonard Thomas, both suffering the effects of malaria, became separated from Duggin, Feebery and Noriega as they carried out an initial reconnaissance. 'I never did a job with the SBS or SAS that went entirely according to plan,' reflected Cyril Feebery. 'However carefully you had thought things through beforehand, sooner or later something would happen that meant you had to start making it up as you went along.'[11]

Despite the intensive training at Athlit there was time to relax with swimming and games of basketball and rugby. (Courtesy of the SBS Archive)

Dowland and Thomas climbed a rocky escarpment in search of a suitable spot to lie up and take stock of their situation, but the effort required exhausted them both. Thomas collapsed. Dowland made his friend comfortable and then descended the hillside to refill their water bottles from a stream. On his return he could find no trace of Thomas. When he did eventually locate Thomas it was clear to Dowland he was in trouble. His breathing was short and shallow and there was no coherence to the words he was mumbling. Dowland nursed Thomas as best he could, dampening his brow with a wet rag and spoon-feeding him stewed apricots. But his tending was to no avail. The 20-year-old Lancastrian died at dusk.

Dowland dug a hole with his small entrenching tool and laid Thomas and his equipment inside, having first removed his rations and ammunition. He said a quick prayer and then struck out east towards the rendezvous beach where Cochran, Killby and the others were waiting.

L–R: back row: Duggie Pomford, Jack Nicholson, Ray Jones and Hank Hancock. Front row: Patsy Henderson and Leo 'Digger' Rice. This photo was taken on Leros in autumn 1943. (Courtesy of the SBS Archive)

On the sixth day of their vigil on the east coast of Sardinia Killby 'saw an Italian patrol and they were clearly searching'. As the soldiers approached the SBS party Lieutenant Cochran attempted to pass them off as Germans on a training exercise. 'But it didn't work,' said Killby. 'From the moment I saw that patrol I knew that the whole show had been given away.'

Killby was convinced they had been betrayed by Louis Tempanyro, and similar thoughts were running through the head of Sergeant Pat Scully. Captain Brinkworth and the rest of the patrol had failed to return from the airfield so Scully did as instructed and set off east towards the rendezvous beach with his two poorly companions. 'That evening we saw a farmhouse so we decided to take the bull by the horns and attempt to get food and water,' recalled Scully. The three men were watered and fed by hosts who 'seemed very friendly', but when the British soldiers stepped outside the farmhouse they found an Italian patrol waiting for them. The trio were stripped of their possessions and thrown in the local jailhouse for the night. The next day they were transported to an army base for interrogation. 'They tried to frighten us with all kinds of threats such as placing thumbscrews on the table and also placing a revolver on the table,' explained Scully. 'They insisted we were not ordinary soldiers but spies or some such thing.'[12]

Despite the attempts at intimidation the interrogation remained within the bounds of the Geneva Convention. Early the next morning Scully and his comrades were taken outside to a parked truck and to his astonishment he recognized one face after another: Captain Thomson, Lieutenant Cochran, Sergeant Cass, privates Killby and Murray, signalmen Schofield and Johnstone.

For the first 15 miles of the journey the prisoners exchanged stories with Captain Thomson, including the sad news that Sergeant Duncan McKerracher and Private Bill Thomas (one of the half dozen Grenadier Guardsmen who had volunteered for the SAS in late 1942) had both died of malaria. Then the truck stopped to collect two more passengers – Corporal Shackleton and Private Gill. 'They told Captain Thomson that they had been in chains for two days,' said Scully, who added that 'most of the boys were sick'.[13]

The men were driven many miles north to Sassari, Sardinia's second largest city and a place rich in culture and history. 'The treatment there was terrible,' commented Scully, although Killby recalled it differently. 'We were very well treated,' he said. 'As I could speak a little Italian I was told to find out if we were going to be shot. So I asked in terrible Italian "are you going to shoot us?" and they said "no, of course not".'[14] On his fifth day of captivity Scully's cell door opened and Sid Dowland was pushed inside.

Sean O'Reilly, 41, loved beer and women, and fighting Germans. (Courtesy of the SBS Archive)

Having buried Leonard Thomas, Dowland had trekked east with the aim of reaching the rendezvous. On his third day he reached the village of Montevicchio in the late afternoon. 'I should really have skirted round the outside of the village,' reflected Dowland. 'But I was still weak and tired and I just wanted to get to the rendezvous. I waited until darkness and when everything appeared quiet I set off.'[15]

Dowland moved slowly through the village, his rubber-soled boots betraying no hint of his presence on the cobbled street. As the dwellings began to peter out Dowland relaxed. Then a dog began barking. Dowland took off into the darkness, darting into an olive grove and running as fast as his weak legs could carry him. When he paused for a rest he heard the sound of more dogs and of their owners. He pushed on and eventually the noises faded, but the chase had shattered his emaciated body. Dowland spent most of the following day recovering and towards dusk he was captured by an Italian patrol.

Dowland told Scully his story, adding that his captors 'had kept him in solitary confinement for three days in an effort to break his morale'.[16] More SBS soldiers arrived in the next few days including Captain Brinkworth, and the remnants of Allan Duggin's patrol. They had reached the airfield, observed the aircraft and then practically wept with frustration as the Italians doubled the guard and reinforced the perimeter with thick coils of barbed wire. There were British commandos on the island and they were taking no chances. By now Duggin was useless with malaria, insisting in his rare moments of lucidity that Sergeant-Major Feebery leave him. Eventually Feebery realised that he and Noriega had no other choice. 'I went through the lieutenant's pockets, taking his maps and revolver,' Feebery remembered. 'His water bottle was half full, so we bound it round his wrist where he couldn't miss it if he woke up and needed a drink.' Feebery and Noriega eased the unconscious officer into his sleeping bag and carried him through the darkness towards a guard post they had passed a short while earlier. 'We lifted the lieutenant onto the grass verge, left him as comfortable as we could and legged it for the coast,' said Feebery.[17] They made it to the rendezvous but found not Lieutenant Cochran's party but a squad of Italian military police, or Carabinieri.

'I never did a job with the SBS or SAS that went entirely according to plan... However carefully you had thought things through beforehand, sooner or later something would happen that meant you had to start making it up as you went along.'

Cyril Feebery

John Verney and Edward Imbert-Terry soon showed up. They had parachuted into central Sardinia several days after the insertion of the seaborne patrols. The patrol reached the target airfield just north of Ottana unimpeded and then split into two with Verney, accompanied by Lance-Sergeant John Scott and Lance-Corporal Bill Brown, attending to the south side. For 45 minutes they tiptoed silently across the airfield placing bombs on six aircraft and in fuel dumps before withdrawing to the pre-arranged rendezvous. As Verney led his two men away from the airfield a German soldier 'appeared unexpectedly on a path and shouted some enquiry about a lorry he was waiting for'. Verney had to make a snap decision, 'to shoot him or not shoot him'. He chose the latter course and instead 'spoke to him politely in German, explaining we were Italians on a night march'. The German went on his way but Verney sensed he departed with the realization of their true identity. As soon as the German was out of sight the British commandos left the path and headed off across country. A few minutes later, at exactly 0400 hours, their bombs began to go off. 'We felt the blast,' wrote Verney. 'We halted halfway up the hill and looked back. Another seven explosions followed in the next two or three minutes. The noises and flashes were terrific.'[18]

According to Verney's account of Operation *Hawthorn* in the first installment of his war memoirs, *Going to the Wars*, published in 1955, he, Brown and Scott evaded capture for 12 days before they were finally apprehended by Italian Carabinieri. In his report of the operation, however, Sergeant Scully states that Verney and his men were captured on 6 July.

The prison in Sassari continued to swell with captured SBS soldiers including Louis Tempanyro. Although the American claimed he had been captured on 7 July, one of the guards informed the British prisoners that he had given himself up on 3 July because 'he

Few soldiers in the SBS were as experienced as Sergeant Jack Nicholson. (Courtesy of the SBS Archive)

was fed up being messed about by the English'.[19] Tempanyro had needed little encouragement to talk, revealing to his inquisitors everything he knew about the mission.

In August the men were removed from their cells and marched on foot towards the coast. At every village they passed through, recalled Dowland, 'people would turn out and give us bread, cheese or apples. They had nothing themselves but they would give you something. They were wonderful.'[20] After more than a week on the move they reached a small port from where they sailed to Naples and an Italian prisoner of war camp.

All except Sergeant Scully. Having contracted malaria in prison, he was then struck down by dysentery and was in hospital when his comrades left for Italy. A month later Scully was well enough to be put on a plane for Italy but no sooner had he landed than Italy sued for peace with the Allies. With the help of the US Army Scully made his way to Tunis by aircraft on 20 September and eventually back to the Special Boat Squadron. Only then did Jellicoe discover the true extent of the shambles of Operation *Hawthorn*.

CHAPTER 4

A CLOSE CALL
IN CRETE

wo weeks after the departure of L Squadron from Athlit, on 13 June
Fitzroy Maclean led his M Squadron north to Zahle, 'high up in the
mountains behind Beirut'.[1] It was a move that suited everyone; Maclean
was pleased to be away from what he considered the more disreputable elements of
the Special Boat Squadron and S Squadron were happy to be free of a unit they
perceived to be too regimental.

   On 17 June there was another round of farewells although these ones, at least
from Walter Milner-Barry's perspective, were more heartfelt as S Squadron were
deployed piecemeal. 'Andy [Lassen] and Ken [Lamonby] left with their troop
leaving a feeling of emptiness behind,' wrote Milner-Barry in his diary.[2]

   S Squadron was further diminished in number when David Sutherland, along
with 12 other ranks, departed for what the SBS war diary noted as an 'unknown
destination'. Tucked into Sutherland's battledress was Operation Instruction No. 166,
marked in capital letters: 'MOST SECRET. OFFICER ONLY'. It began:

> You will plan and carry out raids on the airfields of HERAKLION, KASTELLI,
> PEDIADA and TYMBAKI, in accordance with the 'Outline Plan for Airfield Raids'
> already issued to you … you will command patrols 'B', 'C' and 'D' from the time of
> landing until after re-embarkation. You will remain at the stores dump throughout

OPPOSITE
While on Crete the
SBS ate what little
food they had, all the
while trying to remain
hidden from the
German occupiers.
(Courtesy of the SBS
Archive)

Patsy Henderson took part in the raid on Crete in D patrol under the command of Lieutenant Ronald Rowe. (Courtesy of the SBS Archive)

the operation and will be in communication with your patrols by wireless during the stated period of watch.[3]

Further details followed in the Instruction and it ended with a reminder of D-Day – 4 July.

Sutherland briefed the men as they travelled to Bardia, passing on his experiences of raiding Crete nearly a year earlier and reminding them of the importance of destroying as many enemy aircraft as possible in order to disrupt their offensive capabilities.

By the time they sailed aboard a motor launch from Bardia at 0800 hours on 22 June, Sutherland had split his force into Patrols B and C. The latter, comprising Andy Lassen, Sergeant Les Nicholson, Corporal Sydney Greaves, Private Ray Jones and two signallers, would attack Kastelli. Meanwhile B Patrol, under Ken Lamonby and consisting of lance-corporals Dick Holmes and Billy Whitehead and Private Eddy Sapshead, would make for Heraklion. In addition the third patrol, 'D', led by Lieutenant Ronald Rowe and consisting of Patsy Henderson, Martin 'Gyppo' Conby and Mick D'Arcy, were scheduled to arrive in Crete in four days' time before heading inland towards their target of Tymbiaki airfield. (Pediada airfield was dropped as a potential target for logistical reasons.)

For most of the men on the raid this was their first experience of guerrilla warfare. Only Sutherland and Lassen knew of the challenges in attacking targets deep inside enemy territory. Fresh in the minds of Greaves, Nicholson and Jones would have been the bungled exercise *Bronx* six weeks earlier when they had attacked Latakia without much success. Now they were going in for real and Holmes recalled his 'heart pounding like shit' as they approached the landing beach a quarter of a mile west of Cape Kokinoxos on the southern side of Crete.

The raiders paddled ashore using the launch's dingy and one rubber float and by 0115 hours on 23 June everyone was safely ashore and scrambling up the boulder-strewn shale.

'All surplus equipment was concealed at the rear of the beach, and [the] party moved off to lying-up area,' wrote Sutherland in his operational report. 'The going was extremely rough, and owing to the exceptionally heavy loads carried (between 70 and 80lbs per man) and the fact that the guides were not certain of the route, the party did not reach the lying-up position, approximately two miles from the beach, until just after first light.'[4]

Sutherland established his supply dump, stashing rations, equipment and wireless sets in a series of small caves either side of a small wadi. Lassen and Lamonby led their patrols a quarter mile up the wadi into a deep gorge, whereupon lookouts were posted and water collected from a source located by one of the guides, a Cretan teenager named Janni.

At daybreak Sutherland took a small party back to the landing beach from where they collected the two heavy wireless batteries required by the two patrols. 'After final instructions had been given Patrols "B" and "C" left for the target areas at 1830 hrs,' wrote Sutherland in his report. 'No civilians or enemy were observed throughout the day.'[5]

The two patrols soon discovered that the terrain that had greeted them upon arrival in Crete was even more brutal inland. The ground was steep and rocky, interspersed with thick areas of thorn bushes that slashed any area of exposed skin. Then there was the temperature: bitterly cold at night and unbearably hot during the day.

For the first two days and nights the two patrols trekked north together. 'Our rucksacks were these big Italian packs,' recalled Holmes. 'They had no framework and so we put a groundsheet between our clothes and the pack otherwise they chafed the skin.'[6]

Not long into the 35-mile march north Eddie Sapshead damaged his ankle in a fall. 'Lamonby was all for leaving him behind but I said "no, we will need his

These images show the terrain that confronted the raiding party when they landed on Crete on the night of 23 June 1943. (Courtesy of the SBS Archive)

explosives",' said Holmes. 'So we decided to carry Eddie's pack for him and off we set. As senior lance-corporal [in Patrol B] I carried it first and then Jack Nicholson, from the other patrol, carried it.'

The patrols split after two days, Lassen leading his men north-east towards Kastelli while Lamonby's patrol continued directly north to their target of Heraklion. By this time Sapshead's ankle was stronger and he was able to carry his own rucksack. But by now there were other factors at play. Perhaps it was insecurity, or maybe he was unable to conform to the informal relationship that existed in the SBS between officers and men on operations, but Lamonby had assumed an air of self-importance the moment Lassen departed with his patrol. He refused to consult with the other members of the patrol and when they paused to brew up Lamonby did nothing but to demand the first mug of tea. The mug was thrust into his hands with a forceful reminder that 'we don't have batmen in this unit'.

Eventually B Patrol reached the outskirts of the village of Arkhanes, a couple of miles south of Heraklion. Here they hid up among the rocky hillside, occasionally eating some of their corned beef rations or feasting on a handful of the raisins stuffed into their pouches. At one moment the day was enlivened by the sight of 'a couple of hundred German soldiers drilling in the square below'.

Later Janni, the young Cretan guide, set off on a reconnaissance and returned hours later with the dispiriting news that their target airfield was no longer in use. But the enterprising teenager did have some better news: he had discovered an alternative target a couple of miles west from their hideout, a petrol dump at Peza containing thousands of gallons of precious aviation fuel. That would have to do. Now, having altered the target, all they had to do was sit tight and wait for 4 July – D-Day.

———————

Approximately 15 miles south-east of B Patrol, the men of C Patrol were also counting down the dragging hours, inside a tiny cave within sight of Kastelli airfield. Lassen had dropped the two signallers en route to the target when it proved too arduous for them to keep carrying the wireless and battery (approximately 70lb in total weight).

The patrol's Cretan guide had obtained information from locals about the layout of the airfield and the SBS soldiers now knew that there were eight Stuka dive-bombers on the eastern side as well as five Junkers 88 bombers and a couple of fighters on the western side.

It was also obvious that the Germans had learned their lessons from the previous year when Sutherland and John Duggan had visited the island's airfields; an outer ring of sentries was posted around the airfield, and under the wing of each Stuka loitered a guard.

Lassen was unconcerned by this detail; it just made the mission all the more challenging. Detailing Nicholson and Greaves to approach the target from the south, he and Jones made for the northern side of the airfield with the aim of destroying the bombers. The four raiders carried Lewes bombs that had been invented by Jock Lewes at Kabrit in the summer of 1941. Lewes had been killed in one of the first SAS operations but his eponymous creation lived on and was much loved by the SBS. An individual Lewes bomb was not much to look at, a stodgy lump weighing just 1lb and consisting of plastic explosive and thermite rolled in motor car oil. Added to this was a No.27 detonator, an instantaneous fuse and a time pencil. A time pencil, as one SAS soldier had explained to his diary in early 1942,

Lieutenant Ken Lamonby, Private Sharp, Dick Holmes, Eddie Sapshead and Signaller Viv Schoet, thought to be taken at Mersa Matruh, just prior to the raid on Crete that cost Lamonby his life. (Imperial War Museum, HU 71395)

> … looked a bit like a 'biro' pen. It was a glass tube with a spring-loaded striker held in place by a strip of copper wire. At the top was a glass phial containing acid which you squeezed gently to break. The acid would then eat through the wire and release the striker. Obviously the thicker the wire the longer the delay before

David Sutherland wrote on the back of this photograph that he took it 'of the party a few minutes before the Germans spotted us'. (Courtesy of SBS Archive)

the striker was triggered (the pencils were colour coded according to the length of fuse). It was all put into a small cotton bag and it proved to be crude, but very effective. The thermite caused a flash that ignited the petrol, not just blowing the wing off but sending the whole plane up.[7]

In the company of the Cretan guide, Greaves and Nicholson evaded the beam of the searchlight that darted through the blackness and cut their way through the Dannert fence without a noise. Once on the airfield they headed for a Junkers 88 that had recently landed and placed a bomb on its left wing.★ They did the same to a second Junkers 88 and were about to tackle the trickier problem of approaching the heavily guarded Stukas when pandemonium erupted on the other side of the airfield.

Initially all had gone well for Lassen and Jones. Having infiltrated the airfield without problem the Dane made for the dive-bombers, ignoring his own earlier instructions stating that the Stukas were the preserve of Greaves and Nicholson.

★ From the beginning the SAS/SBS always chose the left wing on the advice of an RAF officer, who had explained that every airfield has spare wings but only a limited number of each.

Almost immediately Lassen was challenged by one of the perimeter guards. He tried to pass himself off as a German but the Italian sensed something was wrong. Lassen sensed it, too, and shot dead the Italian sentry.

The shot brought the other guards running, but in all directions. Lassen and Jones melted into the darkness as Italians began firing on each other. Meanwhile on the eastern side of the airfield, Nicholson and Greaves exploited the mayhem and ran towards the Stukas. Who would notice two more excitable figures on such a night of confusion? The pair furnished two Stukas with Lewes bombs but before they could attend to the rest a lorry roared up and out jumped a dozen Italians to reinforce their nervous colleagues who had drifted away from their guard duties to watch the drama unfolding a few hundred yards to the west. Nicholson and Greaves prudently chose to withdraw, stealing away towards the fence and pausing momentarily to deposit their remaining bombs in a petrol dump.

'I then pulled out a charge, pressed down on the time pencil and pushed the bomb as far under as I could reach, first on the left side and then on the right. Then I made my way to the outside of the pile and pushed two more charges under the barrel of fuel.'

Dick Holmes

Soon the night sky was illuminated with flares and while Nicholson and Greaves slipped off the airfield unnoticed Lassen and Jones were engaged in a fight for their lives. The Dane had always believed in the efficacy of the British Mills Bomb, the hand grenade in a shape of a pineapple that fragmented into lethal shards upon detonation. A tall, strong man like Lassen could hurl the grenade with deadly accuracy more than 50 feet and this he now did from behind a caterpillar tractor. Jones, meanwhile, fired at anything that moved and a lull in the fighting gave the pair the opportunity they needed. Placing Lewes bombs on the tractor, Lassen and Jones sprinted towards the hole in the fence and snuck through unscathed to disappear into the surrounding blackness.

Seconds later the first of the Lewes bombs exploded in a deafening fireball that only added to the disorder sweeping across the airfield. As fire engines raced towards the burning machine, another bomb detonated, then another. Panicked Italians gave up the chase and stood staring in mute horror at the devastation around them.

It took the four men two hours to reach the rendezvous, whereupon they hoisted their backpacks onto their shoulders and hastened south towards Sutherland's base depot. At 1600 hours the next day, 5 July, Sutherland received a 'success signal' from one of the two signallers now reunited with Lassen. The message was a cause for celebration for Sutherland, particularly as on the same afternoon Lieutenant Ronald Rowe and his D Patrol – who had arrived in Crete four days after the other two patrols – had radioed base to report no aircraft on their target airfield at Tymbaki.

———————

A similar problem had presented itself at Heraklion but thanks to the intelligence supplied by Janni, their teenage guide, B Patrol had modified their objective to a large fuel dump 5 miles from their hideout overlooking the village of Arkhanes. In the days waiting for D-Day Janni had observed the routine of the sentries and reported back to the British soldiers, explaining that during the day two guards patrolled the target, one on the petrol dump and another on the adjacent bomb dump. During the night a guard with a dog made three rounds of both dumps.

At 2130 hours on the evening of 4 July Janni guided the four soldiers of B Patrol towards the target. Holmes by now had nothing but admiration for the 'great skill and courage' of his teenage accomplice who remained impassive as he led the raiders

Controlling the Cretans on the beach proved difficult and, in order to prevent them moving off or alerting the Germans to the SBS presence, Sutherland had them rounded up and placed under guard. (Courtesy of the SBS Archive)

down the hillside, across open fields and over the main road that connected Heraklion to Asimi. At 2300 hours they were within sight of the two dumps, and as they observed the target from a vineyard they saw a German officer and his dog pass by.

For 20 minutes they remained among the vines, devising their plan of attack. It was agreed that Holmes and Janni would deal with the petrol dump and the others would take care of the bomb dump, which was surrounded by wire. With that decided, Holmes and Janni 'crept along a narrow gully which opened out on to a flat area dotted with olive trees and there, not more than thirty yards away, was the first dump'. There were three rows of barrels of petrol piled on top of each other.

An SBS soldier rustles up a little supper with the little food he had left. (Courtesy of the SBS Archive)

Holmes estimated there were about 50 in total, each barrel containing 60 gallons. Moving his haversack into a position from where he had easy access to his Lewes bombs, Holmes left Janni in the gully and edged forward towards the narrow opening built into the earthen wall that encircled the dump. Holmes remembered:

> I saw that there was a passage down the middle of the dump and I made my way down this until I reached the halfway point of the pile of barrels. I then pulled out a charge, pressed down on the time pencil and pushed the bomb as far under as I could reach, first on the left side and then on the right. Then I made my way to the outside of the pile and pushed two more charges under the barrel of fuel.

Holmes went about his work with swift precision. 'I was surprised by how calm I was,' he reflected. 'I'd been on Crete in 1941 and had a bit of a do there but this was my first operation with the SBS.'

Having accomplished his task Holmes tiptoed towards the exit and, like a rabbit leaving its hole, stuck his head cautiously out of the narrow entrance in the earthen wall. The German guard and his dog were no more than 30 yards away. Holmes ducked back inside the dump and waited for the guard to pass. 'The sentry was about to continue his patrol,' wrote Holmes in his report, 'when a second guard with a dog came past the dump and the pair began a lengthy conversation.'

Disconcerted by the presence of a second guard and his dog, Holmes stared hard at the barrels of petrol all around and prayed that the two-hour fuses wouldn't go off prematurely. Meanwhile the two Germans continued gossiping, from time to time telling their dogs to stop whining. 'To my apprehensive ears the dogs seemed very restless, as if they knew I was hiding just a short distance away,' said Holmes. 'But neither guard picked up on their dogs' agitation and after half an hour the Germans moved away from the dump.'

Holmes crept back up the gulley and found the rest of the patrol sheltering further back in the vines. To his consternation he learned that although Lamonby had carried out a reconnaissance of the bomb dump the arrival of the two sentries had deterred him from going inside. Eddie Sapshead appeared angry at the failure but Lamonby refused to be swayed, as Holmes wrote in his operational report: 'The officer … decided that, as we had less than an hour left before the bombs went off and we had to cross a main road in order to make our escape, it would be best to leave the area. We distributed our remaining bombs about the area and began to withdraw.'

As they moved away from the dumps at 0015 hours on 5 July the soldiers – with Lamonby and Sapshead still conducting a whispered argument – were joined by Janni, who 'told us that he had left a Union Jack flag in the area of the target so that the Germans would know that the sabotage had been carried by British forces and not take it out on the civilian population'.

At 0110 hours Holmes' handiwork exploded, causing him to perform 'a little dance on the Cretan hillside'. Not long after they reached a cave inhabited by a colony of bats where they spent the rest of the night. In the morning another Cretan guide arrived with good news: flaming streams of petrol had cascaded through the earthen walls and engulfed the adjacent bomb dump, blowing it sky high but adding to the wrath of the Germans. Dozens of patrols were scouring the countryside looking for the 'terrorists' responsible for the inferno.

———————

Back at the dump, Sutherland waited anxiously for news of the two patrols. Every night since arriving on Crete he had despatched reconnaissance patrols and as a result had 'obtained a good knowledge of the area and pin-pointed routes to lying-up places and strategic points in case of enemy action prior to re-embarkation'. On 7 July, he rendezvoused with Lieutenant Rowe's patrol a little way up the coast and arrangements were made for his exfiltration in four days' time.

The following day – 'D plus 4' – there was still no sign of the two patrols and Sutherland hoped they 'were lying up in a good position nearby, and realising the water shortage at the dump, would only join me at the last moment before re-embarkation'.[8]

On 9 July Sutherland felt a rising sense of alarm at the non-appearance of the two patrols. To make matters worse his signaller, Sergeant Beagley, informed him that there was practically no power left in any of the four wireless batteries after three weeks of continuous use.

But dawn on 10 July brought good news. Jack Nicholson and Sydney Greaves appeared with their Cretan guide, the two soldiers full of good cheer and quick to reassure Sutherland that the rest of the two patrols were laid up a two-hour march inland. A short while later a Greek agent working for SOE arrived at the dump with disturbing information: the Germans had shot 50 local men in reprisal for the raids, prompting 25 Cretans who in one way or another had provided assistance to the raiders to attach themselves to the SBS patrols.

Andy Lassen, David Sutherland and Ken Lamonby. This photo was taken minutes before a German patrol chanced upon their beach, leading to the death of Lamonby. (Courtesy of the SBS Archive)

'Suddenly a shout of "Jerries" brought us all to our feet.'

Dick Holmes

The terrain on Crete made the approach to the target airfields arduous and exhausting. (Courtesy of the SBS Archive)

Sutherland decided to send an immediate signal requesting re-embarkation for the following night, 11 July, but no sooner had Beagley began transmitting the message than the wireless went dead. This was a potentially devastating turn of events. Without wireless power they were marooned on an enemy-occupied island and sure to be captured. Their only chance of salvation lay in getting the small No.11 Wireless transceiver from Lassen's patrol, and joining it and its battery to the battery used by Lieutenant Rowe, in the hope that 'by linking them up in series there would be enough power to send the rest of the message'.[9]

Sutherland thus sent two of his men to Rowe's hideout to fetch his battery and another two to Lassen to bring back the transceiver and battery. It was a risk, to despatch four men in broad daylight while hundreds of enemy troops were engaged in a manhunt, but there was no other choice if they were to escape from the island.

Holmes was lying in a small sun-baked gully when Sutherland's two men arrived on their errand. Somehow, perhaps with his victory in the shotput final fresh in the memory, Holmes found himself ordered to carry the battery back to the dump. 'These things were heavy,' he recalled. 'But the man told us we had to get back as soon as possible because the signals sergeant wasn't sure if we had enough juice to signal back to Cairo.'

By 1450 hours Sergeant Beagley had everything he needed to try to send the vital message once more. The tension was excruciating as he linked up the batteries to the transceiver but at 1500 hours he was able to tell Sutherland that the message had been successfully transmitted.

One of the two Germans captured by the SBS on Crete and brought back to Cairo. (Courtesy of the SBS Archive)

Four hours later Beagley received confirmation that the message had been received: a vessel would collect them the following night.

At nightfall Sutherland gathered in B and C patrols and their 25 Cretan companions. The civilians were herded into a gorge and told to keep quiet. The SBS remained in the wadi on the lookout for Germans. Just after first light on 11 July Lieutenant Rowe led his patrol into the dump, reporting to Sutherland that they had been obliged to leave their hideout on account of enemy activity in the area.

Holmes remembered that the day 'dragged interminably' as they waited for the launch to arrive. The sun felt hotter than ever and they were desperately short of water. Some of the Cretans wanted to go off in search of some more but Sutherland ordered them to stay put and suffer under the sun. At 1500 hours a message was received to the effect that the vessel had sailed at 0500 hours and was on schedule to arrive off the beach at midnight. The news proved a tonic and the men began to imagine they might actually evade capture. To celebrate Sutherland made a last supper out of porridge, cheese and biscuits.

'Suddenly a shout of "Jerries" brought us all to our feet,' recalled Holmes. Two Germans were walking casually up the wadi towards the hideout, blissfully unaware of the danger that lay up ahead. The next instant they were 'confronted by a dozen, heavily-armed British soldiers'. Neither put up a fight. Sutherland knew it was unlikely the pair were on their own but while he was organizing a patrol to head down the wadi a group of armed Cretans ran past on a search of their own. Seconds later firing broke out further up the wadi as the remaining two members of the four-man German patrol spotted the Cretans.

The Germans were trapped on a hillside with their backs to the sea but they fought with the desperation of men who knew their enemy did not take prisoners. They were also good soldiers, wrote Sutherland in his report, who 'by skilful use of ground and cover had the better of the Cretans who were completely disorganised'.[10]

Sutherland could barely contain his fury at the actions of the Cretans. It was now approaching 2100 hours, three hours to their arrival of the launch, and a firefight had broken out in their wadi. 'The wind had died down and the noise of the skirmish must have been clearly audible for a considerable distance up and down the coast,' wrote Sutherland, who was aware of the 'grave consequences' should there be more Germans in the vicinity. 'I therefore sent Lamonby and four men down the gully to stop the firing.'[11] Lamonby's orders were to bring back the Cretans, leaving the two most reliable to ensure that the Germans remained trapped on the hillside. He was not to join in the engagement. But once he had overseen the dispersal of the Cretans under the watchful eye of his four soldiers, Lamonby set off in search of the two Germans.

At 2120 hours Sutherland began to lead them all towards the beach. Lamonby had yet to return from the wadi but Sutherland 'concluded as it was dark he had gone straight to the beach'. Once on the beach Sutherland instructed his men to keep a close eye on the Cretans as well as their two German prisoners, then he ordered the wireless sets and equipment to be laid out in six parallel lines as close to the water's edge as possible for quick loading. Sutherland wrote in his report:

> The prisoners and all surplus personnel were retained in the shadow of the western cliff. Patrol 'B' covered the northern exit to the beach, and dump personnel [the men who had remained with Sutherland during the operation] the NE exit. There being no sign of Lt Lamonby I sent out Lt Lassen and the rest of Patrol 'C' with instructions to search the wadi where he was last seen, shouting his name at regular intervals.[12]

AFTER THE RAID

Andy Lassen and commander Young on the voyage back to Mersa Matruh after the successful raid on Crete. (Courtesy of the SBS Archive)

ABOVE Dick Holmes gets some well-earned rest on the return from Crete, an operation for which he was awarded the Military Medal for blowing up the dump at Peza. (Courtesy of Angie English)

RIGHT Some of the Cretans brought off the island by the SBS clean up on the voyage across the Med. (Courtesy of the SBS Archive)

Two of the crew of the motor launch who plucked the SBS off the beach at Crete as the Germans closed in. (Courtesy of the SBS Archive)

Lassen and his men spent an hour and a half searching for Lamonby but at 2345 hours they returned to the beach 'having seen no sign of this officer'.

At 2359 hours Sutherland began signalling the pre-arranged recognition signal out to sea. Holmes and the rest of B Patrol had now joined everyone else on the beach and he remembered staring into the darkness 'fervently hoping' to spot a response. For ten long minutes they waited, and then suddenly over the sound of the surf they heard an engine. Five minutes later the motor launch was visible and within a few minutes the first of the Cretans were being shepherded on board.

By 0100 hours everyone was off the beach, but Sutherland requested that they sail 'slowly round C[ape] Kokinoxos and lay off the mouth of the wadi in which Lt Lamonby was last seen'.[13] Commander Young complied but at 0130 hours, with Lamonby nowhere to be seen, they set sail for Mersa Matruh on the Egyptian coast.

On the 17-hour voyage south the men wound down after their three-week ordeal. After a good sleep they larked about on deck, sunbathing and posing for photographs. They chatted to the two Germans, Heinz and Ulrich, and admired their prisoners' self-loading rifles, a design with which none of the British was familiar.

Down in the wardroom Sutherland discussed with Lassen the likely fate of Lamonby. It was the Dane's opinion that he 'had been wounded and taken away by the Germans for interrogation'.[14]* Sutherland then sent a brief account of the operation by naval cypher over the ship's radio. Middle East HQ replied at once, instructing Sutherland to bring the two prisoners to Cairo for interrogation.

The launch arrived in Mersa Matruh at 1845 hours on 12 July and they set off by road almost immediately for Cairo. At nightfall they pulled off the road. Holmes recalled that 'the prisoners had been issued with blankets and slept in the back of the truck while the rest of us dispersed over a fairly wide area and slipped into our sleeping bags'. No sentries were posted. Holmes woke a few hours later to the smell of bacon. 'I climbed out of my bag and made my way round to the other side of the three-tonners where the smell seemed to originate. The two Germans were crouched down over a desert fire cooking a huge heap of bacon. Ulrich and Heinz had found the firecan, poured on the fuel, lighted it, found the bacon and now breakfast was ready.'

On arriving in Cairo later that day the SBS decided to return the favour. Having dropped their three officers (Sutherland, Lassen and Rowe) at the Shepheard's Hotel, the men treated Heinz and Ulrich to a slap-up feed in Groppi's, arguably the most famous café in Cairo. Holmes recalled that after three weeks on Crete, the SBS were bearded, dirty and unkempt, but the stares they received as they strode into Groppi's 'were nothing compared to the stares accorded the two Germans'. But the exploits of the SBS raiders were already well known in Cairo. Days after the attack, the *Egyptian Mail* newspaper boasted of a 'Smash and Grab Land Raid on Crete Airfield'. The point of the report, other than to lord it over the enemy, was to emphasise that the sabotage had been carried out by British soldiers. 'None of the troops which landed on Crete either asked for or received any assistance from the inhabitants,' lied the paper in the vain hope of preventing German reprisals.[15]

Jack Nicholson and Sydney Greaves then took the two Germans for a beer before officially handing them over for interrogation. Middle East HQ got wind of their unusual dining party and took out their fury on Sutherland. He found it all rather amusing, telling his superiors that at least the prisoners were 'handed over in a positive, co-operative frame of mind'.[16]

---

* Lamonby's fate was only ascertained after the war when it was learned that he had been shot by one of the two Germans he was hunting, dying later of his wounds in a Heraklion hospital. He is buried in Suda Bay cemetery. After the war Holmes went to see Lamonby's parents in Essex to give them a sanitised description of the operation. 'They were nice people,' he remembered. 'He was an only child.'

CHAPTER 5

ARMISTICE AND UNCERTAINTY

Sutherland and his men returned to Athlit on Friday 23 July. Walter Milner-Barry was there to welcome them back, writing in his diary: 'David arrived with some incredible tales of Crete which must have been a fine operation. Stayed up too late talking. The Cretans must be amazing staunch people. From one people they shot 50 hostages, but in spite of this nobody talked. Andy apparently put up an amazingly fine performance. Comic relief was provided by taking 2 German PWs into Groppis for tea in Cairo.'[1]

Holmes recalled that they were all summoned to a debrief at Azzib, headquarters of the Raiding Forces, in the presence of Colonel Douglas Turnbull. Having chewed over Sutherland's report, he concurred with his view that the operation was 'one of the most physically exacting ever undertaken by Special Service troops in the Middle East'.[2] And it had been worth it; only one casualty (Lamonby) at a cost to the enemy of five aircraft destroyed, two petrol dumps and a bomb dump, not forgetting the two prisoners and their innovative new weapon.

Turnbull announced a slew of decorations for the participants. Military Medals for Dick Holmes, Jack Nicholson, Ray Jones and Sydney Greaves, and a second Military Cross each for Sutherland and Lassen. The citation for Holmes' Military Medal, approved and signed on 23 July by General Henry 'Jumbo' Wilson, Commander-in-Chief Middle East Forces, described his destruction of the

OPPOSITE
Not all the SBS men had sea legs, particularly when the wind got up on the Aegean. (Courtesy of the SBS Archive)

Full steam ahead for North Africa. The raiders are transported back across the Mediterranean from Crete no doubt looking forward to their trip to Groppi's! (Courtesy of SAS Archive)

petrol dump and his 'keenness and determination' throughout the operation in general.[3]

The citation for Lassen's Military Cross raised a few eyebrows. The Dane's courage was beyond reproach but Nicholson disputed the sentence that stated that the success of the raid on Kastelli 'was entirely due to this officer's diversion … planes and petrol were successfully destroyed on the eastern side of the airfield since he drew off all the guards from that area'.

Nonsense, claimed Nicholson, who admired Lassen's pluck, even if he was sometimes 'stupidly brave'. But the plain truth was that more aircraft would have been destroyed on Kastelli had it not been for Lassen's imprudence. 'That was no diversion,' said Nicholson. 'It was a bungle, Lassen and Jones were meant to be as silent as me and Greaves.'[4]

> '*There is no time for conventional establishments, but rather for using whatever fighting elements there are…*'
>
> Winston Churchill

Nicholson was not the only man who had reservations about Lassen. Dick Holmes and he didn't get on, a clash of two very strong personalities. 'I certainly respected him,' reflected Holmes, 'but we didn't particularly like each other. Lassen was a very astute judge of character, he could sum up a man pretty quickly, and I think he respected me because I stood up to him if I thought I had to.' Like Nicholson, Holmes was full of admiration for Lassen's commando skills, and never had he met such a killer, but he too considered the Dane 'foolhardy … really it seemed he had a death wish'.[5]

Sutherland was oblivious to how some of the men felt about Lassen. In his eyes the Dane was a man 'of infinite charm and infinite personality … possessed of shrewd common sense and uncomparable [sic] guts. A born leader. He was adored by his men.'[6] Holmes recalled that Sutherland – 'an officer I admired' – did have a weakness for allowing personal friendships to cloud his judgement. It was the case with Lassen, a man he held in the highest esteem, and it was the same with Ken Lamonby. It had been obvious to most from the outset that Lamonby wasn't cut out for the Special Boat Squadron, but Sutherland couldn't – or wouldn't – see that. Though there was no posthumous decoration for Lamonby, in Sutherland's autobiography he eulogised Lamonby as possessing 'all that one admires in a young man – intelligent, adaptable and brave, with an earthy Suffolk sense of humour'.[7]

Karl Kahane was an Austrian Jew who served with distinction in both the SAS and SBS. (Courtesy of the SBS Archive)

There was much news to catch up on for Sutherland and the rest of S Squadron upon their return to Athlit. There was much sadness – but little surprise – when they learned that Tommy Langton had been invalided home indefinitely having failed to recover from illness. As for L Squadron, they no longer existed after the Sardinia debacle and only a handful of men made the long journey back to Palestine. One of them was Doug Wright, now recovered from Malaria, who was transferred to S Squadron.

The news concerning Fitzroy Maclean was more unexpected. From a captain in charge of a small squadron of British commandos, he had been elevated in the space of a few short days in July to become the Prime Minister's political and military representative in Yugoslavia. In his place George Jellicoe had appointed Captain Ian Lapraik to command M Squadron. The 27-year-old Lapraik, who had suffered from tuberculosis for much of his childhood in Glasgow, had started his special forces career with 51 Commando two years earlier, winning a Military Cross in Abyssinia. He had continued serving with the Middle East Commando throughout 1942 and was cherry-picked by Jellicoe while whiling away his time in Malta. Lapraik brought with him to the SBS a young New Zealand officer called Dion Stellin, or 'Stud' as he was known in the officers' mess on account of his success with the opposite sex.

On 25 July, two days after the return of S Squadron to Athlit, momentous events were taking place elsewhere that were to have significant repercussions for the

Special Boat Squadron. In Rome Benito Mussolini was overthrown and arrested, and King Vittorio Emanuele appointed General Pietro Badoglio the new leader of Italy. Twenty years of Fascist rule were at an end and Italy could look forward to an era of peace, or so the majority of the country hoped. But Badoglio was well aware of the danger that lay ahead; thousands of German soldiers were stationed in Italian territory, not just in Sicily and Sardinia, but on the mainland which would be the next objective of the Allies once Sicily was theirs.

Badoglio wisely decided to adopt the politics of one of his country's forbears, Machiavelli, proclaiming that Italy would remain a loyal ally of Germany's in the fight against the Allies. Simultaneously Badoglio instructed the Italian envoy in Lisbon to inform the Allies he was simply playing for time.

As July turned to August, and the Allies continued their advance north through Sicily towards the Italian toe, the diplomatic and military situation concerning Italy grew ever more complex. On 13 August Colonel Turnbull visited Athlit to brief the SBS officers on the latest developments. 'He told us how we were all to be engaged shortly depending on the political situation,' wrote Milner-Barry in his diary.[8]

Turnbull explained that negotiations were ongoing with Italy and that if, as expected, an armistice was agreed, David Sutherland and a small party from S Squadron would land somewhere and carry out a reconnaissance ahead of a main

Billy Whiteside and Dick Holmes wash down The Hedgehog, one of the vessels that helped evacuate soldiers from the Greek islands. (Courtesy of the SBS Archive)

landing by the 8th Indian Division. Milner-Barry would follow in a destroyer with the rest of S Squadron as well as the whole of M Squadron under the overall command of Jellicoe. 'Our role was to keep ahead of the advancing troops, creating as much alarm and despondency as we could, by sabotage and shooting up all kinds,' wrote Milner-Barry.[9] Turnbull did not mention the destination but Milner-Barry guessed it would be Rhodes.

Rhodes certainly loomed large in the thinking of Winston Churchill and his generals. Its airfields were of crucial importance in determining who controlled the Aegean Sea, the stretch of the Mediterranean from Greece in the west to Asia Minor in the east and which linked with the Sea of the Marmara through the Dardanelles.

In the context of the war as a whole the Aegean appeared at first glance an insignificant backwater but it contained three groups of islands that were of strategic importance: the Sporades to the north, the Cyclades in the west and the Dodecanese in the east. It was the last of these that were considered key to the Aegean, with Rhodes, Kos and Leros among the most important islands.

Throughout much of history the islands had belonged to Turkey, even though the inhabitants who worked the arid land were of Greek extraction. That changed after the Italo–Turkish war of 1911–12, a conflict in which the victorious Italians seized control of the three groups of islands with the objective of using them as staging posts for any future drives into Asia Minor.

Thirty years later, when Italy entered World War II on the side of Germany, it was the islands' importance to colonial interests in North Africa, not Asia Minor, which dictated the policy of Mussolini. But at the end of 1940 Britain was winning the war against Italy in North Africa and its navy was also in control of the Mediterranean. Mussolini turned to Hitler for help.

Duggie Pomford and Dick Holmes about to have a shave ahead of a raid. (Courtesy of the SBS Archive)

Erwin Rommel and his Afrika Korps were soon pushing the British back across North Africa but Hitler was also quick to recognize how the Aegean Islands could assist Germany's war machine. Airfields on Rhodes would provide the Luftwaffe with a base from which to attack British convoys steaming towards Malta, while a German presence in the region would also boost the security of the oil fields in Romania.

Britain was alive to the consequences should Germany seize control of Rhodes and the other islands, not just for its shipping in the Mediterranean but also

> *'Our role was to keep ahead of the advancing troops, creating as much alarm and despondency as we could, by sabotage and shooting up all kinds...'*
>
> Walter Milner-Barry

for its control of the Suez Canal in Egypt. Plans were therefore put in place for an invasion of the Dodecanese★ but Germany pre-empted the British plan, invading Greece and then Crete in April/May 1941, and also scoring a major victory in the

---

★ Ironically Layforce, which would provide the bulk of the early SAS and SBS, were to spearhead the planned assault on Rhodes in the spring of 1941.

North African campaign by driving its enemy out of the eastern region of Libya known as Cyrenaica. Britain had no choice but to cancel plans for the invasion of Rhodes and concentrate instead on winning the war in North Africa.

RQMS Evans and Karl Kahane reveal nearly all at Castelrosso. (Courtesy of the SBS Archive)

As August lengthened and negotiations between Italy and the Allies continued, the Special Boat Squadron intensified their training at Athlit. To prevent the men getting too keyed up, the officers ensured there were regular games of basketball and football, and a mobile cinema arrived to help them kill time in the evening. Walter Milner-Barry called up an old friend from his days in the Transjordan Frontier Force, Raymond Cafferata, now deputy superintendent of the Palestine police, who lectured the squadron 'on tactics when dealing with insurgents, such as the army had had to practise in the hills before the outbreak of war'.[10] The talk went down well with the men and Cafferata ended the lecture with a couple of demonstrations on the most effective way of springing an ambush.

Milner-Barry caught up with another old acquaintance a few days later, revisiting the opulent Mount Lebanon resort of Saoufar, a town he knew well from his days working for Shell in the 1930s. He and David Sutherland stayed in the Grand Hotel and later shared an expensive bottle of Chablis over dinner. Best of all, Milner-Barry ran into a string of old girlfriends 'with whom I was able to dance'.[11]

By the start of September General Pietro Badoglio had no more room in which to manoeuvre. Sicily was conquered and now the Allies were ready to advance across the Strait of Messina into Italy. On the third day of the month Badoglio signed the terms of the Italian armistice (the announcement of which was not made public until 8 September) in an olive grove near Syracuse in Sicily, and on the same day the invasion of Italy began with the Eighth Army landing in Calabria, and Paddy Mayne leading the Special Raiding Squadron into Bagnara.

At Athlit, 3 September was a normal day: hard training in the morning followed by a game of football in the afternoon against the Royal Tank Regiment; the SBS won 3–1. The war diary noted that in the evening, 'Major Jellicoe arrives from Cairo'.

Jellicoe had been scuttling back and forth between Athlit and Cairo for much of August attending briefings at Middle East HQ. Since May 1943 the British had

L–R: Freddy Crouch, Jock Cree, Lieutenant Nobby Clarke, Duggie Pomford and Doug Wright have a breather on boat during their destructive campaign of piracy in May 1944. (Courtesy of the SBS Archive)

drawn up seven different plans for the invasion of Rhodes and the other important islands in the Dodecanese, taking into account the strength of the likely German and fascist Italian resistance and the reaction of neutral Turkey, a country that neither Britain nor Germany wished to antagonise.

Churchill had his say, sending a memo on 3 August, in which he said of any invasion: 'There is no time for conventional establishments, but rather for using whatever fighting elements there are …'[12]

By the end of August the British chiefs of staff recognized that they did not possess the resources to overpower the 7,000-strong German division on Rhodes; instead they proposed an invasion of the smaller islands of the Dodecanese. But their thoughts kept returning to Rhodes, and the estimated 35,000 Italian personnel on the island. Surely they could be persuaded to side with the British against Germany? Time was against the British, however, if the Italians were to be talked round before the Germans had time to send reinforcements to Rhodes. Boldness was needed, and General Wilson knew a man whose name was a byword for daring.

On 7 September not only was Jellicoe unaware of the Italian armistice; he did not even know that Middle East HQ had produced another idea for an invasion of Rhodes. He was still working on the assumption that Rhodes had been abandoned and it was the smaller islands that would be targeted. With that in mind Jellicoe,

accompanied by Milner-Barry and Ian Lapraik, motored to Beirut for a meeting with Captain Hugo Ionides, commander of the 1st British Submarine Flotilla.

Ionides and the trio of SBS officers finalised details for a landing by Milner-Barry and an S Squadron patrol on the small Dodecanese island of Levitha. Leaving Milner-Barry to thrash out the details with Ionides, Jellicoe and Lapraik retired to the St Georges Hotel for a spot of dinner. At 2300 hours, as the meal was nearing its end, a military policeman arrived and presented Jellicoe 'with an urgent signal requesting my immediate return to RFHQ'.

Jellicoe left Lapraik to settle the bill and two hours later he was at Raiding Forces HQ at Azzib whereupon he was instructed to catch a flight at 0630 hours from Haifa to Cairo.

The sailors of the Levant Schooner Flotilla were much respected by the SBS for their seamanship skills. (Courtesy of Angie English)

Jellicoe touched down at Heliopolis, just outside Cairo, at 0900 hours on 8 September. A staff car was waiting, as was a summons to attend a conference at Middle East HQ one hour later. Jellicoe grabbed something to eat, had a quick shave, and at 1000 hours presented himself at headquarters. 'At this conference I met and was introduced to a rather bewildered assortment of officers,' recalled Jellicoe, who was informed of the Italian armistice. Surprised by that piece of news, Jellicoe then discovered that to him fell the honour of 'attempting to rally the Italian garrison of Rhodes to resist the Germans'.[13]

Middle East HQ had no definite plan in place to assist Jellicoe in his mission, although he was told that no British military help would be available before 15 September at the earliest. In addition the morale of the Italians was reportedly low and their governor, Admiral Inigo Campioni, had no idea of British intentions for the island. Jellicoe was dumbstruck by the plan's vagueness. Over lunch at the Shepheard's Hotel, he and Colonel Turnbull of the RFHQ were 'equally pessimistic' as to the chances of a successful conclusion. Nevertheless Jellicoe proposed that he lead a small party into Rhodes by parachute to try to make contact with Campioni.

The next few hours were spent rushing around Cairo organizing an insertion for that evening consisting of Jellicoe, a Polish SOE agent called Count Julian Dobrski, whose alias was Major Dolbey, and Sergeant Kesterton, a signaller. But delays in obtaining equipment for the mission led to a 24-hour postponement. Eventually the three men parachuted into Rhodes on the evening of 9 September with Jellicoe carrying three letters for Admiral Campioni from General Harold Alexander, Commander-in-Chief of Middle East Command.

'The drop itself and the events of the next 90 minutes were unpleasant,' wrote Jellicoe with his customary understatement. Not only had they a strong breeze to contend with but they were fired upon by a company of Italian soldiers who presumed they were Germans. Dobrski broke his leg upon landing but was at least able to use his fluent Italian to explain the nature of their mission. Displaying remarkable stoicism, Dobrski insisted on seeing Admiral Campioni before having his injury tended. Jellicoe, meanwhile, unsure if it was Germans or Italians firing at them, removed Alexander's letters. 'I was told I must destroy these letters if I was in danger of capture,' he remembered. 'I thought I was in danger so unable to find anywhere to put them I had to eat the beastly things. They were written on very thick formal paper and proved very indigestible.'[14]

Eventually Jellicoe and his signaller made contact with the Italians and they too were driven to the governor's residence where they were reunited with Dobrski.

Freddie Crouch (left) and Dick Holmes were two east Londoners who often carried out reconnaissance missions together in the SBS. (Courtesy of the SBS Archive)

He told Jellicoe that he had spoken with Campioni and was 'optimistic' that he would side with the British, though Campioni had made clear his displeasure that the British had not thought to forewarn him of the armistice. If they had he could have discreetly manoeuvred his troops into a position from where they could swiftly encircle the Germans. As it was, Campioni had learned of the armistice from the wife of a German officer at the same time as Lieutenant-General Ulrich Kleemann, the competent commander of the German division on Rhodes. Kleemann had wasted no time in sending out mobile columns to occupy the island's three airfields at Marizza, Calato and Cattavia.

Jellicoe had been alarmed by the state of the Italian troops he had passed on his way to the governor's residence and he did not share Dobrski's optimism over Italian intentions. Campioni was jittery, the pressure of his situation weighing heavily on his shoulders, and his state of mind understandably not improved when Jellicoe admitted it would be six days at least before any major British invasion fleet came ashore.

Before retiring to bed for the night Admiral Campioni insisted that Jellicoe and his two companions change into civilian clothes and made it clear that he 'would not allow any British personnel to leave or arrive at Rhodes by seaplane'.[15]

The next day, 10 September, proved one of great frustration for Jellicoe as Campioni prevaricated in the face of the first skirmishes between German and Italian troops. Then, in the late afternoon, Jellicoe sensed a change in the atmosphere at the governor's residence and he managed to extract from Campioni's *aide-de-camp* a confession that the Italians were negotiating peace terms with the Germans.

Recognizing that he could serve no further purpose on Rhodes, Jellicoe left that night on-board an Italian Torpedo Armed Motorboat for the small island of Castelorizzo, 80 miles to the east. Accompanying him was Campioni's chief of staff, Colonel Fanetza, who had been sent by his superior to explain first-hand to the British the invidious predicament faced by the Italian forces on Rhodes. As a token of goodwill, Campioni had furnished Jellicoe with all the available intelligence on the minefields in the Aegean, as well as 'two bottles of Rhodes wine and an excellent picnic basket'.[16]

While Jellicoe was in Rhodes two SBS patrols, one each from M and S Squadrons, had left Athlit for Paphos in Cyprus. Once there they learned of the Italian armistice and received their orders. 'We are to go to Castelorizzo Island, destroy any Germans there, and organise the Italian defence,' wrote Milner-Barry in his diary.

> Councils of War followed, at which there was great argument as to the method of attack. The first plan was to land at midnight on the west end of the island, and march across to the port of Castelrosso [the capital of Castelorizzo], but to my relief, and largely as a result of my intervention, it was decided not to go in like a thief in the night, but to take the bolder course of sailing straight into the port.[17]

Castelorizzo is the most easterly of the Dodecanese Islands, lying just off the Vathi Peninsula on the Turkish mainland, and measuring 4 square miles. The port at Castelrosso is in the shape of an inverted horseshoe, and Milner-Barry found it 'rather a pretty little harbour with some attractive houses'. Less appealing, however, when the SBS came ashore on 10 September, were the local inhabitants there to

CASTELORIZZO

Freddy Crouch sits on a box at Castelrosso having just accidentally shot himself in the hand with a captured German Schmeisser. Duggie Pomford talks to the Sikh soldier on the left. (Courtesy of Angie English)

Castelrosso was an important stopping off point for the SBS on many of their operations in the Aegean, and a chance for them to unwind. (Courtesy of Angie English)

A Royal Navy officer poses with some locals on Castelorizzo. Though they were poor, the Greeks were also generous with food and drink. (Courtesy of the SBS Archive)

The SBS found the islanders, such as these ones on Castelorizzo, to be brave, resourceful and loyal allies in the fight against Germany. (Courtesy of Angie English) greet their liberators. 'They are desperately poor and look half starved,' wrote Milner-Barry, who acting on David Sutherland's orders despatched the M Squadron patrol to secure the wireless stations on the island while he and S Squadron stationed themselves in the port.[18]

The next morning Colonel Turnbull touched down at Castelorizzo in a seaplane to check that all was well, and not long after his departure Jellicoe and Colonel Fanetza arrived in their motorboat. Milner-Barry had his men line up along the wooden jetty to welcome their distinguished guests. 'It was as calm as a mill pond,' recalled Dick Holmes, who was standing next to Doug Wright. Jellicoe was first onto the jetty. Then came Colonel Fanetza, every inch the high-ranking Italian officer in his finest livery. 'Just as he went to step on to the jetty the boat moved and he went straight in the drink,' said Holmes. 'We all pissed ourselves laughing.' Doug Wright heaved the colonel from the water after what Jellicoe described in his report as his 'undiplomatic tumble'. He and his men strove to conceal their amusement but every squelching step of Fanetza's down the jetty was accompanied by the soft sound of strangled giggles.

Jellicoe didn't stay long on Castelorizzo. After breakfast and a quick consultation with Sutherland and Milner-Barry, he and the still damp Fanetza left for the island of Simi, north of Rhodes, where Colonel Turnbull had established his HQ. Not too long after they had left a signal was received from Admiral Campioni ordering the boat back to Castelorizzo but Jellicoe persuaded the vessel's skipper to ignore the request and continue towards Simi. Satisfied all was well, he lay down on deck for

The SBS found the island of Castelorizzo charming but its inhabitants desperately poor and undernourished. (Courtesy of the SBS Archive)

a sleep. When he woke they were sailing into the port of Castelrosso with the smirk this time on the face of Fanetza. It was his duty to obey his admiral's instructions, explained Fanetza, but the fact that the order had been given while Jellicoe was asleep led him to believe that it was an act of revenge on the Italian's part for his humiliation earlier that morning.

Jellicoe's reunion with Turnbull finally took place that evening when the colonel returned in the seaplane just as Colonel Fanetza departed to the relief of the British. Turnbull brought with him bad news: the Italian forces on Rhodes had surrendered to the Germans. No one was surprised by the news, nor particularly despondent, but as Milner-Barry wrote later: 'We certainly did not realise at the time that without the capture of Rhodes itself the remaining islands were virtually untenable.'[19]

Instead there was something of a party atmosphere on Castelorizzo during 12 September. The locals, poor and dishevelled as they were, were determined to celebrate after years of 'groaning under the Italian yoke'. A pig was roasted, toasts were made and for a few blissful hours everyone put the war to the backs of their minds.

The festivities didn't last long. That evening Colonel Turnbull received orders to send S Squadron to the island of Kos, and Jellicoe to Leros. Jellicoe's instructions were similar to those that he had been given before parachuting into Rhodes: namely to discover the intentions of the Italian commander, Admiral Mascheroa, and to reconnoitre a suitable dropping zone (DZ) for a possible parachute insertion.

The two parties left Castelorizzo together late in the evening of 12 September, Jellicoe in his Italian torpedo boat and S Squadron in a British motor launch. After a good night's sleep Jellicoe woke on the morning of the 13th 'with the sun just catching the hills of Kos as we rounded its southern promontory… Kos from the south appeared rocky and austere but as more and more coastline appeared trees, vineyards, houses and eventually the town began to show themselves'.[20] The people of Kos ran down to the harbour to greet the vessels and as S Squadron stepped ashore bunches of grapes were thrust into their hands and there was even the sound of popping champagne corks. Jellicoe sailed on to Leros, leaving behind Sutherland and his men.

Once in Leros Jellicoe was escorted to the residence of Admiral Mascheroa where he encountered a freshly laundered Colonel Fanetza, as 'disagreeable' as ever. The admiral was more amenable, however, and provided Jellicoe with all the intelligence required, which was duly sent to Middle East HQ Cairo. After a tour of Leros to locate a suitable DZ, Jellicoe attended a lavish lunch in his honour before departing by seaplane in the afternoon for Castelorizzo. 'I reported to Col. Turnbull, informed him of the not unsatisfactory situation on Leros and then slept very soundly for 14 hours,' wrote Jellicoe in his report.[21]

CHAPTER 6

THE GERMANS FIGHT BACK

For a small island measuring 25 miles by 6 miles, Kos is steeped in history. Romans, Greeks and Egyptians all enjoyed visiting Kos for its climate and culture. Separated from the Turkish mainland by a narrow channel no more than a mile wide, Kos boasts sandy beaches on its northern coastline. A sharp spine of limestone runs the length of the southern half of Kos, producing a series of steep cliffs overlooking sheltered coves and small bays.

The island was made a free city by the Roman Empire in AD 53 but 1,500 years later another empire, the Ottoman, claimed Kos as its own. The Ottomans' reign lasted until 1912 when Italy took control. Over the next 30 years the Italians constructed an airstrip at Antimachia, the only such facility in the Dodecanese other than the three airfields on Rhodes.

When S Squadron landed in Kos Town (in the far north of the island) on the morning of 13 September they were royally welcomed by the inhabitants with grapes and champagne. But soon Sutherland led his men inland to the flat area of Antimachia where they secured the airstrip from some of the 4,000-strong Italian garrison on Kos. That afternoon a flight of six South Africa Spitfires landed and in the evening 120 men of the 11th Parachute Battalion parachuted on to a drop zone marked out by the SBS. In the days that followed more British personnel arrived to strengthen the island's defences, including a unit from the RAF Regiment, the 9th

OPPOSITE
The SBS accept the surrender of the Italian garrison on the island of Samos in September 1943. (Courtesy of the SBS Archive)

87

Ian Lapraik, seen here in a kilt liberating Kos in 1944, led the SBS in a daring raid on the island of Simi in September 1943, installing himself as 'king'. (Author's Collection)

Indian Field Company and the 1st Battalion Durham Light Infantry.

No longer required on Kos, the SBS moved on to secure other islands in the Aegean in the second half of September, including Kalymnos, Samos, Chios, Simi and Patmos. This last island consisted of a small Italian garrison and when the British arrived to oversee their surrender they were in the throes of a farewell celebration. 'They'd roasted a goat, which we quickly usurped as we'd been living off tinned beef for weeks,' recalled Dick Holmes. As the SBS sat down with the Italians, signaller Viv Shohot eavesdropped on a conversation between a couple of soldiers. Shohot was a polyglot, born in Cairo to a British father and Egyptian mother, and he told Holmes what was being discussed. 'They were whispering about a safe,' said Holmes. 'Well, we soon got all the details and Duggie Pomford forced it open. Inside was a payroll in Lira for about 1,000 troops stationed on Leros. We liberated the lira and took it with us ... it became our kitty and we didn't draw pay for ages!'[1]

By the end of September the British controlled all of the Dodecanese Islands except for Rhodes. On Friday 1 October Walter Milner-Barry 'spent a peaceful day' in Samos including lunch with an SOE agent who also expressed his satisfaction

> '*The future looked bright... Too bright for us to take seriously the warning that an enemy convoy had been observed sailing SE from Naxos.*'
>
> David Sutherland

with the way events had unfolded in September. That evening the SBS left Samos in the hands of a battalion of the Royal West Kent Regiment and the next morning, Saturday 2 October, disembarked in Kalymnos. David Sutherland was waiting to greet Milner-Barry with the news that the island had been designated the HQ of Raiding Forces. The Long Range Desert Group (LRDG) had arrived from North Africa under the command of Lieutenant-Colonel Guy Prendergast and they and the SBS were billeted close together overlooking the town of Kalino.

On Saturday afternoon Milner-Barry, Prendergast and Sutherland set off for Leros to discuss with Colonel Turnbull future operations in the Aegean. British confidence was high and plans were afoot for a combined reconnaissance of Rhodes by the SBS and the LRDG ahead of an attack by a major assault force. 'The future looked bright,' wrote Sutherland. 'Too bright for us to take seriously the warning that an enemy convoy had been observed sailing SE from Naxos.' Sutherland, like everyone else, assumed the German convoy was transporting men and supplies to Rhodes and thought nothing more about it. After a consultation with Turnbull, Sutherland, Milner-Barry and George Jellicoe had a 'frugal fish supper' in a Greek restaurant on Leros and then returned to Kalymnos by speedboat. 'We went to sleep full of plans for the future,' recalled Sutherland.[2]

On 24 September Hitler had hosted a conference at his headquarters to discuss the situation in the Aegean. The information given to the Führer was bleak; with the exception of Rhodes the British controlled the Dodecanese and it was likely they would next seize possession of the Cyclades Islands further west. While some of the officers present advised Hitler to invade the Cyclades before the British had time to land on the islands, Grand Admiral Dönitz was of the opinion that Germany would be better advised to withdraw altogether from the Aegean – including Crete – and instead concentrate its forces in defending the Balkans Peninsula.

Hitler listened to all the advice and then announced his decision: Germany would not withdraw from the Aegean. Quite the opposite. It would seize back the Dodecanese from the British. 'Abandonment of the islands would create the most

Most of the Italians, as seen here at Samos, were only too happy to surrender to the SBS. (Courtesy of the SBS Archive)

Ray Jones, an artilleryman from Birmingham, was awarded a Military Medal for his part on the raid on Crete in July 1943. (Courtesy of Angie English)

unfavourable impression [among our Allies],' declared Hitler. 'To avoid such a blow to our prestige we may even have to accept the loss of our troops and material. The supply of the islands must be assured by the Air Force.'[3]

Kos was the first island the Germans would target, because of its airfield at Antimachia and the second one under construction. The Luftwaffe launched a series of heavy raids on the island in the second half of September, attacking not just the British positions but also the supply ships bringing more men and equipment to Kos. Meanwhile, Germany began its preparation for the invasion by drafting in the elite Brandenburg Division, its nearest equivalent to the Special Boat Squadron.

Two landings would be made by the German forces, one on sandy coastline in the north of Kos and the second close to Kos Town in the east. The time earmarked for Operation *Polar Bear* was the early hours of Sunday 3 October.

———

David Sutherland was woken at 0200 hours on the Sunday 'to find an enemy assault force disembarking on N coast of Cos [sic], midway between the town of Cos and Antimachia'.[4]

From his vantage point on Kalymnos, 8 miles to the north, Sutherland had a grandstand view of the invasion. So did Milner-Barry, who described the events in his diary: 'Morning began with a dawn para [troop] attack by the Jerries on Kos, followed up by a fleet of ships of all kinds bombarding the coast, and occasionally landing troops at different points: overhead continually aircraft.'[5]

A hastily arranged conference was held on Kalymnos, during which Prendergast suggested it might be an idea if Sutherland took S Squadron to Kos to reinforce the garrison. Understandably Sutherland did not think much of that proposal, commenting that 'it was doubtful whether we could have achieved anything by this means being so lightly armed'.[6]

Prendergast saw the sense in Sutherland's thinking and a second plan was agreed: Milner-Barry would land on the south coast of Kos at nightfall and find out what he could about the British defences. In addition Milner-Barry was instructed to try to establish an escape route from Kos to Kalymnos.

By the time Milner-Barry and his 13-strong patrol were put ashore on Kos at 0300 hours on 4 October the Germans were well on their way to securing the island. Pockets of British resistance held out but the majority of the defenders were dead, captured or on the run from the enemy.

The SBS didn't appreciate their role as garrison troops on the islands during the early autumn of 1943 because of the long periods of inactivity. (Courtesy of Angie English)

A group of RAF personnel were milling around on the beach. They briefed Milner-Barry as best they could about the progress of the invasion, including the news that the Germans were in possession of the airfield at Antimachia. Ordering the RAF men into the motor launch, Milner-Barry made arrangements with the vessel's skipper to rendezvous on the same beach in four days' time.

The SBS spent the day concealed in a wadi observing German air attacks on the remaining British strongpoints. There was desultory firing from Kos Town, noted Milner-Barry, but the only major incident of note was the disappearance of Private Ronald Watler during his stint as a sentry.

Throughout the day an assortment of military waifs and strays were rounded up by the SBS and brought into the wadi. Most were British but in late afternoon 'parties of near hysterical Italians' began arriving as the Germans moved across the plains driving them towards the sea. At 1700 hours Milner-Barry ordered his signaller to radio Kalymnos and request a ship to come and collect the survivors. But the radio wouldn't work and so, as the Germans began mortaring the wadi, 'a nightmare scramble over the hills began' as the SBS led the rabble away from the enemy but also away from the rendezvous beach. 'I thought we must be caught,' Milner-Barry confided to his diary. 'But at that moment we found some half-built rafts which the Eyeties had abandoned.'[7] It was decided to patch up the rafts and use them to escape to the Turkish mainland.

None of the stragglers, their morale already low after 24 hours of bombardment, wished to take a chance on the rafts so at 2100 hours Milner-Barry and his patrol pushed off from Kos towards the nearest stretch of Turkish coastline 5 miles to the south-east. The rafts went well initially and spirits soared among the men, in the hope that they would soon be in sight of the Turkish coast. But after a couple of hours the rafts began to sink lower in the water and despite the vigorous paddling of Milner-Barry and his men they were making little progress towards Turkey. After three hours the rafts were no longer seaworthy and the soldiers had no choice but to swim back to Kos.

They staggered ashore on the same stretch of beach from which they had struck out several hours earlier, but to the relief of Milner-Barry there was neither Italian nor German in sight. 'We had no difficulty in finding a large cave, practically on shore, which at least provided shelter, so we could strip off our wet clothes and lie down concealed,' recalled Milner-Barry. One of the SBS men had swum naked back to Kos, discarding everything including his boots. As he sat shivering in the caves his comrades, once they had laughed at his embarrassment, constructed 'a girdle made out of cut up Mae Wests'. It was the only time that night that the men managed to raise a smile. 'It was difficult to maintain morale,' admitted Milner-

Barry, on account of their parlous situation. They had no weapons, many were without boots, and they were cold, exhausted and hungry. All they had for food was one iron ration each, consisting of a hard packet of chocolate and beef essence.

The men got their first break not long after dawn on 5 October when Milner-Barry spotted a local shepherd with his flock. With a combination of hand signals and schoolboy Greek, he 'was able to make him understand our predicament'. At dusk the shepherd returned with lumps of bread and cheese, as well as information about the whereabouts of other British soldiers. That night Milner-Barry led a patrol into the surrounding countryside and rounded up a number of disorientated British soldiers, most of whom were in fact RAF personnel from Antimachia. The following night Milner-Barry and two of his men ventured out again inland, this time returning to their cave with around 50 men, including a number of soldiers from the Durham Light Infantry and eight Italians.

On the night of 7/8 October the motor launch returned to the beach and evacuated everyone except Milner-Barry and two of his men, Lance-Corporal

This soldier wears the hooded jacket which, to one war correspondent, made the SBS seem like 'a band of Robin Hood's merry men'. (Courtesy of Angie English)

Watson and Private Geddes. The pair volunteered to remain on Kos with their officer for a further five days in the hope of rescuing more stragglers. 'I was rather chagrined there hadn't been more volunteers,' reflected Milner-Barry. 'But these two, though among the smallest, had more guts than the bigger chaps.'

It was cold at night on Kos and the three commandos were dressed only in shorts, grey shirt, and khaki stockings, 'so we agreed a roster of lying on the ground side by side, taking it in turns to be the one in the middle for warmth'. Milner-Barry had with him a paperback edition of Thomas Hardy's novel *Jude the Obscure* which proved invaluable to while away the hours, as did Watson's deck of cards.

The next day the shepherd reappeared with more food and the news that a large number of British soldiers were hiding further up the coast, so that night Milner-Barry and his two men went in search of them. The soldiers they were hunting were approximately 60 men from the 1st Battalion Durham Light Infantry, together with some personnel from the RAF regiment and the odd Royal Engineer. They had spent the last week in the hills after the Germans had overrun the airfield at Antimachia, and were busy building a raft to escape to Turkey when Milner-Barry arrived at their cave.

'The SBS Captain informed the group that a small naval craft would arrive at 0200hrs on the 13th October 1943 to attempt a rescue,' recalled one of the infantryman. '[But] it was unlikely that there would be room for all of the men. However that decision would be made by the Skipper of the craft and not by Barry.'[8]

The launch duly reappeared on 13 October and Milner-Barry was the last man to leave the beach having first ensured everyone was on board. As they sailed to Bodrum in Turkey, Milner-Barry sent a signal, reporting the successful conclusion of his mission. Only then did he sit back and relax, and only then did the tension of the past ten days catch up with him. He suddenly felt 'feverish and ill' and the sores on his body that he had accumulated over the past ten days now began to hurt.

It did not much matter at that moment to Milner-Barry that he had been responsible for the evacuation from Kos of 16 officers and 74 other ranks; all he desired was a warm bed. His wish was realised on 16 October when he was flown in Colonel Turnbull's seaplane to Alexandra. There he was admitted to the 64th General Hospital. 'The treatment prescribed was soaking in saline baths and vitamin pills,' he wrote in his diary. 'The food was first rate and I had two helpings of meat for dinner.' To complete his regeneration, Milner-Barry asked for a razor 'to get rid of my beard, now ten days old and of a brindled hue, mixed blood, ginger and grey … a revolting aspect!'

Rodney Hancock, better known as 'Hancock', was the SBS's unofficial war artist-cum-photographer who took many of the photographs in this book. (Courtesy of the SBS Archive)

Unbeknown to Milner-Barry, however, there was one SBS man still on Kos. Private Ronald Watler had vanished on 4 October as he stood guard on the rim of the wadi in which his comrades were concealed. As Milner-Barry had surmised, Watler had been captured after a patrol of Germans ran into him. Rather than risk leading the enemy to the rest of the SBS patrol, Watler had drawn them away from the wadi and across the plains until he was eventually run down and caught. Presuming Watler was just another of the demoralised defenders of Kos, the Germans imprisoned him with numerous other British soldiers and airmen in the island's medieval castle.

On the night of 20 October Watler and a corporal from the Royal Corps of Signals, 'made a rope from electric wire and slipped over the wall' of the castle. Their freedom lasted barely five hours before they were recaptured at first light and returned to the castle. A week later the pair did the same thing, and this time eluded their pursuers. For several days they lived in caves, relying as Milner-Barry had on the kindness and boldness of locals. Eventually one of them directed Watler and his comrade to an old but seaworthy boat, and several hours later they landed at Bodrum on the Turkish coast.

CHAPTER 7

DEFEAT IN THE DODECANESE

The Germans found it hard to believe how easy it had been to take Kos. The expected British resistance had failed to materialise, which emboldened the German High Command. 'Why stop at Kos?' they asked themselves. On 6 October their strategy in the Dodecanese changed from defensive to offensive, and a list of other islands to invade was drawn up, including Chios, Leros and Samos.

Additional shipping would be required to transport soldiers to these islands, and radio stations would need to be installed on Naxos and Simi to facilitate the invasions. What the Germans did not know, however, was that the SBS had beaten them to Simi and were in no mood to relinquish their hold on the island.

Ian Lapraik had led 26 men of M Squadron onto Simi on 17 September, installing himself as 'king' of the island and improving the island's defences by the mounting of a 20mm Breda cannon on a hillside next to an abandoned school. There was a 140-strong Italian garrison on Simi who had done little to endear themselves to the local population during their lengthy occupation. The Greeks wanted their blood, but Lapraik wouldn't let them take it. 'I let them know that wrongs would be righted in due course, that there would be equity for all,' he said. 'But that for the moment the efficient progress of the war rose above all other considerations.'[1]

Lapraik despatched patrols to neighbouring islands to gather intelligence and in the first week of October he himself sailed to Kos on a reconnaissance mission. He did not linger on the island, arriving not long after the first Germans had invaded and departing soon after. En route back to Simi Lapraik bore down on a French sloop carrying 40 RAF personnel under the command of the squadron doctor, Flight-Lieutenant Robert 'Hank' Ferris. The men were ground crew from No.74 Squadron who had set sail from Haifa for Kos on 30 September.

Like it or not, these men were soon on their way to Simi to bolster the island's defences. 'The garrison consisted of approximately 30 Special Boat Squadron men and 100 Italians,' recalled Ferris. 'Our detachment arrived as a welcome reinforcement to this inadequate force, and after a quick meal the men were detailed to duty at the various places. Sick quarters was established in a house near General Headquarters.'[2]

Lapraik was delighted with his reinforcements, so much so that he issued an Order of the Day for their benefit:

For the benefit of the RAF. As you have recently arrived in this area you are naturally unaware of the military situation in general, and in the island in particular, and consequently your actions seem peculiar under the circumstances. Our situation may be compared with that of Singapore when the Japs were only a short distance away and advancing rapidly, i.e. owing to our great strategic importance there is no doubt whatsoever that we shall be attacked. It is merely a question of whether it is tomorrow, or the next day or the one after. Let there be no doubt about it, they will come; therefore we must be prepared. Consequently, it is essential that everyone be absolutely on their toes 24 hours a day. When the guard is called out it will be out in seconds not minutes as was the case last night. When ordered to stand to they will be downstairs and in the bushes like bats out of hell. Everyone must be absolutely on the job all the time no matter what task he is given. We are all doing strange jobs at the moment. We weren't trained as island defenders any more than you were but we have to carry out the task all the same. When you realise that the next island to this, Kos, has been attacked, and almost wound up by the Germans we can understand the gravity of our position so for God's sake let's get our fingers out and get weaving and we'll show these bastards what we are capable of ... lastly, when you hear yourselves referred to as 'the bloody RAF' it is no more derogatory than No. 1 Patrol being referred to as 'that bloody patrol of [Lieutenant Charles] Bimrose's' or No. 4 Patrol being 'those bloody gunners'. So far however you have worked hard and well without moaning so keep it up, but remember – be quick on the job and keep on your toes because if you don't you've bloody had it, believe me.

The Germans came at dawn on 7 October, around 40 soldiers landing at Pedi Bay in the north-east of Simi in two local fishing boats called caiques and a schooner. According to whose account one believes, the Germans either made it ashore unobserved or were allowed to land by the RAF men manning the Breda Cannon and the Bren gun position on the hillside who mistook them for their own men.

> *'Let there be no doubt about it, they will come; therefore we must be prepared.'*
>
> Ian Lapraik

Rodney Hancock, the SBS's unofficial war artist-cum-photographer, recalled that when Andy Lassen woke at first light he looked down at the bay and spotted the boats. 'Who the hell are they?' he roared. To which the aircrew replied: 'Well, they've just sort of landed.'[3] The RAF's version, while admitting that the man operating the Breda cannon was Flight Sergeant Charlie Schofield, 'who wore spectacles on account of short sight',[4] insisted that the enemy were engaged the moment they hove into view. Nonetheless the 40-strong German landing party managed to disembark and seek cover inland, some penetrating as far as the outskirts of Simi town.* While the SBS went off to deal with these Germans, Schofield continued to pour a torrent of fire onto the more timorous enemy, keeping them pinned down just off the beach. Then three Stukas appeared and came in low on a bombing run.

Schofield laughed as the bombs were released, reassuring his comrades that the angle of approach was too tight for the aircraft and that they were perfectly safe because of their position high up in the hills. By now the vibration of the cannon had shattered Schofield's spectacles and the sights had fallen off the overheated weapon. But his eye, short sighted or not, was in and the armourer who had never before experienced a pitched battle, stuck to his gun and displayed exemplary courage that was later rewarded with a Military Medal.

Further down the hillside Lassen was exhibiting similar bravery, which would in due course be recognized with a second bar to his Military Cross. In the days preceding the German landing on Simi, the Dane had been suffering from dysentery and from a nasty petrol burn to his leg. 'Anyone else would have been shipped back,' reflected Hancock, who was one of the men in Lassen's patrol.[5] Also present was Sean O'Reilly, the 42-year-old former Irish Guardsman, who on Simi got his first experience of Lassen's uncanny ability to sniff out the enemy. 'He suddenly stopped by a wall and, sure enough, two Germans were sitting behind it,' recalled O'Reilly. 'We fired over their heads and they surrendered.'[6]

---

* Some British accounts have the invasion party numbering 100 but German documents state that only 40 men made the initial foray onto Simi.

The Germans enter Simi town in October after Ian Lapraik and M Squadron had withdrawn. (Courtesy of John Robertson)

As the SBS entered the narrow streets of Simi Town they came under heavy fire from a German machine-gun position located on a ridge overlooking the village. Lieutenant Bimrose led his patrol forward, the men playing hide and seek with the enemy gunner between the whitewashed houses. Then they were ambushed. A grenade exploded at the feet of William Morrison, one of the Seaforth Highlanders recruited by Fitzroy Maclean, and Bimrose's sergeant was seriously wounded by a burst of small-arms fire. Bimrose was shot in the arm. For a moment he faltered and then, enflamed by the ambush, he charged the enemy 'and personally killed 2 and wounded one'.[7]

Bimrose withdrew his patrol in good order (minus the dead Morrison) and briefed Lassen on the German defences. A short while later, as the citation for his third Military Cross stated, Lassen 'led the Italian counterattack which finally drove the Germans back to their caiques with the loss of sixteen killed, thirty-five wounded and seven prisoners as against our loss of one killed and one wounded'.[8]

Though the citation exaggerated the number of German casualties, there was nothing inaccurate in the description of the German withdrawal in mid-afternoon. But even then the day had yet to run its course for the Germans. On seeing the enemy withdraw to the beach, Lapraik ordered one of the SBS's caiques to set sail from Simi Harbour and drive the fleeing Germans within range of the Bren guns positioned on the hillside. This they gleefully did, and the exposed decks of the three German vessels were raked by machine-gun fire as they rounded the tip of Pedi Bay.

General Ulrich Kleemann, commander of German forces in the Aegean, reacted with fury when he heard of the failed landing on Simi. The next morning at 0800 hours a pair of Stuka dive-bombers screamed out of the sky, dropping their cargo of explosives on Simi Town. These air assaults continued at two-hourly intervals for the rest of the day, inflicting death and destruction on British and Italians and on Greek civilians.

Another SBS soldier, Lance-Corporal Robert McKendrick, was killed in the morning and two dozen civilians were also left dead in the indiscriminate raids. Then in the early afternoon Lapraik's headquarters received a direct hit which also demolished Ferris's makeshift hospital. The doctor crawled out of the wreckage, unscathed other than with a bad wound to his wrist, to be told that though Lapraik was unharmed two SBS were wounded and trapped underneath a pile of rubble.

The pair were Tom Bishop and Sydney Greaves, the latter one of the men awarded the Military Medal three months earlier for his part in the raid on Crete. Greaves was pinned down by a weight of debris on his stomach while Bishop's foot was trapped in the wreckage of the headquarters. The dilemma facing the rescuers was that the rubble was desperately unstable and any attempt to rescue one of the men would almost certainly result in the other dying in a secondary collapse of debris. Ferris, Sergeant Whittle and Lapraik discussed the men's predicament with Porter Jarrell, the SBS medical orderly.

Jarrell was the Canadian-born son of an American physicist. An arts graduate from the University of Middlebury in Vermont, Jarrell had quit his job writing for a New York magazine in early 1942 to join the war effort, though as a conscientious objector he refused to take up arms. Consequently he was posted as a medic to Unit 16 of the American Field Service. Having served with distinction in North Africa, Jarrell was accepted into the SBS in 1943, his new comrades secretly proud of the fact that they had a 'Yank' in the squadron. Jarrell was called 'Joe' (short for GI Joe) and at Athlit he had tried unsuccessfully to convert the men from rugby to American football.

The outcome of the discussion was an acceptance that only one course of action remained: if Bishop agreed to the amputation of his trapped foot, he could be dragged clear and then there was a slight chance that Sergeant Whittle, a pre-war miner, might be able to prop up the wreckage and extricate Greaves. When the proposal was put to Bishop he agreed without hesitation.

What was not disclosed to Bishop was that most of Ferris's medical tools had been lost in the air attack. All he had for the operation was a pair of scissors, a pair of artery forceps, a scalpel and a small saw. In addition Ferris was compelled to carry out the amputation in the most trying of conditions, suspended upside down by his feet into a small chamber at the bottom of which lay Bishop.

Not long into the operation the Stukas returned but Ferris continued his work, successfully amputating Bishop's foot so that he could be brought to the surface. As Bishop was given intravenous blood plasma, frantic work began to retrieve Greaves from beneath the shattered headquarters. Sergeant Whittle burrowed down to his comrade but when he returned to the surface it was to report that Greaves was dead. A few minutes later Bishop died from a combination of shock and bomb blast.

Ferris was subsequently awarded the Military Cross for his 'coolness and courage' in trying to rescue the SBS soldiers. Jarrell was decorated with the George Medal, the citation praising the way he 'entirely disregarded personal risk, crawling along perilous tunnels through the debris to administer morphia, feed and cheer the trapped men'.[9] Many years later Ferris, who after the war opened a doctor's surgery in the Yorkshire Dales, reflected on the incident on Simi: 'They hadn't a hope in hell, but we thought that we had to try something, and operating was the only thing left.'[10]

Lapraik finally withdrew from Simi on 12 October after several more days of Stuka attacks. There was nothing more to be gained from remaining on the island, other than the continued destruction of Greek homes.

———————

While the SBS had been engaged in bitter fighting on Simi, Prime Minister Churchill had been locked in a bitter argument with President Franklin Roosevelt. The American president was being begged by the British leader to help in the fight to defend the Aegean from the Germans. 'I have never wished to send an army into the Balkans,' stressed Churchill in a cable sent on 7 October to the White House. 'But only by agents, supplies and commandos to stimulate the intense guerrilla movement prevailing there.'[11]

But the Americans did not trust Churchill, believing him eager to embark on a Balkan adventure as he had done in World War I with such disastrous consequences. Instead they wished to concentrate solely on maintaining pressure on Italy ahead of the planned invasion of France the following year. Roosevelt replied to Churchill's cable with one of his own, stating: 'It is my opinion that no division of forces or equipment should prejudice 'Overlord' [the codename for the invasion of France] as planned. The American Chiefs of Staff agree.'[12]

Churchill tried again on 8 October, reiterating to Roosevelt the importance of the Balkans theatre particularly with the Soviet forces beginning to threaten the region. But it was to no avail; the Americans saw no strategic importance in the Aegean and as a consequence the British were on their own in the Dodecanese.

By the time Lapraik had abandoned Simi the British had given up any pretence that their strategy in the Aegean was anything but defensive. The hopes they had retained a few days earlier of retaking Kos vanished and instead the focus switched to reinforcing the existing garrisons on Leros and Samos.

———————

Watching the invasion of Kos from his vantage point on the neighbouring island of Kalymnos, David Sutherland received a message to withdraw S Squadron to Leros on the morning of 4 October. They sailed north at dusk, disembarking at the deep water port of Lakki (known to the Italians as Porto Lago) on the south-west coast of the island, and the next day Sutherland had his first opportunity to take stock of his new surroundings. 'Leros is 8 miles long and 4 wide with two narrow mile-long beaches in the middle,' he wrote. 'There are three barren, hilly features, each about 1,000 feet high. In the south-west corner is the all-weather harbour Porto Lago Bay.' Sutherland considered that the island resembled in shape 'a large cowpat trodden on by two feet!'[13] Owing to its rocky and undulating terrain Leros had no airfield, but what the Italians had installed in their 31 years of occupation was a series of formidable coastal batteries overlooking the island's six bays.

At 0900 hours on 5 October a squadron of Stukas attacked Leros at the moment Sutherland was discussing the island's defences with Captain Thomas Belcher of 30 Commando. Sutherland recalled the terrifying scream of the diving aircraft and glimpsed 'a brave man standing up firing a machine gun'.[14] Then his world exploded. The bomb that fell in Porto Lago landed 50 yards from Sutherland, leaving him temporarily deaf, badly shaken and coated in a ghostly white dust. But he was alive, unlike Belcher, two of his commandos and Sergeant Ernest Hawkes of the Special Boat Squadron.

Leros under aerial attack from the Luftwaffe. Even Andy Lassen was scared of Stuka dive-bombers. (Courtesy of the SBS Archive)

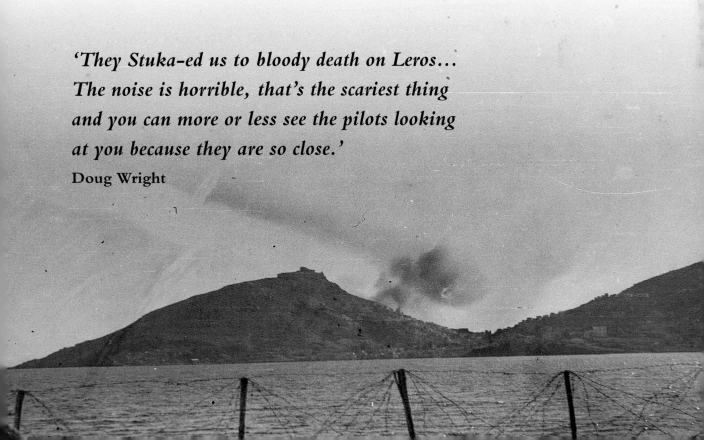

'They Stuka-ed us to bloody death on Leros...
The noise is horrible, that's the scariest thing
and you can more or less see the pilots looking
at you because they are so close.'
Doug Wright

GERMAN REINFORCEMENT OF LEROS

On 13 November the Germans attempted an airborne reinforcement of Leros, as seen here in this dramatic series of photos taken by the SBS.

As the Junkers 52 came in low over Alinda Bay they came under fire from British Bofors guns.

Three Junkers were shot down, and dozens of paratroopers drowned in the Bay.

The ones that dropped onto land came under heavy ground fire.

It was estimated that of 200 paratroopers dropped on Leros on 13 November, only 20 went into action, the rest drowning or dying on the end of their parachutes as they floated to earth. (Images courtesy of Lynne Perrin)

Sutherland was evacuated that evening to the nearby island of Samos but his men remained to endure sporadic Stuka attacks for the rest of the month. 'They Stuka-ed us to bloody death on Leros,' remembered Doug Wright. 'They're terrible things and there's nothing we can do about it. The noise is horrible, that's the scariest thing and you can more or less see the pilots looking at you because they are so close.'[15]

Also on Leros throughout October was Dick Holmes, one of the 12 SBS men tasked with manning the roadblock on the Partini–Alindo Road. It was tedious work, not the sort of soldiering for men of their training, but there were moments of light relief. 'The Germans dropped leaflets on us telling us what would happen if they caught us,' remembered Holmes. 'We used them to wipe our arse.'[16]

Hank Hancock passed the time on Leros by painting a series of watercolours of the island. He had an eye for the landscape, capturing the highlands and dramatic contours of Leros, and the sumptuous sunsets. And as Hancock painted he noted where the scrub was thickest and the boulders largest, so that when the Germans came he and his comrades would be best placed to repel the invaders.

At the start of November Leros was divided into three defensive zones – north, south and central – with the 4th Royal East Kent (The Buffs), 2nd Royal Irish Fusiliers and 1st King's Own Royal Regiment responsible for the sectors.

This force was augmented by Sappers, Ordnance Corps and men of the Long Range Desert Group, as well as the existing Italian garrison. In overall command of the island's defence was Brigadier Robert Tilney, whose fortress HQ 'consisted of a single twisting tunnel blasted right through the peak of Meraviglia', at approximately 650 feet the highest mountain on Leros.[17] Tilney had arrived on Leros breathing fire and brimstone, declaring to the men under his command that: 'No enemy shall set foot in this island unless to be a prisoner of war.'[18] Tilney's plan was to ensure that the Germans could not establish a beachhead but in doing so he deployed his men along too wide a front. Tilney held the SBS in reserve as a rapid reaction force in the unlikely event that the Germans would risk dropping airborne troops onto the island's craggy surface.

Recovered from the wounds caused in the Stuka attack, Sutherland rejoined his men on Leros and prepared for the inevitable invasion. 'Messages were continually coming in warning us of this impending onslaught,' he recalled. 'Consequently tension was high, nerves strained and concentration, in general, difficult.'[19]

After a lull in air raids, the Luftwaffe resumed their bombing runs on Leros in the first week of November with the Italian coastal defences receiving the brunt of the attacks. By 11 November some 30 of the 58 anti-aircraft batteries had been destroyed. On that day Sutherland noted that the Luftwaffe raids were particularly heavy and it was evident that the invasion was imminent.

George Jellicoe was now in command of the 50-strong SBS force on Leros and he could see clearly the hopelessness of the situation. With this in mind he sent Andy Lassen and some of his most reliable men – among them Jack Nicholson, Doug Wright, Dick Holmes and Porter Jarrell – north to the island of Samos. A steady stream of wounded British soldiers had been evacuated to Samos and Lassen's mission was to transport them onto the Turkish mainland just a mile off the island.

Sutherland, meanwhile, departed Leros on the night of 11 November bound for Turkey with orders to contact Lieutenant-Commander Croxton of the Royal Navy and 'make arrangements for the Leros evacuation should it be necessary'.[20]

His patrol sailed from Leros at 2300 hours in a wooden caique, cruising south-east at a leisurely 4 knots. As they passed the island of Kalymnos, Sutherland spotted through the blackness the outline of other vessels heading in the opposite direction. It was the first wave of a German seaborne assault group that had sailed from Kos Town a little before midnight. Their destination was Leros.

This photo was taken from the body of a dead German, perhaps showing a brother (in the Navy) and mother. (Courtesy of Lynne Perrin)

The first wave of the German invasion fleet – 800 troops in total – landed in the north-east of Leros in the early hours of 12 November. They were soon ashore and heading south where the objective was to link up with the second wave who had landed at Alinda Bay. The third blow planned by the Germans was an airborne drop by a battalion of paratroopers from the Brandenburg Division.

The parachute drop was put back several hours because of delays in landing the seaborne troops, a hitch that turned out well for the invaders. Having been engaged in heavy fighting throughout the day, the British defenders appeared to be beating off the German invasion. Then at 1300 hours the first Ju52 transport aircraft appeared overhead. War correspondent L. Marshland Gander described the effect the sight had on him and soldiers around: 'The idea that the Germans would use Paras was so remote from my thoughts that the happenings of the next few minutes had a supremely theatrical and dreamlike quality which almost obliterated the breath-taking surprise.'[21]

Marshland Gander watched in awe as 'twelve or fifteen troop carriers were flying at a height of about 300 feet in line astern across the island's narrow waist between Alinda and Gurna Bays'. In fact there were 40 transport carriers in total, inside which 470 Brandenburgers under the command of Hauptmann Martin Kühne prepared to jump on to Leros. Marshland Gander recalled:

> As I watched fascinated something white appeared under the fuselage of the leading machine… It bellied out into a great mushroom beneath which the dark figure of the parachutist looked absurdly small and helpless … the first man who was probably the group leader had touched ground before the machine gunners on the sides of Meraviglia had recovered from the paralyzing shock of surprise.'[22]

When they had regained their wits the British poured a withering fire into the brave paratroopers jumping from the low-flying aircraft. German casualty figures estimated that 200 were dead before they hit the ground while a further 100 sustained injuries as they fell on to the treacherous slopes of Leros. Nonetheless around 200 airborne troops landed unscathed, 'some 500 to 700 yards away on the slopes on the other side of the road', as George Jellicoe recalled in his operational report.[23]

For ten minutes the two elite units exchanged fire amid the scrubland and boulders. One officer of the Greek Sacred Squadron fighting alongside the SBS was wounded in the leg but other than that there were no casualties. Jellicoe began issuing orders as he spotted the paratroopers attempting to move off towards their objectives. Captain Desmond Holt was instructed to take his patrol towards Navy House, a villa on the western shore of Alinda Bay occupied by the Royal Navy, 'to engage the parachutists', and Captain Bill Blyth was ordered to establish a six-man fireteam on a nearby hillside.[24] Jellicoe then instructed his three machine-gun teams nests to pull back. As they did so Corporal George Walshaw – at 37 one of the oldest men in the squadron – was shot dead by a German sniper.

At dusk on 12 November Blyth reported to Jellicoe at a pre-arranged rendezvous. Holt's patrol, however, appeared without their officer who had been last seen 'advancing by himself in the vicinity of Navy House engaging the parachutists'.[25]* Jellicoe sent out patrols throughout the night and the news brought to him was not

---

* Holt is buried in the Leros war cemetery but Walshaw's body was unaccountably lost, although on 15 November Jellicoe reported his burial, even giving a map reference in his report. Walshaw is commemorated on the Athens Memorial.

good: the enemy had seized an important ridgeline on Leros's narrow waist, in effect severing the British defences in two so that the troops in the north were cut off from the troops to the south.

Early the next morning, 13 November, the Germans dropped more paratroopers onto the island, only this time the British were waiting. Marshland Gander watched as one flaming aircraft fell out of the sky, 'a horrifying spectacle with one solitary parachutist visible dragging behind it, the doll-like figure still attached'. Another crippled Ju52 disgorged its cargo too early and the men drowned in Alinda Bay 'where the silken chutes lingered for a short time like water lilies'.[26]

Jellicoe counted four aircraft brought down and of the 150 or so paratroopers dropped into a 40 mph wind close to Navy House, 'very few of them were able to free themselves from their harness before being dragged over walls, etc.'[27] So negligible had the impact of the German airborne reinforcements been that Jellicoe and his men spent the rest of the day 'resting in the wadi'.

At 0200 hours on 14 November the British launched a counter-attack against the ridgeline occupied by the paratroopers. It failed, and the SBS and the LRDG were then ordered to prevent the Germans pushing north from the ridge. Heavy fighting marked the 15th, day four of the invasion, and the Wehrmacht war diary was pessimistic as to the chances of success, noting: 'The fighting is confused and information scarce, and changes in control by the enemy results in a confused crisis.'[28]

In Turkey, the information relayed to David Sutherland concerning the defence of Leros 'was good … it appeared that even on the 15th the situation was in hand, in spite of the terrific air bombardment'.[29]

It was German air superiority that proved decisive on 16 November. Brigadier Tilney decided to abandon his fortress headquarters and at 0830 hours he sent an uncoded signal to that effect. Jellicoe received it, and so did the Germans. When the

Following the fighting for Leros, this photograph, likely showing the sweetheart of a dead German paratrooper, fell into the hands of the SBS. (Courtesy of Lynne Perrin)

CHAPTER 8

NEW RECRUITS
FOR A NEW YEAR

W alter Milner–Barry had rather enjoyed his autumn. Having recovered from his exertions on Kos, the 39-year-old captain finished his recuperation in Cairo passing one 'gloriously idle day' after another. At the Gezira Sporting Club he watched an excellent game of rugby between a New Zealand Army XV and a team from the South African forces. There were also concerts, dinner parties and agreeable evenings in the bar of the Shepheard's Hotel. It all came to an end on 10 November when Milner-Barry arrived back at HQ Raiding Forces in Azzib to learn that he was in charge of training 37 new recruits to the squadron.

He also discovered the identity of L Squadron's new commander – Major Ian Patterson, a 29-year-old from London who had first encountered the SBS several weeks earlier. On that occasion he had been second-in-command of the 11th Parachute Battalion as they parachuted into Kos on a drop zone marked out by the SBS. Following the fall of Kos the battalion had been earmarked for a return to the UK, a prospect so appalling to Patterson that he sought out Jellicoe in the hope that he might have a vacancy. Jellicoe did, as it happened, following L Squadron's ill-fated foray into Sardinia. Patterson replied that he was hoping for something a little bit more in the way of command than a squadron. 'I'm not sure that would suit me,' he informed Jellicoe. 'I'm rather fond of having my own way, you know.' Jellicoe shrugged. 'You can have it as much as you like,' he said. 'If I don't like you, you'll go.'[1]

Patterson arrived at Azzib in October with neither officers nor men to command. He spent the next few weeks scouring the infantry reinforcement training depots of the Middle East until he had his full complement. By the time Milner-Barry returned to Azzib L Squadron were undergoing the same rigorous training that their predecessors had experienced seven months earlier.

The recruits he was to train, however, were not infantrymen but 37 Royal Marines who had volunteered for the SBS. 'They seemed to be a cheerful lot of chaps and goodish specimens physically,' wrote Milner-Barry in his diary. 'They also appeared almost too well disciplined, at the moment, for SBS troopers.'[2]

Milner-Barry decided he would leave L Squadron training in Azzib and take his force of Marines to Athlit, where the squadron had been based in the spring. Together with Sergeant Pat Scully, fully recovered from his captivity in Sardinia, Milner-Barry established a new camp by the sea and on 13 November he was able to note in his diary: 'Rather a busy morning. Marines on map reading and shooting again and in the afternoon, basketball.'[3]

One of the Marines being put through his paces at Athlit was Ken Smith, a 21-year-old from Portsmouth who had previously served as a gunner on HMS *Penelope* during the invasion of Sicily. It was his sergeant-major, aware that Smith was after a bit more adventure, who alerted him to the SBS recruitment drive in the autumn of 1943. Smith put his name forward and was called for an initial interview with an unnamed SBS officer. 'I was asked if I could swim two miles and if I could speak a foreign language,' Smith recalled. 'I could swim long distances and I'd picked up little bits of French in Algiers. He asked me several other questions.'[4]

Smith was then recalled for a second interview, this time with Major Jellicoe in Alexandria. 'He asked me what school I went to – he knew Portsmouth apparently – and who the headmaster was,' remembered Smith. 'I was one of about 20 who got picked from a few hundred. We didn't know what the SBS was, it was just another Special Service Unit.'

Smith and the other Marines who had passed selection were ordered to report to Cairo, whereupon they were met by Sergeant Pat Scully and another SBS NCO. 'These sergeants found it comical that we marines had so much kit,' said Smith. Scully explained to the Marines that they had one lorry waiting to transport them from Haifa to Athlit so it might be an idea to ditch most of their kit on the train journey north.

The Marines did as advised, flinging most of their kit from the windows into the grateful arms of local children whose curiosity was always aroused by the sight of a train. 'It was comical seeing these Arab kids running around with this marine kit,' recalled Smith. 'By the time we got to Haifa we had our toothbrush, underwear and rifle.'

From Haifa Smith and the Marines were transported in the SBS's solitary truck to Azzib and from there to Athlit where they slept under canvas. The Marines were

Dick Holmes takes the rare opportunity to relax with a book. (Courtesy of Angie English)

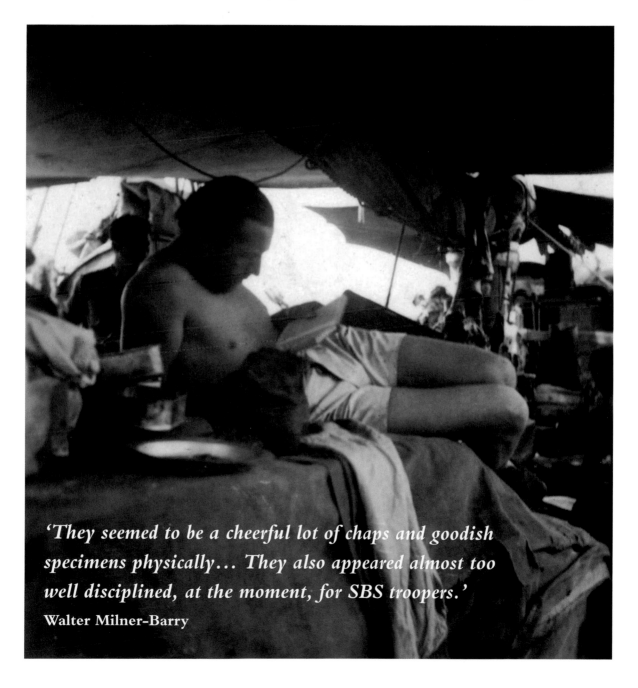

'They seemed to be a cheerful lot of chaps and goodish specimens physically... They also appeared almost too well disciplined, at the moment, for SBS troopers.'
Walter Milner-Barry

A rather assorted group of SBS men and Greek locals find some shade in which to take a break. (Courtesy of Angie English)

all fit, far fitter than the infantrymen recruited by Patterson into L Squadron, but nonetheless the training was tough. 'Every morning we were swimming, [then] forced marches with heavy loads, shooting, map reading, very concentrated and everything you can think of,' recalled Smith. The training culminated with the infamous 45-mile march from Athlit to the shores of Lake Tiberias. 'I was on my hands and knees at the end, crawling to Tiberias in the dark,' said Smith. 'I was so determined to make the unit, and I eventually did.'

As well as the Marines the SBS welcomed two new officers at the end of 1943, a couple of men who came from suitably unconventional backgrounds. Before the war Lieutenant John Lodwick had been a journalist, but craving more adventure he enlisted in the French Foreign Legion and was captured in 1940 during the fall of France. A German prison camp failed to hold his restless spirit and Lodwick escaped to Spain. Further escapades ensued with the SOE before the 27-year-old officer wound up in the SBS.

Lieutenant Jimmy Lees had a military father – Colonel Sir John Lees, a decorated veteran of the Great War – and a maverick mother, who had become an object of embarrassment by the time Lees joined the SBS. Lady Madeline Lees and her husband together with their seven children lived in a large manor house in Dorset which, during the First World War, had been used as a hospital for wounded soldiers. It was here, with Madeline serving as a nurse, that she became a peace activist.

Described as possessing an 'attractive eccentric dynamism', Lady Lees became the long-time lover of Sir Francis Younghusband, the famous explorer turned spiritualist. By 1941 they were publishing pamphlets preaching the virtues of free love and organizing Peace Conferences around the country.

The activities of Lady Lees must have made for some interesting conversations in the officers' mess which, at Athlit, was shared with the sergeants on Milner-Barry's orders.

It was an enjoyable period for Milner-Barry. The weather was good, there were no mosquitoes and the afternoons were taken up with games of football and basketball. There was a camp cinema for the evening's entertainment and Sergeant Scully had even scrounged a gramophone on which was played Handel's *Water Music* most nights. The news from Leros was also 'cheerful' with reports from the LRDG that 'the island could be held'. Apparently Jellicoe and the SBS had given a good account of themselves and 'casualties were small'.

But on 21 November Milner-Barry wrote in his diary: 'Bill Blyth arrived from Leros with v. sad news that Sergeant Hawkes, and Corporal Walshaw were killed in Samos by bombing.'[5] (Walshaw was in fact killed in Leros.)

Blyth also revealed that far from being a glorious victory, the battle for Leros had ended in resounding defeat for the British. Over the next few days the SBS survivors of the Dodecanese campaign arrived back at Athlit in dribs and drabs; Jellicoe returned on 26 November and Lassen, Holmes and the other men of his Samos patrol reached home on 1 December, muttering darkly about what they'd like to do to all Turks.

Once Jellicoe had recovered from his experiences on Leros, Milner-Barry went to see him with a request. 'I pleaded for a separate marine detachment, to be commanded, of course, by myself as the Ancient Mariner,' wrote Milner-Barry. Jellicoe was sympathetic to Milner-Barry's entreaty but gently pointed out that at his age, and with his track record of ailments, he had 'rather outgrown a patrol'. And, anyway, added Jellicoe with rapid tact, he had a particular task in mind for Milner-Barry, whom he now transferred from S Squadron to his HQ staff: 'He wanted me to arrange winter accommodation for all troops in one of the empty TJFF [Transjordan Frontier Force] camps in the Jordan Valley.'[6]

Back from the Leros debacle less than a week, Jellicoe was already planning the next phase of SBS operations and Milner-Barry's job was to oversee their transfer to a new training camp so they could prepare for operations against German forces in the Balkans. On 3 December, Brigadier Eddie Myers of Force

TOP
The SBS Christmas Party in 1943 was at Azzib and attended by Brigadier Turnbull and ENSA star Judy Shirley. (Courtesy of David Henry)

BOTTOM
But the men were more interested in the food than the blonde songbird. (Courtesy of David Henry)

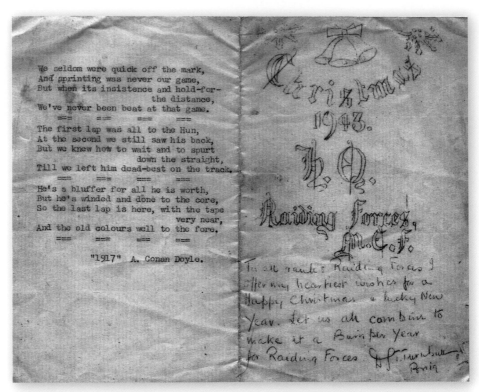

133, the Balkans wing of the SOE, arrived at the camp to lecture the squadron on conditions in the region.

For the new recruits training continued throughout December but for the men who had returned from the Aegean there was leave to be enjoyed in Beirut. By Christmas Day the squadron was reunited in its entirety, present and correct for the visit of Brigadier Turnbull just as they sat down to an extravagant dinner. The brigadier gave a short address, then asked the men to give a warm hand to Miss Judy Shirley, a celebrated radio singer with the BBC Variety Orchestra who was in the Middle East on an ENSA (Entertainments National Service Association) tour. Shirley was blonde, pretty and blessed with a fine voice, but the SBS didn't give a hoot. 'Many of us had just recovered from the hammering we had lived through in the Dodecanese,' recalled Dick Holmes. 'And we looked forward to eating the special meal prepared by our excellent cook, Sgt. Salmon. The officers and the sergeants had just placed our meals in front of us when our intrepid brigadier appeared on the scene, accompanied by Judy Shirley.'

Turnbull announced that Shirley was going to 'reward' the men for their efforts in the Dodecanese with a couple of numbers. 'She began,' remembered Holmes, 'and we eyed our meal, congealing on the plate.' From down the end of the table, Holmes heard someone yell 'Get that cow out of here!' 'The brigadier went very red in the face but decided to withdraw, leaving us to eat our special meal.'[7]

———————

John Lodwick had been in the SBS for only a few weeks but even he, a man who had explored most of the nooks and crannies of military life, was intrigued by what he found in his new unit. 'It must not be imagined that SBS were universally popular,' he wrote in his war memoirs. 'Their discipline was that born of mutual respect, and of this kind of discipline there is little conventional outward evidence and no heel-clicking. The clothes worn by SBS were somewhat odd, the manner of wearing them even more so.'[8]

The men usually wore what they felt most comfortable in. Some soldiers stuck to the standard issue parachute boots, while others preferred South African pattern leather boots with triple pointed mountaineering nails. Dick Holmes was one of the men who possessed a pair of what the SBS called 'Canadian boots' – 'calf length with leather uppers and rubber feet'.

An American war correspondent called Donald Grant, who wrote for the magazine *Look*, was given a tour of Leros by an SBS patrol shortly before the German invasion in November. He described to his readers his impression:

Dressed in sand-colored baggy windproof pants and blouses these taciturn characters unloaded supplies that the navy had brought them, hoisted the heavy bundles on to their shoulders, gestured to me to follow them and set off along the dirt road at a steady pace. As we walked along I realized that I was the only one who was making any noise so that I finished the two hour journey walking on the soles of my feet in an effort to move as quietly as the rest of the group … they were the scruffiest band of soldiers I had ever encountered, carrying an assortment of weapons which they cleaned meticulously as soon as breakfast was out of the way.[9]

Grant said that one of the patrol sensed his surprise at their unkempt appearance and cautioned the American against judging a book by its cover. 'He pointed to a tall, well-built soldier who sported a straggly beard. "Corporal [Dick] Holmes destroyed a fuel dump on Crete a couple of months ago. Awarded the Military Medal. That one, Gunner [Ray] Jones, blew up several planes on the same raid. Got that MM too."'[10]

Whatever it is that these men are doing, they are having a good time. (Courtesy of Angie English)

There were other idiosyncrasies in the SBS than the choice of uniform. As in any military unit, nicknames abounded, but there was little logic in Jellicoe's squadron. Dick Holmes was often called 'Jeff' for reasons he was never able to

> *'It must not be imagined that SBS were universally popular... Their discipline was that born of mutual respect, and of this kind of discipline there is little conventional outward evidence and no heel-clicking. The clothes worn by SBS were somewhat odd, the manner of wearing them even more so.'*
>
> John Lodwick

fathom, while his great pal, Doug Wright, answered to 'Roger' though he had no idea why. Roy Trafford's Christian name was swapped for 'Sammy' and one man was rechristened 'Myrtle', in honour of his sweetheart back in England. In the officers' mess there was more rhyme, reason and respect; Jellicoe was known as 'The Lord', Milner-Barry as 'Papa' and David Sutherland was called 'Dinky' on account of his immaculate appearance.

Sutherland was one of the few SBS officers who deferred to convention, though even he was capable of moments of high irreverence. On Leros in late October Sutherland learned that Andy Lassen had been awarded a second bar to his Military Cross for his actions on Simi earlier in the month. Sutherland thought it would be good for morale if they bestowed the decoration on Lassen there and then, so together with another officer he 'produced an accurate replica of the Military Cross ribbon, using white paper and gentian blue dye, to which two rosettes cut from the silver foil found in every cigarette packet were attached'.

Once the ceremony was over Sutherland, Lassen and every SBS soldier present 'drank everything in sight long into the night and slept like babies'.[11]

Most of the men in the SBS liked to wind down after operations with a drink. Lassen, Sean O'Reilly and Martin Conby all enjoyed a drop, and Holmes and Wright would often hit the town together. On one occasion in Alexandria the pair of them overindulged on Canadian Club whisky. A comment was made from a passer-by to the effect that the men were a rabble, so 'Wright drew his Luger and fired a shot in the air'. Military policemen came running but so did the men's officer, Captain Kingsley 'Nobby' Clarke. 'Nobby explained our situation and suggested they let him deal with us,' recalled Holmes. 'Not liking what they were faced with they agreed.'

CHAPTER 9

PIRACY ON THE HIGH SEAS

T he new year of 1944 saw the Germans in complete control of the islands in the Aegean. Still flushed with their success on Leros, the Wehrmacht's photo journal magazine *Das Signal* crowed that their triumph bore out two indisputable facts:

> In the first place, England's sea power, which is engaged throughout the world's seas, was not able to successfully defend important bases in the Eastern Mediterranean from where it had planned to put increasing pressure militarily. In the second place, however, the quick surrender of many enemy island defenders was a surprise. Contrary to the German soldier who, where fates put him, fights to the last bullet, the soldiers of the Western Powers stops fighting the moment he recognises there is no chance to win the fight.[1]

The Germans could be excused their self-satisfaction. The conquest of the 11 islands of the Dodecanese had been remarkably easy, and with this region under their control they had occupied the islands of the Cyclades and Sporades from the Italians without bloodshed. (Castelorizzo, the twelfth island in the chain, which actually lies in the Eastern Mediterranean remained in British hands.)

For a war machine that had suffered one defeat after another the previous year in Russia and North Africa, there was at least the consolation of triumph in the Aegean.

OPPOSITE
The SBS occasionally stepped on to Turkish land to wash or simply explore the countryside. (Courtesy of Angie English)

HARDING.

A patrol under Lieutenant Dick Harden seized two lighters off Nisiro in February 1944. The original caption misspelt his name. (Courtesy of the SBS Archive)

The question facing the Germans at the start of 1944 was how best to preserve their hold on the islands with the limited resources at their disposal without overstretching their lines of communication.

General Ulrich Kleemann, commander of the German division on Rhodes, made representations to Berlin and consequently received additional troops and a fleet of vessels (barges from the Ems canal and shallow draft cargo ships) with which to transport his men and keep them resupplied across the region.

Retaining the divisional strength on Rhodes, Kleemann divided his troops up elsewhere. Eight hundred men were garrisoned on Scarpanto, an island to the south-west of Rhodes on which was a radar station. Leros received 4,000 troops, Samos 2,000 and Stampalia 200, and Kleemann ordered 150 soldiers to both Simi and Piscopi.

This still left several islands undefended. Kleemann's initial strategy was to install a token garrison on each one, but this proved too much of a burden on their limited fleet of vessels. So instead the general altered his policy, deploying a larger force to garrison single islands for a limited time before moving them on to the next one. Inevitably, however, this meant that some islands would be left unguarded.

The German strategy hadn't gone unnoticed. British agents were scattered across the Aegean and they reported the enemy's movements to Middle East HQ in Cairo. A conference was organized in late December, wrote John Lodwick in *The Filibusters*, and 'it was decided that, with the New Year, Squadrons of SBS working in rotation would resume operations … to make the German occupation an uncomfortable and precarious tenancy of short rations and sleepless nights'.[2]

What the SBS were not told was the ulterior motive for their return to the Aegean. Operation *Overlord*, the invasion of France, was six months away. The Germans expected an invasion and were concentrating troops and materiel in northern France; simultaneously they were being stretched in the east as the Russians continued their advance towards the Balkans. The last thing the Germans now needed was a resumption of fighting in the Mediterranean.

But that was what the British planned, even though the SBS numbered barely 100 men. Jellicoe was instructed to wage war on the Germans, the type of guerrilla war for which his men had been trained. First, the SBS were to focus their attacks on shipping and harbour installations so as to reduce the enemy's capability to move quickly from island to island; then they were to launch hit-and-run raids on the islands themselves, first in the Dodecanese and then moving further afield to the western Cyclades and the Sporades in the north. This would oblige the Germans to draft in more troops to garrison these islands, soldiers the enemy could ill-afford to remove from northern France. In short, as Dick Holmes concedes, 'we were to be terrorists … our job was to terrorize the Germans'.[3]

The SBS were being ordered to act as 'legitimised pirates' but pirates require boats and Jellicoe's men lacked both vessels and seafaring skills. After all, they were soldiers, not sailors, but Middle East HQ knew a man who could help turn them into brigands.

Even by the often-dizzying standards of the British military, Adrian Seligman's eccentricity stood out. The son of an authoress who counted Mahatma Gandhi and the Emperor Haile Selassie as her friends, he had abandoned his studies at Cambridge University in 1936 to spend two years circumnavigating the globe in a 250-ton French fishing barquentine accompanied by a small crew, his 17-year-old wife and a piano. In the first three years of the war Seligman served on minesweepers and then passed himself off as a spy to pilot Russian ships through the Axis blockade of the Aegean to Syria.

By late 1942 he commanded the Levant Schooner Flotilla (LSF), a unit formed by the Royal Navy following the conquest of Crete by Germany in May 1941. Along with Royal Naval vessels, a fleet of Greek caiques had helped in the evacuation of Allied soldiers from Crete. With Axis forces firmly in control of Crete and the other Greek islands, the Royal Navy turned half the fleet over to the SOE, who used them to maintain contact with British agents working in the Eastern Mediterranean and the Adriatic.

The other half of the fleet was reconstituted the Levant Schooner Flotilla and placed under the command of Lieutenant-Commander Seligman. The fleet comprised 12 wooden caiques, sturdily built and weighing approximately 20 tons with vessels measuring from 30 to 45 feet in length. The crew consisted of a skipper, a stoker, a coxswain, a gunner and a wireless operator. There was no wheelhouse so the sailors had to sit on the tiller come rain or shine with their backsides hanging 18 inches over the sea.

On Seligman's instructions each fishing boat was equipped with an Oerlikon 20mm anti-tank (the Swiss-made cannon inspired by a German design from World War I) gun mounted in the bow, two .50 Browning machine guns in the waist at either beam and two .303 twin Vickers.

The men lived on *Takiarkis*, here at anchorage in Turkish waters 1944. Hank Hancock is back row, right, and Corporal Flavell is seated in the middle row to the left. (Courtesy of Angie English)

Seligman liked what he saw of the fleet, except the caiques' 20hp Bolinder diesel engines. These he found too noisy for the covert operations on which the LSF would be deployed, so from Haifa he procured a number of spare 90hp diesel engines intended for a squadron of Australian Matilda tanks. No longer required by the Australians, the engines replaced the Bolinder ones and Seligman wrote in his memoirs that as a result the caiques 'were able to cruise at 6 or 7 knots – only a knot or so faster than their designed speed, but at half throttle or less and therefore in comparative silence'.[4]

Next Seligman needed to find the 70 officers and men to crew the LSF. The former he selected from a detachment of young reservists aged between 19 and 23 while the sailors were volunteers attracted by the prospect of something more exciting than standard naval life. Once the crew were in place Seligman took the unit to a remote stretch of coastline in Western Cyprus where they practised the skills required for clandestine warfare.

One of their main roles during their forthcoming operations in the Eastern Mediterranean would be the landing at night of special forces' raiding parties on Axis-held islands. Consequently the LSF practised navigating on the open sea using small aircraft steering compasses with phosphorescent dial markings; that proved easy enough to master but the challenge lay in locating the entrance to a secluded creek or cove in the dead of night. Relying on recognisable silhouettes to guide them safely to land, the LSF made the final approach in stages, inching forward towards a known rock in line with a cliff or a gap between hills.

The LSF had been active throughout the ill-fated Dodecanese campaign of autumn 1943, transporting soldiers to islands as reinforcements and then returning to evacuate them as the Germans seized Simi, Kos, Leros, Samos et al. They were searching for a new role at the end of the year when they were instructed to facilitate the Special Boat Squadron's legitimised piracy.

Jellicoe selected Ian Patterson's L Squadron to inaugurate the new campaign. Having completed their training by the start of 1944, by which time the SBS had established a new camp at Samakh, a village at the southern end of Lake Tiberias in the Jordan Valley, L Squadron departed for the customary 'destination unknown' on 15 January. They sailed north-west to a remote bay on the west coast of Turkey aboard several motor launches and a 180-ton schooner, *Tewfik*, an 'ugly old tub with temperamental engines and a sea-roll like the swing of a pendulum'. Stacked into the schooner's hold were rations, equipment and nearly 5,000 pounds of explosive.

The incongruous fleet moored in a bay that was heavily forested and closed against the wind on all sides. Among the pine, laurel and storax trees was a small lake of saline water and a stream called the Incedere flowed into the inlet. The Turkish knew the bay as *Degirmen Buku* but to the British it was Port Deremen. To reach the remote bay the LSF had to sail up the Aegean Sea into the Gulf of Gökova, a long narrow gulf, 62 miles in length, with the Bodrum Peninsula to the north and the Datca Peninsula to the south.

Officially the Royal Navy were based in Beirut or Castelorizzo, the one island still in British hands but in reality they had been operating from Turkish waters since the evacuation of Kos. According to John Lodwick 'the Turks had raised no objections, either then or later' despite their neutrality.

In fact the attitude of the Turks was a complex one. Since early on in the Mediterranean war Turkey had allowed both Germany and Britain to infringe upon its neutrality, particularly the latter. The Royal Air Force violated its air space and the army even established a small base at Bodrum. The Germans knew what was going on, or at least most of it, but pragmatism obliged Hitler to turn a blind eye. Germany could ill-afford to have Turkey as an enemy.

The Turkish attitude changed following Germany's triumph in the Dodecanese; Hitler may have been chary of antagonising the Turks but they were similarly concerned that with Germany now in full control of the Aegean, they might be punished for playing host to British forces. Now it was the Germans for whom the Turks did favours; allowing their agents to cross their frontier on their way to spy in the southern regions of the Soviet Union.

In November 1943 Winston Churchill made one final attempt to persuade Turkey to enter the war on the Allies' side. He failed, hardly surprisingly given the situation in the Aegean, and Turkey began to take a harder line in safeguarding its neutrality. The Turks agreed to allow a small number of wounded British personnel to be treated in Bodrum hospital but declared that any other soldiers who landed on their shores would be interned.

This stance presented a potential problem to the Special Boat Squadron. So as L Squadron sailed for Port Deremen, Walter Milner-Barry was despatched to Ankara on a diplomatic mission. He arrived on 27 January and went first to the British Embassy to dine with the ambassador and General Allan Arnold, the British military attaché. 'They asked me about Raiding Forces and the SBS and I waffled away for about an hour,' wrote Milner-Barry in his diary. 'It was a golden opportunity to sell the "firm".'[5]

From Ankara Milner-Barry travelled to Istanbul for a meeting with Commander Vladimir Wolfson, Head of British Naval Intelligence in the Mediterranean. When he returned to the capital a couple of days later there was a letter from Arnold, 'saying he was very sorry he couldn't even get the Turks to agree to our chaps coming ashore for exercise'. The general was most effusive in his apologies, explaining to Milner-Barry that he had tried his utmost to convince the Turks. Still, he concluded cheerfully, not to worry, it just means the SBS 'will have to choose a really deserted spot' in which to establish its base.[6]

A South African officer called Captain Morris Anderson was given the honour of leading the first L Squadron operation. A former member of the Union Defence

At anchor in Port Deremen in Turkish waters in April 1944, the *Tewfik* was the officers' billet for the next stage of SBS operations and described as an 'ugly old tub with temperamental engines'. (Courtesy of Angie English)

Force, Anderson was a 'champion swimmer' and Patterson had every confidence that he and his 11-strong patrol would give a good account of themselves. Their destination was Stampalia at the western extremities of the Dodecanese, and the objectives were listed in the operational orders issued to Anderson:

1. To destroy enemy shipping or seaplanes.
2. To land medical supplies to the Greek population.
3. To destroy the W/T [Wireless telegraphy] station NW of Castello or whichever W/T the Germans are discovered to be using.
4. To destroy enemy and enemy installations.
5. To evacuate any British military personnel who may be on the island.

Stampalia (better known today as Astypalaia) is a strange shape, like a pair of parrots chattering to each other on a perch. Anderson landed on the thin perch in the early hours of Tuesday 1 February. The men concealed their four inflatable boats and scouted a cave, and by first light the men and their supplies were well hidden inside.

The raiders spent the day in the cave until at 1800 hours Anderson, Sergeant Wilson and their two interpreters left for the village of Livadia where they made arrangements for the doctor to collect their medical supplies. The following morning, 2 February, the elderly doctor arrived on a mule accompanied by two younger men. The medical supplies were loaded onto the mule and one of the younger men agreed to post himself on the mountain between the cave and the village and give warning of any enemy approach.

With the medical supplies safely delivered into Greek hands, Anderson switched his focus to offensive operations. Splitting his force in two, the South African explained that the following evening he and Lance-Corporal Nixon would attack enemy shipping on one of Stampalia's islands while Wilson and another party led by Corporal William Asbery would attempt to destroy five caiques at anchor in Marmari Bay.

Asbery was a Scot, short, stocky and very belligerent. His hobbies were war and ornithology. En route to the caiques, under a bright moonlight, he spotted a German floatplane. It was too tempting a target to resist. Cutting through the protective wire that encircled the aircraft, Asbery planted Lewes bombs on the wings and an incendiary device in the fuselage. As the raiders made their escape they were spotted and the Germans began firing with mortars and machine guns. The fire was wild and inaccurate, inconsequential to a man like Asbery who was already eyeing up the five caiques. He and two of his men stripped off in an old chapel close to the beach and then swam out to the vessels carrying their explosives above their head. They laid the last of their charges on two of the caiques, priming the bombs with two-hour fuses, before returning to the beach where they dried and slipped on their uniforms. It had proved all too easy, more like a training exercise than a sabotage mission in enemy territory. As Asbery and his men made

'We were to be terrorists ... our job was to terrorize the Germans.'

Dick Holmes

their escape across the hills they heard a roar and the bay they had left behind was bathed in the glow of half a dozen explosions.

Anderson had been unsuccessful in his mission, but on learning from Asbery that a shortage of explosives had prevented him from destroying all of the caiques in Marmari Bay he decided to finish the job. The next evening Anderson and Nixon blew up the remaining caiques.

Meanwhile the rest of the patrol carried out invaluable reconnaissance across the island, enabling Anderson to make a detailed report on the situation on Stampalia. 'There are about 150–160 Germans on the island with five officers,' he wrote, adding that their commanding officer lived alone in a white house near the harbour and had been on Stampalia since the previous November. Furthermore,

Ferrying supplied from the Turkish mainland towards *Tewfik* and *Takiarkis* in the Gulf of Kos. (Courtesy of the SBS Archive)

wrote Anderson, the garrison strength would soon be reduced to 20 with most of the men transferring to Leros. There was a severe shortage of food on the island with olive oil unavailable for the past six months. There had been an outbreak of malaria the previous autumn and one case of typhoid. There was, however, a lot of scabies and several incidences of syphilis caused by what the report described as bad women.

Anderson concluded his report by stating he had been unable to determine the exact location of the W/T station although he thought it probable it was in the Maltezana harbour area. This was not attacked because of the presence of armed Greek police and because 'having accomplished a certain amount by stealth it was thought better to leave the enemy guessing'.[7]

Encouraged by this opening foray, Patterson sent out other patrols to the islands. Lieutenant David Clark landed on Simi and with his men killed ten Germans; Captain Bruce Mitford sailed north to the islands of

The inquisitive Turks who came to examine the SBS at anchorage could be easily bought off with food or, as here, a spare rifle. (Courtesy of Angie English)

Lisso and Arkhi, wrecked the cable stations on both islands and sank three German caiques. He also captured a schooner containing ten cases of beer, 30 kegs of Samos wine and half a dozen cases of champagne; the schooner was sunk, but not before it had been stripped of its contents. A combined patrol of SBS and LSF under the command of Lieutenant Dick Harden seized two lighters off Nisiro, killing or capturing all those on board.

On 23 February Anderson and his men were once more in action, this time attacking a German outpost on the island Piscopi. Corporal Asbery again distinguished himself and was rewarded with a Military Medal. The citation described how he 'showed great coolness by working himself into a position from which he was able to bomb the Germans with grenades. By this action he killed, amongst others, a German NCO, who was in a position to inflict heavy casualties upon the patrol.'[8]

'They greeted us with "uh-oh, it's that mob with funny hats and funny badges".'

Dick Holmes

The SBS didn't see the point of skiing and they made that patently clear to their instructors. (Courtesy of the SBS Archive)

By the end of February S Squadron were back in camp at Samakh, and Milner-Barry was en route with orders to lead them into action. Following his trip to Turkey, he had been gathering more Royal Marine recruits in Alexandria and organizing the imminent deployment of S Squadron to the Aegean together with the Levant Schooner Flotilla. David Sutherland was in hospital with jaundice and Jellicoe had appointed Milner-Barry to command the squadron in his absence. 'Planning targets in the Cyclades,' wrote a thrilled Milner-Barry in his diary. 'There is certainly great scope and I'm looking forward to it.'[3] At this stage, however, planning was all Milner-Barry could do; Raiding Forces HQ had imposed an indefinite ban on any raids outside the Dodecanese, to the anger of the SBS.

The LSF gave Milner-Barry a lift on one of their motor-launches to Haifa, where he arrived on the morning of 1 March to find George Jellicoe waiting on the quay. Together they 'drove furiously to Samakh' during which time Milner-

Barry was briefed on the latest developments. Captain Bill Blyth would be going on operations, as would the new officer, John Lodwick. The men were pleased to see the return of Milner-Barry. He was old enough to be their father and, although he suffered periodically from a bad back and other ailments, he was straight, sincere and, unlike one or two other officers, never one to shoot a line. 'Milner-Barry was a very, very good officer,' said Holmes. 'No pretence to a fighting man but a nice man and we had a lot of fun with him. At his age he could easily have remained at HQ on the staff but he chose to join us on operations and he proved very efficient.'

On 2 March Milner-Barry, Lieutenant Stefan Casulli and 23 other ranks of S Squadron sailed from Haifa. 'We left at 5pm in some disquiet as there was a gale warning,' wrote Milner-Barry, who had spent the day purchasing last minute essentials – including a pocket chess set. 'Our fears were proved only too well founded, as it blew a gale after dinner, and the boat pitched, tossed and rolled, and did everything but sink. Was not sick but definitely scared as it occurred to me that if we had to swim I should fare ill.'[4]

Andy Lassen skiing at Cedars in early 1944. (Courtesy of the SBS Archive)

Sometimes the men came ashore to cook their meals on Turkish soil. (Courtesy of the SBS Archive)

Milner-Barry and his men survived the storm and arrived in Port Deremen on Wednesday 8 March to find Ian Patterson bragging about two captured P Lighters. 'They had had a daylight engagement, nine of them against twenty two Jerries, and killed, wounded or captured the lot, then navigated the lighters back themselves, a really brilliant feat,' Milner-Barry told his diary.[5]

Patterson had set up his command post on board the *Tewfik*, while most of his men were living in another schooner close by, the *Takiarkis*. Just round the corner of the bay was the command vessel of the Levant Schooner Flotilla, LS9, skippered by Lieutenant-Commander John Campbell. Milner-Barry accepted an invitation from Campbell to dine aboard LS9 and with the assistance of Patterson, sent a signal to Raiding Forces HQ saying that 'unless we could play in the Cyclades it was a waste of time to bring the whole detachment'.[6]

In the meantime S Squadron moved into their new quarters. 'The *Tewfik* was the HQ ship,' said Dick Holmes. 'Our vessel was the *Takiarkis*, which was just up the coast. We cooked on shore and slept in the boat, about 20 of us or so. [John] Lodwick was the only officer, and he had Jellicoe's clerk, Dick Morris, to help write up the reports.'

The Levant Schooner Flotilla had undergone an expansion following the end of the Dodecanese campaign, in men and in vessels. From its base in Beirut

Commander Seligman had increased the strength of the fleet from 12 to 30 caiques and he had also enrolled dozens more sailors. One of the volunteers was 18-year-old Reg Osborn, a Londoner who had become bored of Royal Naval routine. After a fortnight's training he was posted to Dereman as a gunner on caique LS3. 'A lot of the crews were scallywags who didn't fit into big ship navy life and the rather relaxed life on the caiques suited them down to the ground,' he recalled of his shipmates in the LSF. 'In some respects we were a bit like the French Foreign Legion: they were not interested in your past as long as you knew your job and did it to the best of your ability and with the best of heart. Naval discipline in the accepted sense was neither required nor enforced, and they let you get on with your job.'

Dick Holmes (leaning in), Duggie Pomford, Mac Macauly, McClelland and Doug Wright lie up during a recce to Rhodes. (Courtesey of the SBS Archive)

TAKIARKIS

While some of the men have lunch others, such as the one walking the *Takiarkis*'s gangplank, look ready for a swim. (Courtesy of Angie English)

One of the men poses for Hank Hancock in the rigging of *Takiarkis*. (Courtesy of Angie English)

Two members of S Squadron pose for Hancock aboard *Takiarkis*. (Courtesy of Angie English)

Osborn enjoyed life in the Levant Schooner Flotilla. He grew his black hair long, tied it in place with a silk ribbon, and revelled in his piratical appearance. Yet he knew who the real pirates were. 'We were a waterborne taxi service [for the SBS],' he reflected. 'They needed us for our seamanship, there was no mistaking that. They were nice chaps, not all guts and glory, and we had a good rapport but their attitude was "Listen here, mate, you sail this fucking boat!"'[7]

The role of the LSF was to transport small parties of SBS to their target island. 'The caiques were really well built for what they had to do,' reflected Osborn. 'They were pointed stem and stern, shallow bottomed and they didn't take up much draught.' Once the SBS patrol had gone ashore the LSF would sail off to another island and lie low on a secluded stretch of coastline. 'We couldn't hide up near the target because if we'd been spotted by an E-boat or German caique they would then know we were there for a reason and they'd search for the SBS,' explained Osborn. Once they had reached their hideout, the first task was to camouflage the caique. 'It was a ball-aching job but very effective,' said Osborn. 'We dismounted the mast, laid it flat, and covered the boat from stem to stern with this blasted netting. Then using bamboo poles we'd hoist up the netting so that it formed irregular

By the look of things, these men are plucking poultry aboard *Takiarkis*. (Courtesy of Angie English)

shapes. From the air it was difficult to make out the caique against the rocky coastline.' With the camouflage netting in place, the sailors would wait for a wireless message from the SBS requesting collection.

Danger was ever present for Osborn and his crewmates when they sailed the Aegean. The Royal Air Force was in the habit of strafing any caique they saw so to prevent the risk of a tragic accident, the LSF agreed a recognition signal with the RAF. 'To demonstrate that we were British-operated we would haul the jib sail up five times, pause, and then haul it up another five times,' explained Osborn. To reduce the likelihood of attack from the Luftwaffe, the LSF schooners flew the Greek flag with the red and white pennant underneath denoting that the vessel was under German jurisdiction.

The LSF had scant respect for the German Navy, considering their seafaring skills vastly inferior to their own, but nevertheless 'we were constantly keyed up'. Despite it all, however, Osborn considered life in the LSF idyllic compared to the months he had spent serving in the North Atlantic run on flower class corvettes. 'There were plenty of good times out there in the Med,' he reflected, 'but there were no good times in the North Atlantic.'

Lieutenant Keith Balsillie of S Squadron took part in the Santorini raid. (Courtesy of the SBS Archive)

Friday 10 March was a 'lovely day', according to Milner-Barry. The weather was dreamy, Stefan Casulli arrived back from the Turkish port of Bodrum with fresh meat and vegetables, and a signal was received from Raiding Forces HQ promising that they were doing their utmost to lift the ban on attacking German targets in the Cyclades. Milner-Barry even managed to install a telephone line connecting the SBS HQ in the *Tewfik* to the LSF HQ aboard LS9.

In the following days S Squadron settled into their new home. Captain Bill Blyth arrived, together with Lieutenants Keith Balsillie, Nobby Clarke and Jimmy Lees, and 24 other ranks, and Ian Patterson received orders to attend a conference in Istanbul. Milner-Barry went ashore for the first time, to wash in the stream that ran into the inlet, only to encounter a Turkish officer. He demanded to know what the British were doing in their waters. 'I gave the stock reply that we had engine trouble on board but would move as soon as it was cleared,' wrote Milner-Barry. Then, employing all his considerable charm, the Englishman invited him to visit the *Tewfik*, whereupon a bottle of Syrian Arak was presented to the Turk 'to seal our neutral friendship'.[8]

The next day Milner-Barry returned to the mainland, taking with him Bill Blyth and Keith Balsillie. After a wash, the trio 'walked up the valley for a bit, beautifully fresh and green' with not a Turk in sight.[9]

Some of the men of L Squadron relax on board a LSF vessel in March 1943.

> *'In some respects we were a bit like the French Foreign Legion: they were not interested in your past as long as you knew your job and did it to the best of your ability and with the best of heart.'*
>
> Reg Osborn

Bad weather hampered SBS operations for the rest of March, forcing delays and postponements to operations. Then a signal arrived informing Milner-Barry that David Sutherland was en route to Dereman to resume command and that he was to return to England on leave. 'Rather annoying that as I was enjoying my command,' he wrote in his diary.[10]

Sutherland arrived on Sunday 26 March, bringing with him the American war correspondent, Donald Grant, on a day when it rained non-stop. The weather added to the air of melancholy that seemed to pervade the inlet, an atmosphere not helped by a string of misfortunes. A motorboat ran aground in a training exercise, then a launch accidentally rammed the *Tewfik* and, to cap it all, John Lodwick and his patrol returned from an unsuccessful raid on Stampalia. The mission was aborted without a shot being fired after the W/T set, explosives and rations were dropped into the sea during disembarkation.

There was at least some good news to greet the arrival of David Sutherland. Stefan Casulli had just learned that his Belgian wife in Alexandria was carrying his child so a toast was drunk, and then Sutherland locked himself away in the operations rooms to plan how best to reverse the squadron's recent run of bad luck. The opportunity arose when Jellicoe sent a signal informing Sutherland that they had been instructed to destroy the radar station on Scarpanto. It was a long way from Dereman to the target, approximately 125 miles, so Sutherland studied the map and decided that a suitable base from which to launch the attack might be the small islands of Calchi and Alimnia, approximately 40 miles north of Scarpanto.

Sutherland appreciated the risk entailed in the operation. Alimnia wasn't a remote island in the middle of the vast blue Aegean; it was 5 miles west of Rhodes on which was garrisoned an elite German division. Great caution would be needed, so too experience, so Sutherland selected some of his best men for the operation. Captain Bill Blyth was given command of a patrol containing three men with Military Medals. The fourth, Leo 'Digger' Rice, had served with the squadron since the early days and was admired for his sangfroid. Blyth, remembered Holmes, 'was a good man, a pleasant officer and pretty experienced'.

By now the SBS base had been moved to Yedi Atala in the Gulf of Kos and it was from there that the reconnaissance party made their final preparations. They would voyage to the objective in LS24, a converted sponge fishing boat normally captained by Rigas Rigopoulous, a former member of the Greek Sacred Squadron who had decided to put his seafaring skills to good use in the LSF. But at the beginning of April Rigopoulous was instructed to transport a new motor launch to Castelorizzo. His place as skipper of LS24 was filled by Sub-Lieutenant Allan Tuckey, a 21-year-old from St Albans whose law studies were on hold while he served with the Royal Naval Volunteer Reserve.

Tuckey, who was suffering from a heavy cold, introduced himself to Rigopoulous's crew: Demetrios Triandaphillou, Nikolaos Velesariou and Michele Lisgaris. Velesariou was a 35-year-old illiterate born on the island of Kalymnos; the 41-year-old Lisgaris was an experienced sailor who had been serving with the LFS for six months and was on the LS24 when it ferried Sutherland and the American war correspondent Donald Grant to the SBS hideaway.

The fifth crew member of LS24 was the youngest, a telegraphist called Ronald Carpenter from Cranleigh in Surrey. Although he had spent five years in the Royal Navy Carpenter had volunteered for the LSF just the previous month, two days before his twentieth birthday, an occasion he 'celebrated in true sailor fashion'. The same day, 19 March, he received orders to report to HMS *Mosquito*, the Royal Navy coastal forces base, at 1400 hours. Still drunk, Carpenter 'was unable to meet the order', and eventually presented himself at 1700 hours. 'Felt unsteady, but managed it,' he wrote in his diary.[11]

Despite this inauspicious start Carpenter was told to get himself to the LSF base in Beirut. He arrived on the evening of 23 March feeling 'tired, dirty, hungry and exhausted'. His passage on to Yedi Atala was hampered by bad weather and Carpenter's motor launch had to put in at Vathi and wait for the storms to pass. 'I can see myself getting to my schooner … some time next month,' he complained to his diary on 2 April.

Carpenter eventually reached Yedi Atala in the early hours of 5 April. 'Went on board of LS9 at 1000 hours and was immediately sent on to LS24 (Greek sailing boat),' he wrote. 'Only with the Old Man [Tuckey] and me as Englishmen. He is a decent chap, so that we got on all right. Four Special Boat Squadron men and their officer came on board at 1600 hours and at 1630 we started off on our operation. Everything seems to have to be a rush for me.'

The operation instructions issued to Captain Bill Blyth by David Sutherland state that their objective was to 'recce the islands of Calchi and Alimnia'. (Courtesy of SAS Regimental Archive)

CHAPTER 11

CAUGHT, QUESTIONED, VANISHED

They sailed west out of the Gulf of Gökova before LS24 rounded the Datca Peninsula and headed south-east towards the Loryma Peninsula (known in ancient times as the Bozburun Peninsula). Now their voyage became hazardous. The German Navy patrolled these waters and Carpenter could feel the tension heighten as they sailed at 7 knots towards a small bay near Loryma. 'In order to get here we had to pass between Rhodes and Simi, both occupied by the enemy,' he wrote in his diary. 'So we steamed straight through under the Turkish flag, which seems rather cheap but was safer.'[1]

They arrived in the bay at 1615 hours on 6 April and were met by an agent from Force 133 who provided them with the latest information concerning the islands of Alimnia and Calchi. Tuckey informed his crew that they would leave for Calchi at 2000 hours that evening; Captain Blyth told his men the same thing. Final preparations were made.

Perhaps Carpenter familiarised himself with the Vickers K machine gun he was required to operate in the case of enemy contact, one of two such weapons fitted on LS24 along with an Oerlikon 20mm cannon. As a telegraphist he had had next to no training in its use, either in the Royal Navy or with the LSF. He was also equipped with a Lancaster pistol, a multi-barrelled sidearm that had been popular

OPPOSITE
Leo Rice was an Australian and a very experienced operator. This was one of a series of portrait photos taken on Leros after an SBS patrol had returned from a reconnaissance of Rhodes in November 1943. (Courtesy of the SBS Archive)

with Victorian army officers in the British Raj. It was a strange choice of weapon for Carpenter to carry, stranger still compared with what Blyth and his men carried.

Even though they were ostensibly on a reconnaissance mission, the five SBS were armed for trouble. Stashed on the deck of LS24 was a German Schmeisser sub-machine gun, a Tommy gun, a Bren gun, three rifles and three US carbines. Each man also carried two grenades, two Lewes bombs and 12 spare magazines for their particular weapon. In the SBS it was possible to choose your own weapon. Most men carried a Smith & Wesson revolver and then selected a machine gun or a semi-automatic carbine depending on the mission and the level of resistance they expected to meet.

As the men lounged around on deck, their hooded sand-coloured windcheaters done up tightly to protect against the wind that whipped across the bay, the trepidation would have been high. None more so than for Private George Evans, the newest recruit to the SBS.

Evans had joined the squadron two months earlier from the Sherwood Foresters. Evans was an Eastender by birth, born in Plaistow to a railwayman and his wife, but he had spent his formative years in the Midlands after his father was transferred to Derby. By the time Evans enlisted as a driver in the Sherwood Foresters in January 1939 he had grown into a fine-looking man of 6 feet 2 inches: handsome, adventurous and a heartthrob with all the local girls.

In July 1942 the Evans family received a telegram informing them that their George had been reported missing following the fall of Tobruk the previous month. For two months his parents and two sisters had no further news; then on 4 September they received another telegram, this one from George. It said simply: 'Please don't worry all well and safe.' Following this, the war office provided more detail:

No DIV/II/CAS/SF
Army Form B. 104–80B

Infantry Record Office
York
1.9.1942

Sir
With reference to previous notification I have to inform you that a report has been received from the War Office to the effect that (No.) *4976245*
(Rank) *Private*
(Name) *Evans. Augustus. George*

(Regiment) *1st Bn Sherwood Foresters*
is now *located in Cairo having escaped from Tobruk.*

I am
Sir
Your obedient Servant[2]

When Evans next wrote to his family he explained, 'it's not possible to write all my travels now but I will tell you all about them when I come home'.[3] Instead Evans asked for news of home, and of old girlfriends. He didn't mention that he had been awarded the Military Medal for his daring escape from the German entrapment at Tobruk. 'Evans not only escaped alone but showed the most remarkable endurance,' explained the citation for his medal. 'He walked slowly on through the enemy confident that he would arrive in the end, and finally, by remaining under Australian artillery fire under great privation, was able to bring back useful information. A courageous effort.'[4]

Evans had volunteered for the SBS in early 1944 and had been accepted without hesitation on account of his service record. He was one of three soldiers on LS24 with a Military Medal. Ray Jones, an artilleryman from Birmingham, had been awarded his for his part in the raid on Crete the previous July, and George Miller had won his while serving with his parent regiment, the Royal Armoured Corps, earlier in the war. 'Miller was a very strong personality and well thought of by his patrol,' remembered Dick Holmes. 'I did a lot of training with him in Beirut in the latter part of 1942 and early 1943 and was very impressed by him.'[5]

Miller was 23, so too Jones, Evans and Leo Rice, the Australian known to his friends as 'Digger'. Their officer was 31. Captain Bill Blyth – he had been christened Hugh William but preferred his middle name – had been commissioned into the Scots Guards in 1933 and was immediately put on the officers' reserve. He spent the rest of the decade farming, receiving his call up papers shortly before the outbreak of war. For the first three years of the war Blyth served as an instructor in the Scots Guards, and it was probably here that he encountered David Stirling for the first time. Such was the impression made on

Second Time Reported Missing

Hero of a 400-mile desert trek for which he was awarded the Military Medal, 23-years-old Private Augustus George Evans, of the Sherwood Foresters, has been officially reported "missing, believed prisoner of war."

The news has been received by his parents, Mr. and Mrs. A. T. Evans, of 6, Dorchester-avenue, Chaddesden, and is the first information they have received either from or about their only son for more than a year.

Pte. A. Evans

Pte. Evans has been reported "missing" before, after the fall of Tobruk, in 1942.

Later, his parents were notified that he had escaped, and that he had been located in Cairo. This was the occasion when his exploits gained him his award, his desert march occupying nine weeks.

An old boy of Nottingham-road school, Pte. Evans joined up in January, 1939, and in July of that year was posted to Cyprus. Later he was sent to North Africa.

He was previously employed at Ley's Malleable Castings Co., Ltd.

George Evans, far right on the front row, in early 1944. The soldier second from left in the back row is Ray Jones, another member of the Alimnia Patrol. (Courtesy of the Evans Family)

Blyth by Stirling that when he finally got the overseas posting he craved, to the Infantry Training Depot in Haifa in January 1943, he 'immediately requested to join the 1st SAS Regiment'.[6]

He arrived at Kabrit at the end of January, around the time Stirling was captured in Tunisia, and to Blyth fell the burden of trying to bring order to the administrative chaos left behind by the SAS commander. In the subsequent 15 months Blyth proved himself as a special force officer, lacking the offensive ardour of an Andy Lassen or Ian Patterson perhaps, but displaying a quiet efficiency and resolve during the debacle on Leros.

While Blyth was receiving from the Force 133 agent the latest intelligence on enemy movements in the Aegean, the Germans were being given some information of their own. One of their agents in the region had learned that a unit of British commandos were bound for the islands of Calchi and Alimnia. On hearing the intelligence General Kleemann, the German commander on Rhodes, ordered two landing groups to be formed from the 1st *Küstenjäger*-Abteilung, the coastal raiding unit of the Brandenburger Regiment.

In the early hours of 7 April four caiques left the west coast of Rhodes 'escorted by two attack submarines of the German navy',[7] and deposited a force of Brandenburgers on Calchi whose orders were to establish strong points in anticipation of a British landing. On returning to Rhodes, the fleet collected a second landing force and at 0630 hours set sail for Alimnia. This time they were escorted by a motor launch, *Malona*, from the Rhodes Flotilla.

———————

LS24 sailed out of the small bay at 2000 hours on 6 April, heading in a south-westerly direction towards the island of Calchi. Travelling at 7 knots per hour Tuckey expected to cover the 50 miles in around seven hours.

An hour and a half later the vessel had left behind the relative safety of the Turkish coast and was headed towards Rhodes. 'Everybody at battle stations,' wrote Carpenter in his diary. 'Sighted two enemy E-boats when we were between Rhodes and Simi but we were lucky, they did not see us.' At midnight it was Carpenter's turn on watch. 'This was a good reason for taking advantage, to climb over the gun and to sit down in the dinghy with the Lanchester [sic] and to do nothing other than … '[8]

The diary came to an abrupt stop, almost certainly because Carpenter was called away from his lookout duties to decode a message that was sent from David Sutherland at 0034 hours. Carpenter decoded the message and handed it to Tuckey: change of plan, they were first to reconnoitre Alimnia and then Calchi.

LS24 reached Alimnia at 0200 hours and Blyth and his four men were put ashore onto a small jetty in a cove on the south side of the island. Alimnia was small, just 3 square miles, but its 60 inhabitants considered that its green and hilly interior made their island one of the prettiest in the Dodecanese.

The SBS stepped ashore expecting their thorough reconnaissance to last several hours, possibly the whole day. LS24 should have sailed away from the jetty to await the message from Blyth requesting collection, but Tuckey was inexperienced and his crew tired after the night sailing. Blyth might also have been in some part responsible for the decision of Tuckey not to leave the area and return later at a pre-arranged hour. The orders given by Sutherland to Blyth stated that 'the method and route of recee will be decided before leaving Loryma in conjunction with the CO LS24'.[9] Instead of leaving the area and hiding up on a remote stretch of coastline, Tuckey camouflaged the vessel and then he and his men lay down to rest and await the return of the commandos.

At approximately 0700 hours the small German fleet of four caiques (*Caesar*, *Fritz*, *Dora* and *Otto*) and the motor launch sailed into the cove and spotted

'Everybody at battle stations… Sighted two enemy E-boats when we were between Rhodes and Simi but we were lucky, they did not see us.'

Ronald Carpenter

300 yards to starboard 'a very well camouflaged motor sailing ship'.[10] The lookout of the LS24 had already shouted a warning and as the Germans altered course to investigate the five seamen ran from the boat rather than open fire with their cannon and two heavy machine guns. It was the German crew on board *Caesar* who fired the first shots, raking LS24 with cannon fire as Tuckey and his crew took up defensive positions on the jetty. Carpenter threw his diary and code book into the water as the British and Greeks returned small-arms fire. Another one of the four German caiques brought their cannon to bear on the pier and two of the Greeks were slightly wounded. Realising the hopelessness of their situation, Tuckey ordered his men to surrender.

The SBS patrol heard the commotion as they made their way over a ridge of high ground on Alimnia called Point 123. According to a German report, a soldier on board one of the caiques spotted a figure 'eastwards of Point 123'. From their vantage point the British soldiers would have been able to watch events unfold in the cove; they were also able to spot a possible means of escape. On the eastern side of the island a small fishing boat from Calchi had just landed containing Nikita Tsouroutis, Davelis Tripolitis and Moskamberis Halkiti and the 1,100lb of fish they had caught. They were on the island to purchase a sheep from a local farmer.

The SBS patrol moved quickly down the other side of Point 123 and then Sergeant Miller approached the men alone and asked for a lift to Turkey. The fishermen advised waiting until dark but Miller shook his head and explained that the island would soon be crawling with Germans. They had to leave now.

The three fishermen agreed and ushered the soldiers on board. There was little room on the boat but the five men were told to lie down side by side before being covered with a heavy tarpaulin. At 0830 hours the boat began its voyage towards Turkey, unseen by the dozens of Germans fanning out across the hills in search of the commandos.

Meanwhile the five British and Greek seamen had been herded onto the motor launch and were now on their way to Rhodes to be interrogated. As the vessel approached the island of Makri, a thin mile-long strip of uninhabited land between Alimnia and Rhodes, its skipper spotted a fishing boat sailing north-east towards Turkey. The motor launch changed direction and then fired a shot across the bows of the boat. 'There was no question of fighting,' recalled Davelis Tripolitis, one of the three Greek fishermen. 'We couldn't outrun them. We were just a small, wooden fishing boat. They could have blown us out of the water.'[11]

Within minutes the Germans had boarded the fishing boat and discovered Blyth and his men hiding under the tarpaulin. The men were dragged to their feet and, together with the three Greeks, bundled onto the launch. The fishing boat was then sunk.

Once in Rhodes the three fishermen were separated from the others and taken for questioning. The ten men who had arrived at Alimnia a few hours earlier on board the LS24 were handed over to Major Curt Kronsbein, operations officer of the Rhodes division, whose HQ was a plain grey stone building on Demokratias Street in Rhodes Town. Also given to Kronsbein was Carpenter's code book and diary retrieved from the sea by a sharp-eyed German.

Blyth and Tuckey were immediately separated from their men and driven to Demokratias Street where they dined with Major Kronsbein. It was all a convivial affair. Afterwards they were taken to different cells and questioned separately with

Sergeant Helmut Viebrock acting as translator. Before the war the 31-year-old Viebrock had taught English at the university of Marburg. He was the author of a book entitled *Experience and Design of Beauty in the Poetry of William Wordsworth* and Blyth was astounded by the excellence of Viebrock's English, considering it of the standard 'usual only amongst the highly educated British'.[12]

Both men declined to answer any questions other than to give their name, rank and number.

Blyth and Tuckey slept in their cells and the next day, just before midday, Blyth was put on an aircraft and flown to Athens at the behest of the Interrogation and Counter-Intelligence branch of Army Group E. Tuckey was driven to Rhodi prison and imprisoned with the other eight men. Three days later the four SBS soldiers were flown to Salonika where they were met by Oberleutnant Straud and Sonderführer Helmut Poliza of Army Group E's Interrogation and Counter-Intelligence branch.

None of the soldiers had revealed anything to the Germans since their capture but Nikolaos Velesariou and Michele Lisgaris had 'talked freely'.[13] So too Ronald Carpenter, who was in a most unenviable position. The Germans had his diary.

Ray Jones (foreground) and his comrades proved 'obstinate' during their interrogation, giving the Germans the barest of information. (Courtesy of the SBS Archive)

They therefore knew all about his birthday celebrations, about how he had missed an interview because he was drunk, and how he was young and inexperienced in this type of warfare.

At some point early on in Carpenter's interrogation he would have been made aware of an edict issued by Hitler in October 1942. In his Commando Order, the Nazi leader instructed his forces that all captured Allied commandos or similar units were to be handed over to the Sicherheitsdienst (SD, the intelligence service of the Schutzstaffel, or SS) so that they could be 'annihilated to the last man'.[14]

Carpenter was almost certainly informed that unless he co-operated this was the fate that awaited him. The young telegraphist agreed to tell the Germans everything they wished to know. Within a short space of time Carpenter had revealed that the joint LSF/SBS base was in Turkish waters and that the crews of the LSF were a mix of Greek sailors and British seamen. Then he explained in detail the recognition signals used by the flotilla.

The Germans were delighted. Unable to contain their excitement, the Wehrmacht radio service in Athens broadcast a triumphant communiqué on 11 April in which they gloated that 'British and Greek commandos attempted a raid NW of the island of Rhodes. They have all been mopped up.'

The High Command within Army Group E was furious that subordinates had disclosed details of the raid over the wireless. Alerted to the fate of their comrades, the SBS would inevitably change their recognition signals and move their base. An angry telephone call was made to Helmut Poliza on 14 April, admonishing Interrogation and Counter-Intelligence branch for releasing details about the men's capture and demanding to know the progress of the commandos' interrogation.

So far Poliza's strategy had followed the guidelines issued to the Counter-Intelligence branch the previous year, in which it was stated: 'Experience shows that questioning is most effective when the prisoner does not realise what is happening but has the feeling that he is having a pleasant unforced conversation.'[15]

Poliza replied that though the SBS men were proving 'very obstinate' he had managed to extract the home addresses of Miller, Rice and Jones, possibly having told them that a cable would be sent to their families via the Red Cross informing them of their wellbeing. Rice and Jones had also given snippets of information about their military background, the sort of inconsequential details that were probably teased out of them as Poliza lit their cigarettes. Evans played the Germans at their own game, replying to their friendly questions with a series of fibs. There were 1,000 men in the SBS, he told Poliza, exaggerating tenfold the real strength of the unit. These were split into several detachments and the location of the squadron HQ was variable.

George Miller alone of the prisoners refused to be engaged in conversation. Perhaps he realised early on his mistake in telling his captors he lived on the Lewis Estate in Camberwell, south London. Thereafter 'he declined any questions having military content, despite repeated attempts'.[16] The only thing Miller would say, as all the men said, was that the three Greek fishermen on Alimnia had been coerced into hiding them on their boat. After six days of captivity, the three men were released.

The last question put to Poliza concerned the prisoners' *Sonderbehandlung* ('special treatment'). Had a date yet been set? Poliza replied that 'the people are to be handed over to the SD tomorrow morning [15 April] but are to be further interrogated. The date for the special treatment will be decided by the SD.'[17] *Sonderbehandlung* was the Nazi euphemism for liquidation.

For reasons unknown the four SBS men were not handed over to the SD on 15 April. They remained in Salonika, where they were joined by Allan Tuckey and Ronald Carpenter and subjected to more persistent questioning. Carpenter was continuing to co-operate with the Germans and had even agreed to testify that Turkey had knowingly allowed British forces to infringe its neutrality.

Tuckey was proving altogether more unhelpful. While he was happy to discourse on a number of subjects with his inquisitors, describing the British Labour party as a 'necessary evil', labelling Americans 'a nuisance and boring' and lauding the leadership skills of Winston Churchill, Tuckey became reticent when the conversation turned to military matters. 'He expressed himself with vagueness and avoidance instead refusing concisely to make statements about items to be kept secret,' complained Oberleutnant Straud, his interrogator, who didn't much care for the Englishman. 'He talks in an ironical, often conceited manner and makes demands

George Miller, MM, was unflappable and another of the men specially chosen by Sutherland for the mission to Alimnia. (Courtesy of the SBS Archive)

with respect to his treatment,' continued Straud in his report, adding bitterly: 'He belongs to that class of young intellectual Englishmen who show their self-confidence by ironical and sarcastic superiority.'[18]

The Germans had not had much luck either with Captain Bill Blyth. A week after his capture he had revealed nothing of consequence, merely telling the Germans what they could have worked out for themselves. His interrogator wrote that Blyth was 'an experienced professional soldier who avoided important statements' during questioning. Ominously, however, Oberleutnant Lochner, a 26-year-old German of Greek extraction who was tall and thin with slicked-back black hair, believed the British officer was 'well informed of the structure, force-distribution and deployment possibilities of the Raiding Forces'.[19]

Acting on this statement the Germans ordered a Dr Mueller-Faure to subject Blyth to a more forceful interrogation at Stalag 7A, a prisoner of war camp in Moosburg, southern Germany, where Blyth was flown from Athens. The exact nature of the interrogation was not revealed but in similar scenarios in 1944 a SAS lieutenant captured in France was beaten 'until the whites of his ribs showed', while another officer was put in the *Schaukel* position; his ankles tied to his wrists and an

Standing lower left is Lieutenant Stefan Casulli killed in the Santorini raid in 1944 and top right is Captain Anders Lassen. (Imperial War Museum, HU 71434)

iron bar then passed through his elbow and knee junctures before he was suspended from a step ladder.

Whatever the methods of Mueller-Faure, they were effective. Blyth began to talk. He described how the SBS was split into three Squadrons – L, S and M, the letters denoting the names of the commanders. He revealed what weapons the squadron carried, how they trained with boats and he described the unit's badge as a 'suspended winged perpendicular sword with the motto underneath "Who Dares Wins".[20] But what Blyth did not reveal, despite the best efforts of Mueller-Faure, was names. Jellicoe, Sutherland, Lassen, Patterson, Lapraik, none of them passed his lips. Nor did the location of Raiding Force HQ. It was in Palestine, he admitted, 'by a lake', but he didn't know the name of the lake.

Back in Salonika, the Interrogation and Counter-Intelligence branch of Army Group E sent a telex on 26 April in which they said that further questioning of the prisoners had proved 'fruitless'. They asked whether now was not the time to hand them over to the SD. The reply came the following day, 27 April, from Lieutenant-Colonel Von Harling, the senior intelligence officer. He said that Ronald Carpenter and Michele Lisgaris were to be kept alive in the event that Hitler decided to challenge Turkey on its neutrality. As for the remaining prisoners, they were to be handed over to the SD 'for any further interrogation still of interest to them, and for subsequent special treatment in accordance with the Führer's order'.[21]

Also on 27 April a telex was sent to Colonel Otto Burger, commandant of Stalag 7A, ordering him to hand over Captain Blyth to the local SD 'in accordance with the Führer's order No: 003830/42g top secret of 18/10/42'.[22] Burger ignored the instruction, as he had a similar demand the previous week.

In the following weeks Army Group E forgot about the whole Alminia incident. Then on 22 May a bureaucrat somewhere remembered that Carpenter and Lisgaris were still being held prisoner. A telex was sent to General Walter Warlimont, Deputy Chief of the Armed Forces Operations Staff, asking for guidance. It took Warlimont nearly two weeks to reply but on 4 June he sent a telex saying: 'The British wireless operator Carpenter and the Greek sailor Lisgaris, captured off Alimnia, are no longer required and are released for Special Treatment.'[23]

CHAPTER 12

VENGEANCE

On 16 April, the day Captain Blyth was being brutalised at the hands of Dr Mueller-Faure, David Sutherland received word from Raiding Forces HQ that the operational ban in the Cyclades was lifted. Immediately Sutherland disappeared into the operations room inside *Tewfik* to consult his charts. 'My plan,' he wrote, 'was to attack Mykonos, Ios and Thira simultaneously, priority targets to be shipping and communications.'[1]

By now the SBS knew that Blyth and his men had been captured. 'We heard the news from the Greeks,' recalled Dick Holmes, a reference to the three fishermen released after six days of interrogation on Rhodes. Although the SBS had no indication as to the fate of their comrades, Holmes said they had a pretty good idea of what would happen. 'We were never told what to do if captured. We had no interrogation training, but we didn't really expect to be captured. It was more likely we would be shot.'[2]

Consequently, said Holmes, 'we were not so keen on taking prisoners'. Doug Wright agreed. The disappearance of the Alimnia Patrol triggered a change in philosophy among the SBS. The days of treating prisoners to ice cream in Groppi's was over. 'There was a lot of killing in the Dodecanese,' said Wright, who himself was reputed to have killed eight of the enemy with his bare hands. 'Sometimes we'd

OPPOSITE
M Squadron enjoying some down time between raids in the summer of 1944. (Courtesy of the SBS Archive)

May 1944: Martin Conby, John Lodwick, Sean O'Reilly, Hank Hancock, Tig Harrison, (middle) Lynch, Porter Jarrell, Mick D'Arcy, Bartie, Jock Cree, Grainger Laverick, (front) Malorie, Patsy Henderson. (Courtesy of the SBS Archive)

bring one back for interrogation but mostly we'd just kill them. We didn't really have much respect for them, the Germans.'[3]

One German, Obergefreiter Adolf Lang, had had the good fortune to be captured before news of the Alimnia Patrol reached the SBS. He told his captors everything, including what he knew of German troop dispositions on the island of Santorini (Thira, to the Greeks), where he had been stationed for the duration of December 1943. 'The garrison consisted of 20 Germans and 30 Italians,' explained Lang, who then pointed out on a map of the island the location of the barracks and radar station.

Sutherland told Lassen to visit Santorini. There were three objectives in the operation order issued to the Dane on 19 April:

(i) To destroy, capture or entice enemy shipping in Santorini.
(ii) To destroy enemy communication and personnel on Santorini island.
(iii) To attack other opportunity targets as they occur.[4]

The island itself, the southernmost in the Cyclades, had already been reconnoitred by Lassen who described it as crescent-shaped, 'ten miles by three. Sheer, sombre cliffs of black, volcanic rock.'[5]

The 19-strong party landed at Santorini in the early hours of 23 April 1944 after a three-day sail from their Turkish base. The force was divided into two patrols: 'P' led by Lassen and 'Z' commanded by Lieutenant Keith Balsillie. The raiders hid in a cave overlooking the inland village of Vourvoulos during the day, while Lieutenant Stefan Casulli and their Greek interpreter went into the village to obtain intelligence.

> *'The operations were well planned and carried out in a highly professional way at all levels.'*
>
> David Sutherland

Shortly before midnight the raiders moved off. Balsillie's target was the wireless station at Murivigli while Lassen and his men headed a mile south to the main barracks that were in an old bank.

Included in Lassen's patrol was Sammy Trafford. He recalled that at one point their Danish captain called a halt to their approach 'and made everyone swallow two tablets of Benzedrine pills, watching them go down before taking two himself. He wanted us wide awake. He was a good organiser, a hitman and a killer.'[6] Another of the raiders, signaller Billy Reeves, remembered that 'Lassen's motto on prisoners that night seemed to be "don't take any".'[7]

Dick Holmes is dead to the world but Mac Macauly doesn't look too happy at being woken, though at least this time it wasn't the Germans interrupting their sleep. (Courtesy of the SBS Archive)

Lassen issued last minute instructions to his men. Once inside the barracks they would move methodically through the building in pairs, one man throwing in a grenade, the next raking the room with machine gun fire from the side of the door. 'We succeeded in getting the main force into the billet unobserved, in spite of barking dogs and sentries,' Lassen wrote in his report. 'The living quarters comprised twelve rooms.'[8]

Lassen was paired with Sergeant Jack Nicholson who was armed with a Bren gun. 'That was the only time I was in action side-by-side with Lassen and it's one of the reasons I'm trying to forget the war,' recalled Nicholson years later. 'It's no fun throwing grenades into rooms and shooting sleeping men. That garrison could have been captured.'[9]

Stefan Casulli and Sean O'Reilly were operating together but the young Greek officer lacked Lassen's precision. As O'Reilly hurled a grenade into the first room they encountered, Casulli stepped into the doorway and was hit in the chest by a burst from inside the room.

The call went out for the medical orderly, Sergeant Frank Kingston, but the 24-year-old was himself a casualty after the unexpected return of a German patrol. Kingston had been shot in the stomach as he waited outside the billet, and Sammy Trafford and Jack Hughes were also wounded in the exchange of fire. The German patrol began working their way closer to the entrance of the billet, forcing the SBS back inside the building. Suddenly Nicholson emerged from the bank, firing his Bren gun from his hip in short, deadly bursts. At the same time an Italian fascist leapt 40 feet to his death from an upper floor window. The two simultaneous events unnerved the German patrol, who panicked and fled.

Lassen led his men to the rear of the building where they smashed and shot their way into the billet. Nearly all the enemy encountered on the ground floor were killed. On the upper floors terrified men barricaded the stairway and fired wildly at the assailants below.

Eventually Lassen ordered his men to withdraw. Casulli was dead but Sergeant Kingston was carried away on a gate borrowed from a vineyard; however the medic bled slowly to death en route to the rendezvous with Lieutenant Keith Balsillie. His patrol had suffered no casualties in the successful destruction of the wireless station.

Lassen arrived back at the SBS base on 29 April, ten days after his departure. In the interim Lodwick and his patrol had called on Mykonos, an island in the north of the Cyclades that had been a popular tourist destination before the war. They landed at Lazaretto Bay just before midnight on 22 April and the following day, a Sunday, gleaned information on the disposition of the German troops on the island.

There were only nine of them in total, seven billeted in Mykonos town and two stationed in the lighthouse at the end of a spit.

The attack commenced at 0530 hours the next morning, the SBS having first observed the target from behind the garden wall of the villa that served as the billet. 'The sentry was seen on the balcony and from 40 yards Pct [parachutist] Lynch shot him through the fifth rib on the right side,' Lodwick wrote in his operational report. 'The sentry, subsequently identified to be the Unteroffizier I/C died in two minutes. We then rushed the lower balcony, three grenades, two No.36 and one phosphorous, were thrown up the stairs and the Germans, who later declared that they had sprung out of bed at the first shot, replied with two more, a small piece from one of which went into my behind.'[10]

Lodwick and his men spread out around the villa and orders were shouted for the Germans to surrender. There was no response from inside. The SBS shot the aerial off the roof so their enemy had no recourse to the wireless. 'The attack now developed into a siege,' wrote Lodwick.

Lodwick had despatched three local men to deal with the two Germans in the lighthouse with explicit orders not to kill them. The Greeks obeyed their instructions and now arrived at the villa with two very frightened young Germans. 'I took one

Members of M Squadron, who replaced S Squadron in June 1944 and focused their energies on the Sporades, the islands in the north of the Aegean. (Courtesy of Angie English)

of these prisoners to the garden wall and ordered him to tell his comrades that unless they surrendered immediately we would burn the house down with the aid of a dump of petrol in its grounds,' recalled Lodwick. 'The Germans surrendered immediately.'[11]

'Lassen's motto on prisoners that night seemed to be "don't take any".'

Billy Reeves

Lieutenant Kingsley 'Nobby' Clarke was sent on a tour of the islands with instructions from Sutherland to spread alarm and despondency at every available opportunity. With him went some of the most hardened men in S Squadron: Dick Holmes, Doug Wright, Duggie Pomford and Alan Sanders who, on being asked by Jellicoe the previous year why he wished to join the SBS, had replied that it was to escape the bed-bugs that infested the barracks. Also with the patrol was Fred Crouch, a 26-year-old former Metropolitan policeman who, like Holmes, hailed from east London. 'Freddy was a great guy, steady as a rock, and a very good soldier,' recalled Holmes.

The first island visited by Clarke's patrol was Ios in the south of the Cyclades, known to be lightly defended. Clarke and Pomford broke into a billet and surprised two Germans getting ready for bed. The pair were brave men, leaping at the intruders and trying to kill them with their bare hands. Unfortunately they had the misfortune of taking on Pomford, one of the best amateur boxers in England. Neither German survived.

Meanwhile Dick Holmes, Doug Wright and Fred Crouch had been sent by Clarke to capture three Germans known to be living in a billet on another part of the island. 'We were to lay an ambush for these three Germans,' recalled Holmes. 'I told Doug that I'd shout "hande hoch" but as soon as I did he was to open up with the Bren and shoot the bastards.'

John Lodwick wrote his version of events in *The Filibusters*, describing how the Germans saw the SBS men approach and grabbed some local children for human shields, and using them for protection made their escape. This was not what happened. 'In fact they [the Germans] just came into the village with a young Greek boy walking next to them,' explained Holmes. 'So we let them pass into the village and when they returned without the boy we got them.'

Clarke and his men then destroyed the island's telegraph station and blew up a cache of 75mm shells. With Ios subdued the patrol set sail for Amorgos, 15 miles east, having learned that approximately 30 Germans had recently left the island for Santorini (they were despatched to help hunt for Lassen and his men, who had already escaped). The only man left on Amorgos was the officer in charge, Lieutenant Schiller, who was taking advantage of the solitude to spend time with his Greek mistress. Called upon by Clarke to surrender, the German refused. 'He was a stupid little man and he wasted a great deal of my time,' wrote Clarke in his report.[12]

While Clarke eliminated the disobedient German, Holmes, Crouch and Sanders were sent to Nisiro with instructions to find out what had been happening on the island since Patterson's L Squadron had visited two months earlier. The three men carried out a thorough reconnaissance, noting that the majority of the German troops on Nisiro were garrisoned to the north in Pali. They sketched the position of three coastal guns and learned that the Germans were 'short of food [and] they confiscated goats and cheese from local inhabitants'. Furthermore, some German engineers had visited Nisiro on 6 April to 'ascertain possibilities of mining sulphur'.

The second purpose of the mission to Nisiro was to capture a German for interrogation. 'The Greek who was guiding us put us in a cave at the end of a gully,' remembered Holmes, who removed his boots before slipping into his sleeping bag. Early the next morning the soldiers were preparing to move out of their cave when a German appeared at the entrance. 'He probably heard our voices,' reflected

Dick Holmes, seen here on one of the Dodecanese Islands, likened the campaign of warfare carried out by S Squadron in May 1944 as 'terrorism'. (Courtesy of Angie English)

'Mac' Macauly (centre) bandages the wrist of Duggie Pomford after he had been wounded by shrapnel from a grenade during an island raid. Lieutenant Nobby Clarke watches. (Courtesy of the SBS Archive)

Holmes. 'We were armed to the teeth, bearded and a pretty frightening sight. He turned and ran, trying to drop back behind a terrace – there were lots of terraces – but Al Sanders hit him twice in the back with his Schmeisser.' Holmes spotted another German running for his life. 'I opened up with the Bren. I'm not sure if I hit him but we didn't hang around to find out. We escaped.'

On 1 May Clarke returned to Amorgos. By now ten of the German garrison who had sailed to Santorini had returned to discover that their officer, Lieutenant Schiller, was nowhere to be found in their billet at Katapola Port. 'The ten Germans now on the island had taken over the village school but we knew the lie of the land,' recalled Doug Wright. 'I positioned myself on a flat-topped roof to give covering fire with the rest of the patrol behind a wall on the other side of the school.'

Wright, a left-hander, was approximately 300 yards from the target with the rest of the patrol, which now included five members of the Greek Sacred Squadron, spread out around the school. The attack commenced with a Greek soldier hurling a grenade through one of the school windows. This was Wright's signal. 'I fired ten Bren gun magazines loaded with a good mixture of ball, tracer and incendiary and armour piercing,' he remembered, 'raking all the windows and doors of the building.'

Immediately after Wright ceased firing Duggie Pomford dashed forward, throwing a grenade through a window and then firing a quick burst from his Tommy gun. Clarke called on the Germans to surrender. Instead they chose to burst out of the building, guns blazing as if they were Wild West bandits fleeing a botched bank raid. Two of the ten escaped in the darkness; the rest were shot dead. 'It wasn't possible to take many prisoners,' reflected Wright, who was awarded the Military Medal for his part in the attack as its success was 'to a very great extent due to the work of this NCO'.

At Raiding Forces HQ in Azzib, there was widespread delight at all the destruction being wrought on the islands. An Intelligence Report, written in the first week of May, described April's activities and ended with the following:

> Tribute is paid many times to Raiding Forces, agents and Greeks alike in the captured German orders from Mykonos, but none so gratifying to all concerned as the phrase: WIR BEFINDEN UNS IN FEINDES LAND written across the middle of a page of security instructions. Translation (approx.) 'WE ARE LIVING IN AN ENEMY COUNTRY'.[13]

May continued where April had left off as far as the SBS was concerned. Lassen led a patrol to Paros – just 70 miles south of the Greek mainland – with the intention of destroying an airstrip in the throes of construction. But the target was well guarded and Lassen, no doubt mindful of his experience on Crete the previous July, aborted the attack. Nonetheless they did not leave the island empty-handed; an officer and three soldiers were killed in a raid on one billet and a similar number of enemy soldiers disposed of on a second assault.

On the nearby island of Naxos Nobby Clarke was again creating havoc with his patrol. A single German garrison containing one officer and 17 men was attacked on 22 May. Once again devastatingly accurate bursts of fire from Doug Wright's Bren terrorised the Germans, and as on Amorgos Duggie Pomford 'conducted himself with coolness and complete disregard for danger', for which he was awarded a bar to his Military Medal.[14]

Hank Hancock took this photo of Dick Holmes on board *Tewfik*. (Courtesy of the SBS Archive)

DOWN TIME

The SBS revelled in their piratical acts in 1944 and this was reflected in life at their Turkish hideout where they lived on their wooden schooners. (Courtesy of Angie English)

ABOVE **M Squadron relaxing between raids in the summer of 1944.** (Courtesy of the SBS Archive)

Anders Lassen (front) shortly before departing on the raid to Santorini, which eye-witnesses recalled as a 'bloodbath'. (Courtesy of the SBS Archive)

Those left alive surrendered, including one sergeant who provided much amusement on the sea voyage home. 'Every five minutes he would stand up, give a Nazi salute and shout "*Heil Hitler*",' recalled Wright. 'He was a fine figure of a man but completely brainwashed.'

Though Clarke's patrol were on their way back to their base in Turkey there was still great danger in the Aegean. 'On the way back the motor blew so we had to sail across,' remembered Holmes. 'On a couple of occasions German aircraft came in low to investigate us but fortunately some of the boys had taken to wearing the German peaked caps and we carried a lot of German weapons so that fooled the pilots. It was pretty nerve-wracking but the Levant [Schooner] crew were cool customers.'

At the end of May S Squadron received orders to return to Palestine. Sutherland, who not wishing to miss out on the action had led a raid against the island of Saphos, totted up the squadron's scorecard in the previous two months: three caiques captured and 12 sunk or damaged; three wireless stations destroyed and 11 more captured; three cable stations destroyed and dozens of enemy soldiers killed or captured. In addition 25 tons of much needed food had been distributed to the malnourished inhabitants of the islands. On the debit side, the SBS had suffered two fatalities (Lieutenant Casulli and Sergeant Kingston) and Bill Blyth and his four men were in enemy hands. 'I reflected as we sailed quietly south back to Beirut how special these officers and men were,' recalled Sutherland. 'The operations were well planned and carried out in a highly professional way at all levels.'[15]

Donald Grant, the American war correspondent who had arrived in Turkish waters with Sutherland in March, had accompanied the SBS on one raid to see first-hand their skill in guerrilla warfare. He subsequently described the experience in a radio broadcast made on 22 May: 'One cold morning, with spring fresh on the mountainside, where nimble-footed goats stepped over wild flowers, a British patrol took me with them while they ambushed and killed the commandant of a certain German garrison walking with his young bodyguard along a narrow gravel road.'[*]

Grant then described how on patrol,

> … no-one washes because the water is scarce and no one ever takes his clothes off at night. There is considerable variation in uniform, but all are dirty, greasy and torn. About the only common garment to all Raiding Force men is a strangely hooded jacket, which makes them appear to be a band of Robin Hood's merry men, stepped out of a story book, complete with knives slung at their belts.[16]

---

[*] This was on the island of Piscopi when a patrol led by Keith Balsillie killed the commandant after luring him from his office with a present of a 'big, fat pig' for his lunch.

CHAPTER 13

GERMANY ON THE RUN

The storm of carnage that had swept through the Aegean in the first months of 1944 frightened the Germans. Though the division garrisoned in Rhodes was of a high calibre, many of the reinforcements that had been drafted in to defend the other islands at the end of 1943 were of an inferior quality, men who were recovering both physically and emotionally from their experiences on the Russian front. Promised that the Aegean would offer them sun, sea and serenity, they were terrified by the bearded British pirates who visited upon the islands a whirlwind of violence. 'Gone for ever were the days when the German defenders would be found in bed,' wrote John Lodwick. 'The German defenders now slept increasingly in slit trenches with barbed wire for their eiderdown.'[1]

In May 1944 the Germans felt compelled to fortify the Aegean Islands with an additional 4,000 soldiers at a time when they could ill afford to divert troops from other fronts. Into this maelstrom of reinforced steel sailed M Squadron, sent north to replace David Sutherland and his men. They were led not by Ian Lapraik – unavoidably detained in Alexandria – but by his second-in-command Stewart Macbeth, a former *aide de camp* to General Kenneth Anderson, commander of the First Army in Tunisia. According to Lodwick, Macbeth 'was a young man of a type so far unknown and very badly needed in the SBS ... tactful, possessed

By the end of the summer of 1944 the SBS left the Dodecanese in the capable hands of the Greek Sacred Squadron, some of whom are seen here. (Courtesy of Angie English)

considerable charm of manner … the unit's professional diplomatist, smoother of ruffled feathers and envoy extraordinary'.[2]

Macbeth, aware that the Germans had strengthened the islands, decided upon a change of strategy. Instead of focusing their energies on the Cyclades and the Dodecanese, M Squadron would concentrate on the Sporades, the islands in the north of the Aegean. Captains Jimmy Lees and Charles Bimrose led patrols into these islands where for two weeks they carried out reconnaissance missions. Here the SBS had their first encounter with ELAS, the left-wing guerrilla fighters who in time would prove to be as awkward as they were courageous.★

Meanwhile Lieutenant Bob Bury was also having difficulties with the Greeks, who mistook his caique and his men for Germans on numerous occasions as they toured the Sporades searching out targets. Eventually, however, the Greeks, recovering from their surprise of finding British commandos so far north, advised him to visit the island of Pelagos. The small German garrison was billeted in a monastery, Bury was told, which turned out to be true. It was a 16th-century post-Byzantine monastery located on top of a hill overlooking the sea on the eastern

★ ELAS, the Greek People's Liberation Army, was the military arm of the predominantly communist National Liberation Front EAM.

side of the islet. As they approached the monastery the Greek guide spotted what he took to be a monk, until the monk removed a grenade from his greatcoat and hurled it in their direction. The sentry was killed and the monastery sacked.

Other than the raid on Pelagos the Sporades did not strike Macbeth as a fertile hunting ground so in late June he decided to return to the Dodecanese. A ten-man patrol under Lees was ordered to Kalymnos, the scene of a ferocious attack by John Lodwick two months earlier in which he had blown up the cable station and sunk ten caiques moored in the harbour, one of which was the pride and joy of the local Gestapo chief.

Among Lees' patrol was Ken Smith, embarking on his first operation with the SBS. He remembered that the landing on the west coast of Kalymnos was a harbinger of things to come. 'I got one foot ashore and the chap in the boat went to offer me the battery but the ship lurched and the battery went in so we had no [radio] contact.' Nonetheless they pushed inland, climbing a hill until they reached a cave whereupon Lees divided the patrol. 'He said to me and my mate, Bill Mayall, "go off tonight and recce Vathi on the other side".'[3]

Smith and Mayall struck out east over the rugged interior of Kalymnos and by dawn they were in position overlooking the harbour of Vathi. 'We watched them round the clock,' Smith recalled. 'Changing guard, queuing up for breakfast, movement of transport, despatch riders coming and going, swimming in the bay, where guns were, any useful intelligence.' At nightfall they returned to the cave and informed Lees that the harbour was strongly garrisoned with scores of troops. Smith and Mayall were next ordered to carry out a similar reconnaissance on the little village of Chorio in the southern heartland of the island. 'As we were trying to get into position above Chorio we could hear bells,' remembered Smith. 'It was this Greek girl taking the goats to pasture. We were trying to hide from rock to rock, and we found ourselves in full daylight, right alongside the road, but lucky enough there wasn't many people around.'[4]

Little of interest occurred during the day, and one of the few entries Smith made in his notebook was a brief exchange of gunfire from the direction of Vathi. In fact the shots were the result of a contact between an SBS patrol and a couple of Germans too inquisitive for their own good. Informed by a local boy that he had seen suspicious figures on the hillside, the two Germans came to investigate themselves rather than first calling for reinforcements. One of the two was shot dead from a distance of 10 yards. The other fled and in his haste to escape slipped and fell over a cliff to his death.

Smith and Mayall knew that the gunfire, whatever its cause, would bring out the Germans. As they broke cover and began making for the SBS hideout they could see the enemy moving across the hills all around. For hours the pair moved cautiously from rock to rock and from shrub to shrub, evading the frequent German patrols that passed close by. Eventually they reached the cave and for the two days the men laid low until 'it had seemed to quieten down'.[5] Eventually Lees considered it safe enough to lead his men to the beach where they were picked up by a LSF caique in the dead of night.

'Gone for ever were the days when the German defenders would be found in bed… The German defenders now slept increasingly in slit trenches with barbed wire for their eiderdown.'

John Lodwick

A few days later the SBS returned to Kalymnos. They came ashore at Vathi on the evening of 1 July, a 25-strong force consisting of SBS and Greek Sacred Squadron. At once they came under accurate mortar fire from a German garrison who now knew never to underestimate the audacity of their foe. As flares illuminated the night sky the British began taking casualties.

Despite valiant attempts to reach the houses that lined the seafront, the invaders were beaten back by the mortar barrage and the well-directed small-arms fire from inside the buildings. Eventually the SBS withdrew to their vessels leaving behind three wounded men. Ian Lapraik arrived in the Gulf of Kos a few days later and was withering in his assessment of the botched attack. 'The approach and attack were reasonably sound,' he wrote. 'The withdrawal, however, I do not consider to have been in any way satisfactory.'[6]

Lapraik resolved to restore the reputation of the SBS with an operation that would far exceed any other in scale and daring, and which would disabuse the Germans of the notion that they might be returning order to the Aegean.

The target was Simi, that old friend of the SBS, but to reach the island the raiders would first have to eliminate a pair of formidable obstacles in their path. These were two German destroyers berthed at Porto Lago in Leros, one of which was the *Turbine*, an Italian vessel that had been commandeered by the Germans and converted into a torpedo boat. The SBS lacked the skills to destroy the destroyers so Lapraik requested help from Brigadier Turnbull at Raiding Forces HQ. He in turn contacted the Royal Marines Boom Patrol Detachment, a unit formed two years earlier that had scored a noticeable success at the end of that year in a raid on enemy shipping at Bordeaux that gave rise to the legend of the 'Cockleshell Heroes'.

A section of this unit had been posted to the Middle East in early 1944 and they were only too glad to accept the assignment. Three canoe parties paddled silently into Porto Lago and with the aid of limpet mines sank an ammunition ship and two escort vessels, causing serious damage to the *Turbine* and the second destroyer. Both ships were towed back to Athens for repairs, much to the satisfaction of Lapraik who sent Macbeth to Simi on a reconnaissance in the first week of July. Upon his return Lapraik and Turnbull, who had decided to lead the attack in person, sailed from Yedi Atala towards the island in a flotilla comprising ten motor launches and two schooners and 220 soldiers, 139 of whom were from the Greek Sacred Squadron.

Duggie Pomford dresses up as a German while onboard one of the SBS caiques. By this disguise the SBS managed to avoid attacks by the Luftwaffe. (Courtesy of the SBS Archive)

Turnbill split his force into three. 'Main Force', under his command and with Lapraik as his second-in-command, would attack Simi Town in the north of the island, the objective being to neutralise the German HQ in the medieval castle overlooking the harbour; Stewart Macbeth and 'South Force' had the task of assaulting the monastery of St Michel in the south of the island; Captain Charles Clynes, a 26-year-old Northern Irishman, would lead 'West Force' against the caique yard that lay in the harbour close to Simi Town.

Ken Smith was in West Force. 'We spent the whole night climbing up [the hill overlooking the harbour] with 3-inch mortars,' he recalled. By dawn they were in position watching two 'Ems' barges and a couple of German caiques sail out of the harbour. 'We saw the convoy leave and as soon as they were out of sight the first mortar landed,' said Smith, part of a Bren gun crew with instructions to target a coastal gun on the other side of the harbour. 'As dawn broke we couldn't see the gun, it was too well camouflaged. But they gave themselves away because as dawn broke the men – about ten of them – began to move around and stretch, and then amble down to the house in the harbour.'[7]

A member of the Levant Flotilla Schooner. (Courtesy of the SBS Archive)

The SBS's Bren guns began firing, cutting down the Germans and sending those unscathed scurrying back to the house. Clynes called a halt, and then sent in the Greek Sacred Squadron to mop up the last of the German resistance. 'All I can remember, then,' wrote Clynes subsequently, 'is a general surge up the slope and two small and pathetic white handkerchiefs waving at the top of it. I ordered a "Cease fire" all round and began to count my prisoners.'[8]

The two barges had not sailed far from the harbour before they were confronted by five of the British motor launches. More white flags were waved. With the harbour in the hands of the invaders, Smith was ordered to take his Bren gun and help out at the castle where a fierce firefight was in progress. As Smith scrambled towards a suitable firing position he came under fire himself. 'Someone opened up on me, bullets whizzing down,' he recalled. 'I dived to ground and got my head against a rock and I could feel the vibrations of the bullets hitting the rock.'[9]

By 0900 hours Turnbull's Main Force had advanced to within 800 yards of the castle ramparts, but despite a combination of mortar rounds and cannon fire from the motor launches, the Germans showed no inclination to surrender.

In the south of Simi, meanwhile, Stewart Macbeth's South Force had blasted the Germans out of the monastery and pursued them down to the edge of the island. The Germans were trapped; it was either give up or jump to their death. Having received an assurance from Macbeth that they would not be handed over to the locals for summary execution, the Germans surrendered.

Back at the castle the British were making little headway. Recognizing that a change of tactic was required, Brigadier Turnbull sent a petty officer from one of the captured Em Barges into the castle to inform the garrison commander of the hopelessness of his position. The naval officer returned with an encouraging message; the Germans were willing to parley. Having first given a brief demonstration of the firepower at his disposal, Turnbull then sent one of his young lieutenants, the German-speaking Kenneth Fox, into the castle, along with a more senior representative of the invasion force, Lieutenant-Commander Leslie Ramsayer, the naval liaison officer from Raiding Forces HQ.

For three hours the men discussed surrender terms, with the British growing ever more irritated by the prevarication of the German commander. So Turnbull gave him an ultimatum: surrender or die. The demand had the desired effect. Minutes after the last of the German garrison had laid down his weapon, three Messerschmitts roared overhead and dropped a stick of anti-personnel bombs on the harbour. The German commandant was reported to have shaken his head and with a wry smile said to Turnbull: 'I radioed for them five hours ago … that's what comes of being late.'[10]

The attack on Simi was a resounding success for the SBS. For the loss of two Greek officers who drowned as they came ashore, the invasion force had killed 21 enemy troops and taken a further 151 prisoner. Lapraik celebrated by ordering breakfast for everyone, Germans included, in the harbour yard. Then the British and Greeks embarked on an orgy of destruction, sinking 19 German caiques at anchor in the harbour, blowing up everything from gun emplacements to wireless stations and throwing tons of supplies into the sea. That evening, just before midnight, the raiders returned to their base, their prisoners loaded onto the two barges. The following morning the Germans launched a counter-offensive, sending in a flight of bombers before landing a large number of infantry. The soldiers stepped ashore to find nothing but bacon rinds and 21 bodies.

The destruction of Simi was the last act of the SBS in the Aegean. They were required elsewhere and the Greek Sacred Squadron was now perfectly capable of harassing the Germans unaided by their British allies. 'For the present you will confine yourself to reconnaissance,' Lapraik instructed the Greek commander. 'But in September, raiding activities will be resumed upon a much larger scale.'[11]

M Squadron returned to Palestine in July to learn that the squadron was about to depart for Italy in preparation for operations in Greece and Yugoslavia. The SBS were sorry to say goodbye to the Greek islands after nearly a year of operations in which they had learned to respect and admire the people: poor and downtrodden, but generous and brave. 'The Greeks on the whole were very good,' reflected Holmes. 'They were reliable and could be trusted. It was impossible to land on one of the islands without the islanders knowing so it paid to be on good terms. We'd usually leave a case of corned beef to keep them happy and sometimes buy a sheep with a gold sovereign, but they were nearly always willing to help despite knowing the consequences if caught.'[12]

CHAPTER 14

INTO THE BALKANS

The Special Boat Squadron were no longer under the command of Brigadier Turnbull, who remained with Raiding Forces HQ in the Gulf of Kos, but instead answered to Land Forces Adriatic (LFA), commanded by Brigadier George Davy.★

The LFA was based at Bari, on the east coast of Italy, and for a couple of weeks the squadron remained in the city while a suitable base was found. Doug Wright, Duggie Pomford and four other members of the squadron kept fit in Bari by sparring with an NCO in the US Army. His name was Joe Louis, the then reigning heavyweight champion of the world. 'Six of us did three minute rounds with him,' recalled Wright, himself a decent light heavyweight amateur before the war. 'He didn't hit us, that was the condition that we sparred with him!'[1]

The new home of the SBS was in the town of Monte St Angelo on the spur of the Italian boot. Situated at 2,500 feet above sea level, the town was in the Gargano Peninsula, a 'barren waste of granite and virgin forest which provides the only topographical relief in 800 miles of Italian Adriatic coastline'. The Long Range Desert Group were already in the town, a chance for the SBS to renew old acquaintances and receive thorough briefings on the situation across the Adriatic in Yugoslavia and Albania.

★ In autumn 1944 the islands of the Aegean began toppling like dominos as the Germans were ousted, either with a fight or in some cases with barely a shot being fired.

OPPOSITE
Members of the Greek Sacred Squadron, who took part in the audacious raid on Simi, in July 1944. (Courtesy of Angie English)

Des Marshall, one of L Squadron's signallers, on leave in Beirut in the autumn of 1944. (Courtesy of Ian Layzell)

On the evening of 27 August Andy Lassen and 11 men, including a signaller and a Royal Engineer corporal, crossed the 100 miles of Adriatic that separated Italy from Yugoslavia in a fast motor launch. 'We were all carrying two rucksacks,' recalled Dick Holmes. 'One contained our own kit and the other fifty pounds of plastic explosive, so there wasn't much room on board.'[2]

The explosives were to be used to blow up a railway bridge over a gorge inland from Gruda, a village approximately 20 miles south of the port of Dubrovnik. 'According to our intelligence there should have been ten partisans and a couple of mules waiting for us when we arrived,' said Holmes. 'But there were no mules and the partisans couldn't carry our explosives so we had to carry them.'

The route inland was treacherous, particularly at night. Steep ascents criss-crossed with narrow, crumbling footpaths. Weighed down with their packs the raiders' progress was slow and tortuous. 'It took us a couple of night marches to reach the bridge,' recalled Wright. 'But finally we reached a mountainside from where we could see the target.'

The region was known to be rife not just with Germans but with their barbarous allies, the fascist Ustashi, whose predilection for savagery surpassed even that of the Nazis. In 1942 the Gestapo compiled a report in which they described how the 'Ustashi committed their deeds in a bestial manner not only against males of conscript age, but especially against helpless old people, women and children'.[3]

The next day the SBS kept the bridge under surveillance, noting the timings of trains and any other activity. The following evening, 30 August, they made their way down to the bridge. 'To our delight we discovered that the Germans had already drilled holes ready for its demolition,' recalled Wright. 'They were planning to blow it once they'd retreated north.'

The SBS soldiers attached electric charges to each of the bridge's abutments while a corporal from the Royal Engineers made a junction box with a primer cord to each charge. It took only a few minutes but the minutes felt like hours to the saboteurs as the sapper inspected the 500lb of explosive.

Once the wiring from the charges to the plunger was in place, Holmes and Lassen crouched behind a large rock 200 feet from the bridge. 'On the count of three I pressed down on the plunger but nothing happened, there was no proper connection,' recalled Holmes. 'I tried again but the same result.' Lassen ordered Holmes to clean the plunger, believing that to be the source of the problem. 'I unscrewed the terminals and polished and replaced the wires,' recalled Holmes. 'We pressed once more and again there was nothing.'

By now the air was blue with Lassen's profanities. Ignoring the insults, the engineer scrambled down to the bridge to implement plan B. Running a safety fuse from the detonator back to the rock, he struck a match and assured the SBS that this method was fail-safe. 'But after three minutes the bridge was still standing and Lassen was starting to get impatient again,' explained Holmes. 'He wanted to go down and have a look for himself. Then suddenly the whole lot goes up and great chunks of masonry begin raining down on us. One bloody big piece flew past over head. It's amazing no one got killed.'

Unlike a lot of photos taken by the wartime SBS, Albert Layzell scribbled details on the back of this snap to remind himself 'who', 'where' and 'when' … (Courtesy of Ian Layzell)

The SBS men did not stay to admire their destructive handiwork. 'The job itself was easy,' reflected Wright. 'It was afterwards when it was tricky.' Leaving behind a thick pall of yellow dust the British raiders hurried high up into the mountains until they reached the sanctuary of the partisan HQ. 'There were a couple of young women among them who made us a big cauldron of delicious stew,' remembered Wright. 'Then we got our heads down and slept like babies.'

In his official report on the blowing of the bridge, Lassen wrote that 'on the morning of 2 Sept 44, this [partisan] HQ was surrounded by 400 Ustashi and Germans and fighting began. Lt [Jim] Henshaw with five men defended one ridge. Later a withdrawal was ordered and carried out successfully.'[4]

Both Wright and Holmes have different recollections of the morning events. 'We ran,' recalled Wright. 'That's the only way to do it. Hit and run, that's how we operated. We don't want to lose highly trained men. There was no point in fighting. You've got to at times but no point in sticking your neck out when you're only ten.'

A patrol from L Squadron poses near Kozani, Albania, as they chased the Germans north out of Greece. (Courtesy of Ian Layzell)

Holmes remembered that they were woken by a shout from a breathless and terrified partisan. 'Ustashi!' he blurted out and, turning to the British, he added 'Very bad.' In the grey dawn light Holmes saw between 50 and 75 Germans and Ustashi advancing up the mountain towards their hideout, the officer in charge blowing a whistle and exhorting his men to move more quickly.

Lassen ordered his men to take up defensive positions along the rim of a hollow. 'He decided to engage the approaching enemy troops to the disgust of the rest of us,' reflected Holmes. 'I believe he was anxious to impress the partisans … we had done what we had been asked to do. Nothing would be gained by staying to fight.'

Holmes said that the subsequent myth of a heroic last stand was perpetuated by an SBS sergeant 'who was not even there'. What actually happened was that as the enemy advanced ever closer the partisans bolted. Holmes spotted their departure and passed the news on to Lassen.

'He didn't believe me at first but he rushed up just in time to see the last of our friends disappearing round a bend in the path,' explained Holmes. 'As soon as he realised we were on our own he gave the order to get the hell out. We took to our heels, leaving our rucksacks behind. During the course of our hasty retreat Doug Wright fired a burst from his Bren gun and I loosed off a short burst from my Tommy gun. These were the only shots fired.'

'We split up into twos and were given a rendezvous four days later,' said Wright, who paired off with Holmes as they ran further up the mountain. 'We were up in the hills for three or four days with no food,' added Holmes. 'I had, as we all did, a mixture of oatmeal, sugar and chocolate but … no utensil to put it in.' Eventually they encountered the partisans again who gave them some roasted potatoes and told Wright that the two women who had fed them a few nights earlier had been caught by the Ustashi and 'chopped to bits'.

The partisans rounded up the British raiders (all except the Royal Engineer who never made the rendezvous) and guided them to the pick-up beach in the early hours of 6 September. 'We hid among some bushes and signalled out to sea,' said Holmes. 'A searchlight suddenly sent its beam out to sea and caught in it was a small boat. We assumed it was our launch and quickly decided that it would not risk collecting us that night.' Holmes felt his spirits plunge. His feet were in agony from all the marching through the mountains of the previous week and because he had been compelled to leave behind his rucksack he had had no change of socks for days. 'Suddenly we spotted a boat coming towards us and a voice called out "SBS",' said Holmes. 'We recognised George Jellicoe's voice. It heaved to and we were ferried aboard in inflatable dinghies.'

The men crowded below and within moments most were asleep. When Holmes woke his feet were so badly swollen that he had to cut off his socks in strips. Back at their base in Italy he went to see the squadron medical officer, 'and got a little testy when he made a stupid remark concerning changing my socks more often'.

More S Squadron patrols were inserted into Yugoslavia in September but none met with much success, nor much help from the locals. 'Yugoslavia was a difficult place to operate and bridges were about the only things we could attack,' said Holmes. 'The Yugoslavs didn't want us there, Tito didn't, and they were uncooperative and suspicious.'

L Squadron in less demanding circumstances, making the most of a rest period in Greece. (Courtesy of David Henry)

The job itself was easy… It was afterwards when it was tricky.'
Doug Wright

There was another factor that mitigated against SBS operations. They were no longer fighting an enemy from island to island but were engaged in a war on a continent; lines of resupply were therefore more problematical and means of escape also presented a greater challenge.

The officer who adapted most quickly to this more demanding environment was Captain Ambrose McGonigal, a Southern Irishman who had recently joined the squadron along with Lieutenant Ian Smith. Both men arrived with splendid reputations, having won four Military Crosses between them for commando operations in Europe. Smith was a 24-year-old from Somerset who had represented the army at rugby and survived the shambles at Dunkirk in 1940. That convinced him of the need to leave the infantry as soon as possible if he was to have a chance of surviving the war. 'I think I had an easy time, usually sleeping dry and warm and getting regular food,' he said of his experiences in the special forces. 'The only difference is that if an ordinary soldier had been caught he would have been a POW, whereas if we had been nabbed then the consequences would have been very unpleasant.'[5]

Smith was surprised to find David Sutherland doing so well for himself in the SBS. The pair had been in the same platoon at Sandhurst five years earlier and Smith had Sutherland down as the type of officer to thrive in a spit-and-polish regiment. But here he was, second-in-command of the SBS, and greatly admired by his men. Nonetheless, reflected Smith, 'I sometimes felt he did not quite enjoy all the jokes and inconsequential behaviour that abounded'.[6]

At the start of September Sutherland sent McGonigal and his eight-strong patrol into southern Yugoslavia, close to the border with Albania, with orders to harass and delay the Germans as they retreated north from Greece towards Italy. The Irishman soon realized that the best method of establishing a working relationship with the partisans 'was to tell them absolutely nothing about his plans'. That way there would be no interference. If the partisans had any doubts as to the British commitment to kill Germans they were dispelled by McGonigal. Throughout September he waged a vicious war with the enemy, ambushing convoys and on one occasion springing an ambush on a platoon of Germans in a defile. Twenty were killed in the initial hail of bullets. 'The remainder,' recalled McGonigal, 'threw arms, ammunition, even water-bottles away, and ran as hard as possible.'[7]

McGonigal had with him Robert Eden, a member of the Special Operations Executive, who one night learned of a troop train that would be passing along a stretch of remote railway in a couple of days' time. In a joint attack with the partisans, the SBS ambushed and derailed the train. 'The enemy evacuated the train and we

Albert Layzell was a Welshman who joined the SBS in 1944 just in time for the drive into the Balkans. (Courtesy of Ian Layzell)

pursued them down the railway line where they took cover in a wood at the side of the line,' remembered Eden, 'and it was now hand-to-hand fighting.'[8]

The Germans were slaughtered in the wood. When the battle was over 37 of their number had been killed or wounded. McGonigal had lost one of his men, Private Ellis Howells, a 25-year-old from Swansea who had followed his officer into the SBS from 12 Commando. The next day Howells was buried and 'the local population of a man attended his funeral as a mark of respect'.[9]

McGonigal's achievements illuminated an otherwise bleak period for the SBS. 'We were stepping into a full-blown Balkan Civil War,' reflected Sutherland,

'We were stepping into a full-blown Balkan Civil War
... with Royalists and Communists fighting each other to
the death in Albania and Yugoslavia.'

David Sutherland

'with Royalists and Communists fighting each other to the death in Albania and Yugoslavia.'[10]

Sutherland decided that the squadron's cause would best be served if he was on the ground alongside his men rather than back in southern Italy, so he parachuted into Albania and based himself just south of the town of Permet close to the border with Greece. Waiting for him were some of the squadron's most experienced operators, including Duggie Pomford, Stud Stellin and Jimmy Lees. They looked as Sutherland soon felt − exasperated at the sullen truculence of the communist partisans in the area. Sutherland was informed by their interpreter that the partisan leader 'does not like your arrival on the scene as this will spoil his personal standing with his political and military superiors'.[11] Sutherland was advised to move his men further north, which he did the following day, finding the Albanian peasants infinitely more agreeable than the partisans. They were fed royally at each village, plied with 'spectacular meals of veal and poussin with rare Albanian steaks soaked in wine'.[12] Of the enemy there was no sign; most had already fled north so the SBS contented themselves with shooting ducks in the marshland: less dangerous and infinitely more delicious.

The bountiful food in Albania was one of the few pleasures of the squadron's operations in the Balkans that autumn. The men, Sutherland remembered, 'longed for the sound of Greek voices again, and for the feeling of trust and co-operation' which they had experienced in the first half of the year.[13] In fact the SBS were about to become reacquainted with the Greeks but the bond of friendship they had developed with the islanders in the Aegean was to be broken on the mainland as the internecine conflict that had caused so much mistrust in Yugoslavia and Albania spread to Greece.

OPPOSITE
Young women, such as this Albanian partisan, often proved braver and more reliable than their male counterparts. (Courtesy of the SBS Archive)

CHAPTER 15

THE NAZIS' GREEK TRAGEDY

By September 1944 the Third Reich was on its way to defeat. Squeezed on two fronts, Germany began recalling its troops from the Balkans to defend its border from the Soviet troops rampaging westwards. As German soldiers streamed north from Greece, up through Albania and Yugoslavia, Winston Churchill demanded that his chiefs of staff act quickly to ensure that British troops beat their Soviet allies into Greece. The problem faced by Britain was a lack of resources; with so many soldiers fighting their way up Italy or across France, there simply were not enough troops in the Mediterranean theatre to meet Churchill's insistence that a force of 5,000 march on Athens. The Americans were not interested in helping either, so instead the British turned to its air force and special forces to seize a series of key objectives while they waited for additional troops to arrive from elsewhere.

First into action was M Squadron, now led by Andy Lassen following the transfer of Ian Lapraik to the Greek Sacred Squadron. M Squadron was part of 'Foxforce', commanded by Lieutenant-Colonel Ronnie Tod of No.9 Commando. Foxforce consisted of commandos, SBS, Greek Sacred Squadron, LRDG and the Raiding Support Regiment. Tod was answerable to the 2nd Special Service Brigade that came under overall control of Brigadier Davy's Land Forces Adriatic.

On 15 September Foxforce occupied the island of Kythira, 6 miles south of the Peloponnese, the large peninsula in southern Greece. The island was a good base from which to launch operations on the Greek mainland and the British established a naval base on the south of the island. From here the SBS and LRDG began reconnoitring the islands in the Bay of Athens.

Meanwhile L Squadron was handed the task of seizing the airfield at Araxes in the north-west of the Peloponnese. This would allow air support to be provided for all subsequent land operations in Greece. After an initial reconnaissance of the

'It was great… The welcome we received was unbelievable. There were women everywhere wanting to kiss us!'
Doug Wright

airfield had been carried out by Charles Bimrose, Ian Patterson and his 58 men of L Squadron dropped by parachute onto Araxes on 23 September. The following day the main force – codenamed 'Bucket Force' – landed on the airfield in a fleet of Dakotas – with George Jellicoe and Walter Milner-Barry among the 450 personnel. Patterson, meanwhile, had already despatched a couple of patrols in the direction of Patras, a port 20 miles east along the coast, which was still in German hands.

The patrols reported that Patras was garrisoned by approximately 900 Germans and 1,600 Greeks from a collaborationist security battalion. Establishing his HQ just outside Patras, Patterson deployed his men on the high ground overlooking the port and through a combination of perpetual movement and concentrated mortar and small-arms fire convinced the enemy that they were faced by a considerable force. Then, in the company of a local Red Cross representative, Patterson entered Patras under a white flag. The German commander listened to what Patterson had to say but conveyed the impression he was 'playing for time'. So the British turned their attention to the 1,600 Greek collaborators, all of whom were terrified as to their fate if the port fell. Jellicoe gave them his word that if they surrendered they would not be handed over to their left-wing compatriots. The Greeks dithered. Jellicoe gave them a deadline – surrender by 0600 hours on 2 October or else answer to the communists. Jellicoe was pessimistic about the chances of their compliance but at the appointed hour 1,600 Greeks gave up the fight.

As the Greek collaborators streamed out of Patras, Charles Bimrose raced into the port hoping to catch the Germans before their withdrawal. The majority of the enemy had already put to sea when the convoy of SBS jeeps arrived at their HQ; those that had not were engaged by Bimrose and his men, the British causing 'much confusion and damage, and inflicting many casualties' on the German stragglers.[1]

Despite Bimrose's pugnacity the Germans made what the SBS considered an orderly withdrawal from Patras on the night of 3 October. Milner-Barry and George Jellicoe entered the port at 0800 hours the following morning, accompanied by an ELAS Brigade Commander. From their jeep flew the flags of their respective nations. 'Terrific reception,' Milner-Barry wrote in his diary. 'Carpet on the streets, flowers and lovely girls on balconies.'[2]

A sizeable press corps followed the SBS into Patras and one American correspondent wrote that 'Major Earl Jellicoe, son of the famous British admiral, commanded the Allied forces into Patras'. It was hoped, added the correspondent, that the fall of the port 'might clear the way for a major Allied operation in Greece that could result in the liberation of the entire country within two weeks'.[3]

To expedite such an ambition, Patterson set off in pursuit of the Germans who had sailed out of Patras heading east up the Gulf of Corinth towards the Corinth Canal. In a convoy of jeeps the SBS roared along the headland overlooking the gulf, a captured field gun hitched to the back of Patterson's vehicle. Whenever the

The communist graffiti behind these men of L Squadron in Athens gives a clue to the trouble brewing within Greece following the German withdrawal. (Courtesy of Ian Layzell)

THE MOVE THROUGH GREECE

LEFT
Albert Layzell, second left, and his L Squadron comrades during the advance through Greece. (Courtesy of Ian Layzell)

BELOW
It wasn't all work for the SBS in Greece, and there was plenty of time to take a jeep and play the tourist, (Courtesy of Angie English)

RIGHT
Two soldiers from L Squadron at their billet in Athens. (Courtesy of Ian Layzell)

LEFT
Even though the political situation in Greece was to cause problems for the SBS, the locals proved very hospitable, as seen by this tavern owner and his wife. (Courtesy of Ian Layzell)

German fleet came into view, Patterson loosed off a few shells. 'It was not altogether satisfactory as the Germans had removed the [gun] sights,' he recalled later. 'However, by a process of hit or miss, we succeeded in inflicting casualties; many of them due, I have no doubt, to shock.'[4]

Patterson reached Corinth on 7 October, exchanged desultory fire with the Germans on the other side of the canal and then accepted the surrender of another battalion of Greek collaborators. From Corinth, the SBS advanced as far east as the town of Megara, where Patterson divided his force. Bimrose led a section north towards Thebes with orders to continue the harassment of the Germans. There were several contacts in the days that followed and during one of these Lance-Corporal James Carmichael was killed. Another patrol commanded by Lieutenant Keith Balsillie sailed across the Bay of Salamis on a reconnaissance. When Balsillie stepped off his caique and onto the Piraeus, he unwittingly became the first soldier of the Allied liberating army to reach the outskirts of the Greek capital.

Balsillie returned to Megara to find that Jellicoe had arrived, as had a company from the 4th Independent Parachute Brigade. On hearing Balsillie's report of his foray into the outskirts of Athens, Jellicoe was ordered by Land Forces Adriatic HQ to see for himself the situation in the Greek capital. Milner-Barry accompanied

The SBS enjoy a tourist trip around Greece. (Courtesy of the SBS Archive)

The depth of bitterness between the communist EAM and the Royalist EDES took the British by surprise. (Courtesy of Ian Layzell)

his commander, the pair of them deciding that such a momentous occasion required aggrandising: 'It was agreed that George should be a brigadier and myself a full colonel,' wrote Milner-Barry. 'So we donned the necessary emblems.'[5]

It was the late afternoon of Friday 13 October as the two officers, accompanied by three bodyguards, set off 'rather timidly' in a motorboat. Once across the bay they made contact with Ian Patterson near Eleusis, about 10 miles north-west of Athens. Patterson and Jellicoe commandeered a pair of bicycles and headed towards the Greek capital with the rest following in cars. The odd convoy received a rapturous welcome as they entered Athens.

'Tears, shouts, kisses, handshakes, blows on the back, dragged into the houses and nearly suffocated,' wrote Milner-Barry. 'Made a speech from a balcony, shouting "Zeto to ELAS", when I ought to have said "Helas", meaning "Up with Greece", rather than "Up with ELAS". I don't think the loss of an "H" was remarked on in the excitement.'[6]

The rest of L Squadron followed a few hours later. One soldier, Corporal 'Windows' Hill, remembered that he and some of his men were ordered to guard the Athens power station in case of a German sabotage attack. But there was no assault and when Hill made it into the city centre the next morning he and his comrades were set upon by 'two girls [who] rushed out, seized us and took us off to a party that was still going on at dawn the next day'.[7]

Milner-Barry, Patterson and Jellicoe spent the night in one of the finest hotels of the city, recovering their breath and preparing for another round of festivities. Saturday, wrote Milner-Barry, 'proved an unforgettable day of ceremony in which we felt like cinema stars' as Athens officially celebrated its liberation.[8]

In the days that followed Milner-Barry attended church services, dances and dinner parties, and on Tuesday 17th he took tea with Princess Andrew of Greece, sister of Louis Mountbatten (and mother of the Duke of Edinburgh). Though Milner-Barry found the princess a little deaf, her hospitality could not be faulted: English tea, cucumber sandwiches and a delicious plum cake.

Meanwhile L Squadron had already left Athens behind and was pushing north towards Lamia, one section by caique and another by road, chasing the German rearguard. Augmenting the SBS was the 4th Independent Parachute Battalion, a unit from the RAF Regiment and a battery of 75mm guns. Numbering nearly 1,000 men in total and codenamed 'Pompforce', they were under the overall command of Jellicoe, no longer a brigadier but recently promoted – officially – to colonel.

From Lamia 'Pompforce' headed north towards Larissa, driving past the detritus of a large-scale retreat without ever catching sight of their enemy. Finally they made contact with the enemy just south of the town of Kozani. Jellicoe split his force in two, the paratroopers skirting around Kozani and pushing on to Florina, which lay close to the borders with Yugoslavia and Albania, while the rest of 'Pompforce' crushed German resistance at Kozani. The town was swiftly captured and the SBS hurried north on their dwindling supplies of petrol to link with the paratroopers at Florina.

Consequently L Squadron had to patrol the streets in December 1944 to prevent EAM fighters killing their rivals, though this photo is clearly staged. (Courtesy of Ian Layzell)

Here the SBS at last had a chance to unwind, drinking beer, sightseeing and seeking out souvenirs. One soldier found a copy of Hitler's *Mein Kampf* in what had been the HQ of the German Feldgendarmerie (military police) and numerous cameras were retrieved, allowing the SBS to capture for posterity their drive through Greece.

Milner-Barry arrived in Florina on 1 November and the next day received a signal 'instructing us not to go into Yugoslavia or Albania, presumably as a result of a pact with the Russians'. The order was a blow and Milner-Barry confided to his diary that he feared the squadron would turn into an occupational force. Fortunately news of a more uplifting nature reached Milner-Barry later that day: 'Andy Lassen, after some considerable patrol success, is in Salonika in sole charge!'[9]

The photo of this unidentified SBS sergeant was taken by Duggie Pomford in 1945, as the unit prepared to carry out raids on the Adriatic Islands. (Courtesy of Lynne Perrin)

Lassen had sailed from the island of Kythira on 30 September, disembarking at Poros, on the eastern tip of Peloponnese. Here he met an old acquaintance, a naval liaison officer called Martin Solomon, who asked if Lassen could get him to Volos, a port in eastern Greece. Lassen agreed, transporting Solomon to Volos and then prising permission from HQ to continue his exploration of Greek waters as far north as Potidea. Lassen was now just 30 miles south of Salonika. The temptation to remain in Potidea was too great and, having acquired a jeep and a large supply of petrol, Lassen set off on the afternoon of 26 October to see what lay between him and the second most important city in Greece.

With Lassen went one of his Greek soldiers, Jason Mavrikis, who recalled an incident as they stopped close to a wood to answer the call of nature. 'We heard strange voices [from the wood],' remembered Mavrikis. 'We approached carefully. There was a large German armoured car and three or four Jerries were having a conversation near it. We

'But for Lassen and his band, Salonika would not have been evacuated as soon as 30 October 1944… His solitary jeep and few troops were seen everywhere; behind the enemy's lines, with ELAS and in the mountains. Their numbers and strength were magnified into many hundreds.'

British Intelligence report

surprised them without firing a shot, destroyed the car's engine and took two of them with us on the jeep back to Potidea.'[10]

Late in the next day, 27 October, Lassen drove north a few miles to Polygyros to discuss the situation with ELAS. Some reports have stated that Lassen's relationship with ELAS was by now very strained, a consequence of the death of Lieutenant Bob Bury a month earlier. Bury had been shot by Greek resistance fighters as he carried out a reconnaissance on a caique; though it was an accident Lassen was furious at the loss of one of his best officers. But Mavrikis remembered his rendezvous with ELAS passing off amicably. The coffee was doubtful but otherwise Lassen, accompanied by Lieutenant Aled McLeod, whose schooners had transported the SBS this far north, got all the assistance they required. The Greeks pinpointed areas on sea and on land where mines had been planted. In return Lassen told Mavrikis to reassure ELAS that they were the vanguard of a large Allied armada sailing north. 'We had to play that big bluff and convince everybody of the forthcoming invasion of northern Greece by the Allies in the hope of stopping the Russian march to enter Greece,' said Mavrikis.[11]

The next day, armed with the information supplied by ELAS, the 35 men of M Squadron pushed north towards Salonika. 'Lassen seemed to please himself most of the time in Greece,' remembered Doug Wright. 'He had no time for ELAS. They were too scared to enter Salonika because they knew the Germans were preparing to blow up the place. So Lassen decided we'd go in. He got hold of a fleet of fire engines and in we went, guided by a farm boy who knew where the Germans were.'[12]

The boy told the SBS that the west of the city was clear of Germans; it was in the east that they were assembling, ready to withdraw in a large convoy having first sabotaged a number of key installations.

Lassen ordered his men to dismount from the engines and divided them into two patrols, one under his command and the other led by Lieutenant James Henshaw. 'I was in Henshaw's patrol,' recalled Wright. 'We entered the city, got

AN 'L' OF A GOOD TIME

FROM TOP TO BOTTOM

This set of photos belonged to Jack Emerton of L Squadron and show him and his comrades in late 1944. Here they relax with a beer.

Washing a dog who doesn't seem that impressed with his clean coat.

Somewhere in Greece.

(Images Courtesy of David Henry)

round the back of them [the Germans] and opened fire. I must have fired a dozen magazines of Bren gun as they were stood there. When they started throwing flares up, we pulled out leaving behind a lot of their dead and wounded.'

Estimates put the number of enemy casualties at 60 while the SBS came through the engagement unscathed. Lassen and his men reboarded the fire engines and drove through the centre of Salonika, marvelling at their reception and the sight of a myriad of Union Flags fluttering from windows and lamp posts. 'It was great,' recalled Doug Wright. 'The welcome we received was unbelievable. There were women everywhere wanting to kiss us!'

As early as 1 November the news was being reported on the front pages of British and North American newspapers. 'British Units in Salonika', ran the headline in one American paper, adding that 'British forces entering the seaport … were received enthusiastically by the populace'.[13] Though the Germans had succeeded in destroying several important installations before their withdrawal, leaving a 'black pall hanging over the city',[14] a subsequent British Intelligence report said of the SBS action: 'But for Lassen and his band, Salonika would not have been evacuated as soon as 30 October 1944. The town would have suffered greater destruction. His solitary jeep and few troops were seen everywhere; behind the enemy's lines, with ELAS and in the mountains. Their numbers and strength were magnified into many hundreds.'[15]

Aboard a Greek vessel. (Courtesy of David Henry)

CHAPTER 16

ADRIATIC OFFENSIVE

The winter of 1944 was not kind to the SBS. A series of misfortunes befell the squadron, including the death in separate aircraft accidents of Dick Morris, who had been with the unit for nearly two years, and of Ian Patterson. Milner-Barry felt desperate when he heard the news of Morris's death, confiding to his diary that 'apart from the fact that he was an exceptionally nice fellow, he was due to go back to England and I contributed to inducing him to stay an extra month'.[1]

Patterson's loss was felt keenly by Jellicoe, although he too was soon to depart the squadron for a staff college at Haifa. David Sutherland replaced Jellicoe as commanding officer and Ambrose McGonigal took over L Squadron in place of the deeply mourned Patterson.

Sutherland assumed command of the SBS at a time when their future was uncertain. The weeks leading up to his appointment had been trying for the squadron with L Squadron acting as glorified policemen in Athens. There were demonstrations on the streets of the Greek capital in protest at the government of 'National Unity', and EAM were fomenting trouble. L Squadron began patrolling the streets to deter communist fighters from shooting members of the pro-British Royalist National Republican Greek League EDES. But the fighting soon escalated and the SBS were targeted, on one occasion a bomb being thrown through the window of their billet that killed a Royal Engineer. As Civil War loomed the British drafted in the 4th Indian Infantry Division, much to the relief of the SBS.

The rest of the SBS spent December in Crete, a familiar location for a number of them, although by the end of 1944 the 13,000 or so Germans left in the north-west of the island were weary and ragged. They were still armed, however, and Lassen's orders when he arrived in Crete in early December were to observe from a distance the enemy and to ensure adequate food supplies for the civilian population. Lassen was not going to observe the enemy himself – that was what his subordinates were there for – and it fell to Lieutenant Ian Smith to spend most of December in a cave overlooking the German positions, where he and his patrol played cards to while away the hours. 'When the spirit moved us we made small expeditions to see the enemy at close quarters,' he recalled. 'But they like ourselves were essentially looking forward to the end of the war, and they had no aggressive intentions.'[2]

Lassen lived in Heraklion, where he divided his time between the city's brothels and the top-class hotel he had designated his billet. David Sutherland flew in for Christmas, acting as Santa with a rucksack full of beer, whisky and cigarettes. They celebrated Christmas in style with the local brass band hired to play and a limitless supply of food, alcohol and women. Sutherland recalled it being 'the most extraordinary party' with Lassen once again 'a great example of how to live up to the limits in all respects'.[3]

Back in Italy, at their base in Monte St Angelo, Milner-Barry was warding off the cold with games of basketball. On 11 January it snowed and the men of S Squadron stood and stared. 'A lovely sight which I hadn't seen in five years,' wrote Milner-Barry in his diary. Two days later, to further insulate against the cold, Milner-Barry and Jimmy Lees went to Foggia on a wine run, returning with 'a dry white for the Officers, at 40 lira a litre, and a sweet white for the men's canteen, at 30 lira, both very drinkable'.[4]

The rest of the month passed slowly, if agreeably, for Milner-Barry. Then on 27 January he was informed that Stewart Macbeth was returning to England and he was to replace him as David Sutherland's second-in-command. 'So I packed my kit with a heavy heart and moved into Bari,' said Milner-Barry. Once in Bari at Land Forces Adriatic HQ he learned that 'something was in the wind about our movements which would involve quite a lot of work … operations looked promising'.[5]

The operations that Milner-Barry helped plan were to involve what Sutherland described as 'those jagged splinters of land off the Croatian coastline which rejoiced in such names as Krk, Rab and Pag, Lussin and Olib'. Unlike in the Aegean, the islands of the Adriatic were heavily wooded with good lines of communication

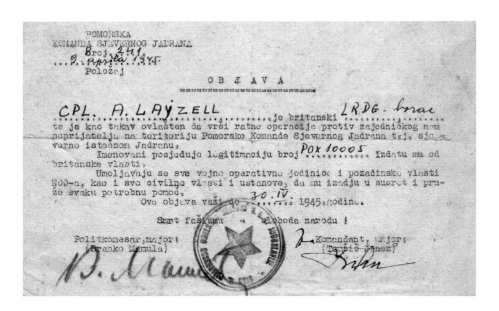

This 'permit' to operate was issued by the Yugoslav Adriatic authorities in April 1945 to Albert Layzell of L Squadron, though it incorrectly identifies him as a member of the LRDG. (Courtesy of Ian Layzell)

and even metalled roads. Furthermore they were garrisoned by the same Germans who had been stationed on the likes of Santorini, Mykonos and Amorgos. As Sutherland warned his men they were therefore 'well aware of both the strengths and the weaknesses of the raiding forces now about to attack them'.[6] The Germans constructed their defences accordingly, strewing mines across beaches and exposed ground, digging deep gun emplacements and encircling important installations with coil after coil of barbed wire.

David Sutherland led S Squadron (now under the command of Captain Kingsley Clarke) across the Adriatic and established his HQ in Zara, a little port a few miles north of Dubrovnik. They received a cold reception from the Yugoslavs, many of whom were now openly hostile to the presence of British soldiers in their country. The feeling was mutual. 'There were no friendly partisans in Yugoslavia, you didn't know who you could trust,' recalled Dick Holmes.[7]

Without the co-operation of the partisans, the SBS had to carry out thorough reconnaissance of the area in which they were being asked to operate. Captain Kingsley Clarke sent his intelligence officer, Lieutenant Conlon, and three men to the small island of Olib on 20 February. Equipped with rations for 14 days, their instructions were to 'establish a W/T link between Olib island and S Sqn, 1st SBS HQ at Zara with a view to collating information regarding the German held islands of Cherso, Lussino, Rab and Pag'.[8]

In fact Conlon and his three men remained on Olib for a month, radioing back vital intelligence to Zara about enemy strength and movements on the neighbouring islands, intelligence that Sutherland decided to cross-check.

On 24 February Ambrose McGonigal and three men landed on Unie, to the north-west of Olib, with the objective of using it as a vantage point from which to observe the neighbouring islands of Cherso and Lussino to the east. But on the second day of his reconnaissance McGonigal took advantage of a cooperative partisan group and rowed the couple of miles to Lussino to see the situation for himself. Landing on the northern part of Lussino, McGonigal spent an hour climbing to the top of a hill covered in thorn bushes and low scrub. It was worth the effort. From the peak 'it was possible to obtain a good view of the bridge and the town of Ossero'.[9] McGonigal spent two hours on his observation point before moving on to reconnoitre the village of Neresine.

His interest piqued by McGonigal's intelligence, Sutherland planned a bigger reconnaissance operation at the start of March involving three two-man canoe parties. Party No.1 comprised Captain Jimmy Lees and Corporal Allen with orders to explore Cunski in the centre of Lussino; Party No.2 consisted of Lieutenant Allan Lucas, a New Zealander who had joined the SBS the previous December, and Lance-Corporal Hank Hancock, and had the objective of reconnoitring Neresine; Party No.3 comprised Lieutenant Brian Gallagher and Sergeant Dick Holmes, whose objective was Ossero.

Each party was instructed to pay particular attention to six points:

a) Number of enemy troops
b) Map references of enemy positions (defensive)
c) Number and type of guns manned
d) Location of any possible mined areas
e) Position of troops billets
f) Approach routes to enemy held areas.

A motor launch transported Holmes and Gallagher most of the way before the pair paddled ashore in a canoe, landing on a rocky beach at 2220 hours on 2 March. Both men felt a degree of trepidation, but for different reasons. Holmes was in his third year of guerrilla warfare and wondering how much longer his luck could last. The war, in Europe at least, was all but won but would his luck hold? 'In the Balkans there was little we could do to influence the war and we wanted now just one thing: to survive,' he reflected. 'Yet I had to go on reconnaissances right up to the end of the war and that was no joke.'

For Gallagher the mission to Lussino was his first SBS operation. So Ambrose McGonigal paired him with Holmes in order that he could learn from one of the best operators in the unit. 'Gallagher was very green but a hell of a nice guy and

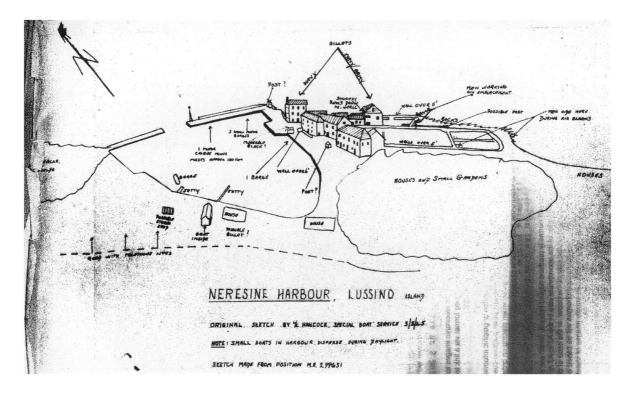

NERESINE HARBOUR, LUSSINO ISLAND

ORIGINAL SKETCH BY L HANCOCK SPECIAL BOAT SERVICE S/S/B.S.

NOTE: SMALL BOATS IN HARBOUR DISPERSE DURING DAYLIGHT.

SKETCH MADE FROM POSITION M.R. 2.99631

I thought a lot of him,' said Holmes. 'He came to us late but he didn't pretend to know anything.' Gallagher put himself in the hands of Holmes, bowing to his greater experience and knowledge.

Shortly after they had struck off north Gallagher, a South Wales Borderer, received his first lesson in planning a reconnaissance mission of this sort. 'The paths marked on the map [were] unreliable as overgrown by thick bushes,' he commented in his report. 'Consequently going was very slow.'[10]

They halted at 0345 hours, rested until 0800 hours and then resumed their march after a quick breakfast. By mid-morning they were looking down on Ossero from a pine-covered slope. Gallagher wrote in his report that the sound of woodcutters in the distance was audible but otherwise it appeared they were alone on the mountain. They observed the town for a while and then sat down to a lunch prepared by Holmes. Suddenly two civilians appeared through the trees. 'No word was exchanged and the civilians, probably Yugoslavs, did not seem surprised or interested,' wrote Gallagher.[11] Nonetheless, the moment they were gone Holmes advised his officer that they should move their camp a quarter of a mile south on the reverse side of the mountain.

For the next 36 hours the pair observed the target and noted down everything of interest. In the afternoon of 4 March, just as they prepared to set out for the

Hank Hancock put his artistic skills to good use in producing this map of Neresine Harbour prior to the SBS raid in February 1945. (Author's Collection)

rendezvous at Neresine with the other two patrols, Gallagher asked Holmes if he could have some of his water. 'He'd run out because he'd been making so much tea,' said Holmes. 'I said "no, it will teach you a lesson about conserving water."'

———

Meanwhile back at Zara plans were afoot to despatch a much larger patrol to Lussino following the capture of two Italian deserters. They informed McGonigal that their unit at Villa Punta would surrender en masse if they received a guarantee of merciful treatment. McGonigal decided to send a small force of men to deal with the Italians. Ideally he would have sent one of his experienced officers – Jimmy Lees or Stud Stellin – but with both out on operations, McGonigal ordered the inexperienced Lieutenant Donald Thomason to lead the mission. 'It was a rushed job with a new officer on his first raid,' said Corporal Ken Smith, who also recalled

Q Patrol rests at Unie after the raid on Villa Punta. L–R: Lieutenant Allan Lucas NZ (holding mug) and troopers Fenn, Ginger, Partridge and Goldie. (Imperial War Museum, HU 71356)

his patrol had a new sergeant in Jock Cameron.[12] Smith was one of the more experienced members of the patrol, along with a fellow Marine called Tommy Kitchingman, a 'good footballer and a great lad' in the opinion of Dick Holmes.

When McGonigal issued his operational orders to Thomason it was clear that surrender was not the priority of the mission. His task was to 'attack and destroy the occupants of Villa Punta … and bring away any prisoners and equipment captured'.[13] To aid in their destruction of the villa, the 21-man patrol loaded onto their transport a 5-gallon can of petrol.

Smith remembered standing on the jetty in Zara waiting to board the motor launch with the Italian guide close by. McGonigal and Thomason appeared and within earshot began a discussion. 'I heard the senior officer say "kill the f'ing lot of them",' recalled Smith. 'This Eyetie heard this and immediately ran forward and said "no need to kill". And right away I could see we were in for problems because no way was he going to show us where his mates were knowing we were going to kill them.'

On reaching Lussino the patrol began their trek towards the target. 'I wasn't too happy about the progress of it,' said Smith. 'It was this officer's first raid and the sergeant [Cameron] was a little bit careful.' With the Italian convinced he was being led to his death he started 'pretending he didn't know the path to his billet'. Tempers began to fray, the men quarrelling with each other and their petrified guide. Finally Thomason rounded on Smith and accused him of undermining his authority. 'About 3 in the morning we were going round in circles and this officer … turned round in frustration and said "well, corporal smith, what would you do?"'

Smith replied that they should 'get them to surrender' rather than wiping out the villa. The SBS pressed on but the guide was leading them astray. As the night sky began to lighten the raiders aborted the mission.

On 9 March the SBS returned, only this time McGonigal was leading the operation with Jimmy Lees his second-in-command. There were 27 men in total, including Lieutenant Conlon and his party who had been collected from Olib en route to the island. Shortly after arriving on Lussino McGonigal received intelligence that the garrison at Villa Punta had been reinforced with German soldiers and '4 two man patrols are posted in the village guarding the approaches to the villa'.[14]

McGonigal issued instructions. A patrol led by Lieutenant Jones-Parry would advance along the coastal path to the south side of the villa while the main force would approach through the village, eliminating the patrols before launching a frontal assault.

By 0200 hours the target was within sight and no sign of the enemy had been spotted.

Jones-Parry led his patrol southwards but almost at once a challenge rang out. When the British failed to give the password the sentry began firing at the shadowy figures. 'Fire returned,' wrote McGonigal in his report. 'Enemy driven back into house and house surrounded.'[15]

The enemy were surrounded but in no mood to surrender. Their response to McGonigal's call to lay down their arms was a withering burst of machine-gun fire. The SBS replied in kind and a fierce firefight erupted that lasted 20 minutes as the

British gauged the strength and disposition of the enemy inside the villa. At 0230 hours McGonigal ordered the storming of the building, directing Jones-Parry to clear the ground floor and Lieutenant Thomason and three men to neutralise the first floor; Captain Lees and his patrol were held in reserve.

Jones-Parry led his men forward into the villa. Once inside he 'saw two or more persons moving about in the corridor. I threw a grenade but it was a dud, so I threw a phosphorous bomb and opened fire. I went in. I went up to a door and listened. No sound, very dark. Rushed in, paused. No movement. I went into a second room.'[16]

Tommy Kitchingman followed his officer into the room. It was dark. There was a scuffling noise. 'Are you all right?' Kitchingman asked Jones-Parry. 'At that moment there was a burst of machine-gun fire from some point in the room which we must have overlooked. I was hit in the arm and chest. Kitchingman collapsed. He had received the burst through the head.'

Jones-Parry ducked out of the room, changed magazines, then fired a burst from round the door, 'traversing along the wall and floor'. Sergeant McDougall helped his officer from the villa and led him to where McGonigal had established his command post. 'I am certain I got the man,' Jones-Parry told his commander, 'as there was no reply, only groans.'[17]

Meanwhile Thomason was displaying similar courage in clearing the first floor of the villa. The three soldiers who had accompanied Thomason inside the villa had all been wounded as they bounded up the stairs towards their objective. Thomason, 'unaided and in the face of intense fire … fought his way onto the first-floor landing and engaged the enemy in the first-floor rooms'. Such was Thomason's fearlessness that McGonigal recommended him for an immediate Military Cross, the citation for which described how 'three times this officer withdrew, replenished with ammunition and returned to the attack until the enemy were silenced'.[18]

McGonigal ordered Lees to lead his patrol into the villa to support Thomason. As they ran towards the building Lees told Ken Smith, a sergeant and another soldier to 'get over to the other side of road, past the house, and guard it against enemy further up the road while [Lees] went in to see if he could capture them'. Smith and two other men ran past the house as Lees disappeared inside the villa. 'I remember getting under the trees on the side of the road with the sergeant and then I felt a stickiness in my hand,' said Smith. 'It was blood from my arm where I'd been hit.'

As Smith clamped a field dressing to his wound Lees fought his way up onto the first floor where Thomason was still engaging the enemy 'with complete disregard for his own personal safety'.[19] Lees burst into one room and was shot by a German concealed behind a sofa.

'Back at the house there were cries and screams and a lot of firing,' recalled Smith, as the British began to subdue the enemy. 'By 0300 hours all resistance ceased,' wrote McGonigal in his report. 'The house was a complete wreck inside from Lewes bombs used by ourselves and from blast bombs used by the enemy in house fighting.'[20]

The victory had come at a heavy price. Lees and Kitchingman were dead and eight men were wounded. McGonigal counted seven enemy dead but estimated that several more were buried under the 'rubble covering the floors and the stairs blown away from one flight'.[21]

Smith considered himself fortunate to have received just a flesh wound to his arm; his friend Bill Mayall was in a much worse state. 'Leave me,' he begged Smith. Ignoring his friend's pleas, Smith helped hoist Mayall onto a door and he was then carried back to the beach.

Milner-Barry learned of the raid the following day. Lees had been a close friend and Kitchingman was a 'very good marine'.★ He spent the next few days visiting the wounded, angry that they had been sent to hospitals in Bari, Barletta and Trani. 'God knows why they had to be split up,' he wrote in his diary, 'but hospital laws must be obeyed.'[22]

Marine Thomas Kitchingman was a valued member of the SBS, who was killed during the raid on Villa Punta in March 1945. (Courtesy of Paul Ogden)

Smith was one of the men visited by Milner-Barry in hospital. He told him about the attack and the surprise of finding Villa Punta garrisoned not by a few pusillanimous Italians but by a squad of very determined Germans, evidently drafted in after word of the first unsuccessful attempt to attack the villa had reached the enemy.

Brigadier Davy was undeterred by the casualties incurred during the attack on the villa. It had achieved its objective. A few days later the SBS was instructed to launch a similar raid on the bridge at the Ossero, which linked the islands of Cherso and Lussin and was of such strategic importance to the enemy that they guarded it with 80 men and several light anti-aircraft guns. The Balkan Air Force had tried to destroy the bridge, so too the Royal Navy, so now the task was placed in the hands of the SBS. The operation was not well received by the veterans of the squadron. If a navy and an air force could not destroy it, what chance did 38 soldiers have? 'It was just something for us to do,' said Doug Wright, an opinion shared by Dick

---

★ A couple of years after the war Kitchingman's mother and two sisters holidayed on the Lees' Dorset estate. Lady Lees made a pilgrimage to her son's grave in Belgrade War Cemetery in 1949.

'Three times this officer withdrew, replenished with ammunition and returned to the attack until the enemy were silenced.'

Military Cross citation for Lieutenant Donald Thomason

Holmes, who considered the objective 'dicey'.[23] The presence of three medical orderlies as they sailed from Zara at 1530 hours on 18 March further exacerbated the sense of foreboding.

McGonigal split his force into two – the 'Main Party' and a four-man 'Folboat Party'; the latter, led by Dick Holmes, were to land by canoe and make their way to a rendezvous point close to the bridge where they would link with the Main Party once they had dealt with the garrison. Holmes had had a dress rehearsal two days before the attack proper. Initially everything went well but when the canoeists returned to the rendezvous point the motor launch had vanished, 'so we were forced to paddle about twenty miles across open water to an island off the coast'.

The men were finally picked up on the morning of 18 March, hours before they were due to sail from Zara. Two of the soldiers were too exhausted to go out again so McGonigal reduced the Folboat Party to two – Holmes and Private 'Lofty' Lecomber.

At 2030 hours on 18 March the pair were back in a canoe heading for the target beach. The Main Party sailed on, coming ashore shortly before midnight. McGonigal split his force into patrols – K Patrol under Lieutenant Ian Smith; P Patrol under Captain Anderson, J Patrol under Lieutenant Gallagher and Z Patrol under Captain James Henshaw.

They reached the target after a three-hour march. Smith was ordered to investigate a church while Sergeant Doug Wright was told to reconnoitre the main road through the village. Wright bumped into an enemy patrol. He killed four of the five Germans with his Bren and the fifth fled for his life back up the road. The gunfire alerted the Germans and four well-sited machine guns opened up on the British. McGonigal ordered his men to advance but as Ian Smith's patrol neared the bridge they found 'barbed wire, great coils of the stuff to roof top height, there was no way we could get through that'.[24]

Anderson's patrol had encountered the same defences and so too Henshaw's. Wright rejoined Henshaw and together they loaded a PIAT anti-tank weapon. 'We ran into some Germans on a street and they started firing so we had a go back at them with the Brens and the PIAT,' remembered Wright. 'I was on the PIAT and Henshaw was reloading for me when he was shot.'*

---

* According to McGonigal's report Henshaw was killed by a grenade although this seems unlikely as Wright was uninjured.

As Henshaw was carried out of the firing line, McGonigal ordered Smith's patrol to find a way through the wire to the bridge. 'We tried to find a way round but wherever we went there was this wire,' he wrote later. 'I suppose we must have been about 100 yards from the bridge when we more or less ran out of ammo. I fired five sten mags [magazines] at what I'm not sure.'[25]

Meanwhile Holmes and Lecomber were experiencing problems of their own. Having been thwarted in their initial attempt to land by the appearance of a German patrol on the beach, the pair eventually came ashore further up the coast and were still making their way towards the rendezvous when the battle began.

McGonigal was still trying to force a way through when the Germans opened up with two 20mm Oerlikon cannons, wounding three SBS soldiers in the first salvo. Even a man of McGonigal's bellicosity now realised that to press the attack was unwise; at 0350 hours he ordered his men to withdraw.

The men were despondent when they disembarked at Zara. Wright in particular was furious with the futility of the operation. 'Henshaw was shot just at the end of the war but it would have made no difference if we'd blown the bridge,' he reflected. 'I was sad about his death. He was a good officer.' Sutherland shared the men's disquiet and ordered an end to such operations: 'In view of the strong precautionary measures being taken by the Germans almost everywhere I decided that raids of this nature could only produce diminishing results.'[26]

The SBS were based at Monte St Angelo in the spring of 1945, allowing the men to practise swimming in the Adriatic. (Courtesy of the SBS Archive)

CHAPTER 17

ANDY LASSEN'S BIG WAR

Sutherland's decision had ramifications for M Squadron. Andy Lassen and his men had been scheduled to participate in operations on the islands, but Land Forces Adriatic now considered they would be better deployed in Italy as part of Brigadier Ronnie Tod's 2nd Special Service Brigade (he had been promoted brigadier at the end of 1944).

The brigade had spent the winter advancing north from the warm climes of the Aegean to the misery of the Lower Romagna in northern Italy, an area so flat and wet it had earned comparison with the Netherlands or, for English soldiers, with the Fens. The Allied front line began in the east in front of Lake Comacchio and followed the course of the Senio River to Castel Bolognese and Highway Twelve. Brigadier Tod and his brigade held the line south of Comacchio, situated between Rimini to the south and Venice to the north on Italy's north-east coast.

The muddy waters of Lake Comacchio were on average only two feet deep, and home to eels but little else. A thin strip of sand, known as 'the spit', separated the eastern edge of the lake from the Adriatic Sea and several small islands were dotted across the lake that stretched for 4 miles at its widest point and 20 at its longest.

The lake posed a problem for the Allies. It blocked their advance north and Lieutenant-General Mark Clark of the American V Corps wanted it seized. The Germans wished to hold it, and had sewn mines into the shores and built several

OPPOSITE
Anders Lassen, one of the most famous faces of the SBS. (Topfoto)

Freddy Crouch, S
Squadron, had a
premonition of his
death at Lake
Comacchio. (Courtesy
of the SBS Archive)

deep and well-concealed machine gun nests on the north, west and east shores.
'On the south lay the neck of the spit, a strip of commando-held territory,' wrote
John Lodwick. 'Then the high banks of the Senio river where it joined the lake.
From behind these banks German sentries lay watching, their fingers upon Very
light pistols.'[1]

At the end of March Lassen received orders to lead M Squadron to Comacchio
having been granted permission by Sutherland to augment his unit with some men
from other squadrons. 'He selected four men from my patrol,' remembered
Lieutenant Ian Smith. 'As far as I recall they were mostly ex-policemen …
[including] trooper [Fred] Crouch and corporal [Edward] Roberts.'[2]

M Squadron set off in a convoy of trucks carrying with them their folboats.
In his haste to depart Italy Lassen forgot his pet dog, Dog Tom, a scrawny animal no
one else much cared for. On arriving at Comacchio Lassen sent a signal asking for
Dog Tom to be despatched north but the animal was never sent: it had been shot.

The news unsettled Lassen, who recently had started to exhibit signs of
restlessness. John Lodwick believed that Lassen 'was somewhat tired of the carnival',[3]
although others believed the Dane's edginess stemmed not from war weariness but
from inactivity. Killing Germans was his drug and if the fix was removed, Lassen
became irritable and bored.

Since the liberation of Salonika in late October 1944, Lassen's energies had
been channelled into debauchery. But he soon tired of the women and wine: 'Even

when he was on leave, it was as if he knew that he had challenged faith too much and had to fill these brief hours with the life that was about to run away from him,' recalled Porter Jarrell. 'His existence had become a race with death.'[4]

Lassen's frustration increased throughout the spring of 1945 as he heard accounts of fierce battles in Lussino and Ossero while he was stuck in Bari. 'Andy often talked about participating in the "Big War" as distinct from the small raids for which the SBS were trained,' reflected Dick Holmes. 'With us he felt he was a big fish in a small pond.'[5]

Lassen hoped Comacchio might provide him with a taste of 'big war'.

Lassen was ordered by Tod to paddle out onto Comacchio and find channels deep enough to transport the commandos' Goatley floats, engine-less vessels that could each accommodate ten men and their equipment. One of the SBS men was Corporal Ken Smith, now recovered from the wound sustained in the Villa Punta attack: 'We used to go out each night in our canoes,' he recalled. 'Now on the lake, on the right was the spit, a narrow neck of land that separated the lake from the sea and that was where the Germans had some machine gun battalions.'[6]

It required a steady nerve and a lot of skill to paddle unseen across the water. 'What we had to be careful about was the phosphorous on the paddle,' recalled Smith. 'So we had to make long gliding strokes to make as little noise and phosphorous as possible.'

The SBS patrols reconnoitred the lake at night and at the first hint of dawn they laid up, dismantling their canoes and concealing them among the reeds in the

A Commando Forward Observation Post at Lake Comacchio, giving some idea of the flat, exposed terrain that Lassen and his men had to operate. (Author's Collection)

marshes where they remained during daylight. 'I remember the mossies at dawn would come over and they raised an almighty noise, like bombers going overhead,' said Smith. 'We had mossie cream and at dusk they would come over again and settle on us. At dark we would paddle off again.'

Once the commandos had seized the southern promontory of Comacchio, Clark began to prepare for the next stage of the assault, which would entail sending the No.2 and No.9 Commandos to secure a bridgehead on the north shore of the lake. Appreciating the hazardous nature of his task, Brigadier Tod instructed the SBS to create a diversionary raid on the German positions on the eastern shore in the hope of fooling the Germans into deploying troops from the north shore to repel the assault.

Ken Smith recalled the conversation between Tod and Lassen: 'We sat round in a small circle and the brigadier said to Lassen "I want you to spread your chaps out tonight, right along the front, get ashore, and make as much commotion as possible to give an impression of a big landing." Lassen kept interrupting him … "But I can take Comacchio." The brigadier said "I don't want you to, just spread your chaps out."'

The night before the diversionary raid, 8 April, an SBS patrol reconnoitred the shore between Comacchio and Porto Garibaldi where Lassen planned to land. A stiff headwind made the task impossible and the failure heightened the men's feeling of dread: compounded by poor terrain, poor reconnaissance and little time to add to their knowledge of the eastern shore. Fred Crouch confided to Hank Hancock that he had a premonition of his death; even tough veterans like Sean O'Reilly and Les Stephenson felt a clawing sense of doubt about the operation.

Lassen split his small force into three patrols having handpicked the men from those who had volunteered for the mission. His own patrol, 'Y', comprising himself and ten men, would be first onto the spit. E Patrol, composed of seven soldiers under the command of Lieutenant Turnbull, would then land a little further north and join them. Meanwhile a third patrol led by Stud Stellin (and including Ken Smith) would discharge numerous thunderflashes and other explosive charges to fool the enemy into believing the main assault was underway.

The SBS had to endure an excruciating delay to their mission as they waited for the commandos to drag their landing craft across the mud to the channels. Everyone was tense. Then at 0430 hours on 9 April Lassen and his ten-strong patrol set off in some small local fishing boats accompanied by two Italian fishermen who knew the lake well. Turnbull's six-man patrol followed a short while later.

Once ashore Lassen (leaving the fishermen with the boats) and his men crossed a canal that ran parallel to the lake. So far so good. Now they advanced up the road that ran between Comacchio and Porto Garibaldi, alongside which was a railway line on a low dyke. To the west of the dyke was the canal and to the east a floodplain.

Lassen led the way, trotting noiselessly along the road with Private Fred Green at his side. The rest of the patrol were a few yards behind, invisible in the darkness. A quarter of a mile down the road a challenge was issued by a soldier from the 162nd Turkoman Division. Green stepped forward and replied in Italian that they were fishermen from San Alberto, on their way to work. 'I said this three or four times,' recalled Green subsequently. 'There was no reply, and then firing began.'[7]

Shoving Green to the ground, Lassen returned fire at the checkpoint. So did the rest of the patrol. The engagement was brief and the two sentries surrendered. Green escorted them back up the road towards their canoes while the rest of the patrol pressed on. A few yards further a machine gun opened up from a well-concealed firing point, 'built from stone and covered with sods and entered through an arch like the mouth of a small tunnel'.[8]

Lassen gave a sharp blast on his whistle, roared 'forward, you bastards!' and charged the enemy machine gun, hurling a grenade as he ran. Having destroyed the emplacement, Lassen continued up the road towards two more machine guns that were now firing short bursts in his direction. The Dane sprinted up the left hand side of the road, withdrew another grenade, and threw it with pinpoint accuracy at the first emplacement. Two more grenades followed in quick succession and the machine gun fell silent.

The rest of the patrol tore after their leader, just as a flare lit up the road. Another machine gun thumped into life and Stan Hughes and Corporal Edward Roberts from E Patrol were killed. Braving the fire Sean O'Reilly tried to reach Lassen but was stopped by a bullet to his shoulder. Sergeant Waite fell too, crawling to the side of the road and continuing to lay down suppressing fire despite the wound to his leg. Someone noticed Fred Crouch was missing.

Lassen is the only member of the British SAS or SBS to have been awarded the Victoria Cross. (Author's Collection)

Some of the survivors from the ill-fated raid on Comacchio recover in hospital: Back row (l-r) unknown, Hank Hancock, Mick Conby and Trooper Randell. Front row (l-r) unknown, Corporal Pollock, Sergeant Ronald Waite, Sergeant Sean O'Reilly and Sergeant Patsy Henderson. (Imperial War Museum, HU 71362)

and paddled like hell. I could see little mortar bombs coming each side of us and the zimming of machine gun fire.'

From the bow of the boat Bimrose screamed instructions – 'hard to port, hard to starboard' – as the pair zig-zagged across the lake in a frantic bid to escape the German mortar rounds. 'I was like the engine room' reflected Smith, who turned 22 that same night.

When they returned to their base on the swamp road 5 miles north of Comacchio, Bimrose handed Smith a bottle of whisky. It was a gift, not just to celebrate his birthday, but to give thanks for their survival.★

———

The day after the successful Allied crossing of Comacchio, 13 April, Bimrose returned to the lake with Milner-Barry. 'We embarked in an assault boat with outboard attached and after numerous breakdowns got into our folboat and made cautiously for the islands,' wrote Milner-Barry. They found no sign of the SBS, living or dead. On the way back they bumped into Brigadier Tod who told Milner-Barry 'M [Squadron] had done very well and that he would look after them'.[12]

★ Bimrose was awarded a Military Cross for his actions this night, the citation describing how he 'drew much fire onto his canoes … and in spite of great danger remained within range creating a diversion until absolutely satisfied that the main attack was going in successfully'. (National Archives, WO373/14)

But it was Milner–Barry who saw to the needs of M Squadron. On 14 April he addressed them, explaining 'that they had done a most important job of work' in aiding the capture of Lake Comacchio. He asked what they required in the way of resupplies and promised it would be delivered soon. 'They are an exceptionally nice lot,' Milner–Barry wrote in his diary, 'thanks largely to Bimrose, I suspect.'[13]

Before he left the area, Milner–Barry paid a visit to the bedside of Sean O'Reilly. The Irishman was in good spirits, smoking like a chimney and asking for some whisky. His reaction was typical among the men of M Squadron. Lassen was dead, Crouch too, and others, but life went on.

Ian Smith grieved more for the two men from his patrol, Fred Crouch and Edward Roberts, than he did for Andy Lassen. In early 1945 he recalled that the officers' mess in the SBS was 'split between those who wanted to have one last go and those that took the view that they had been at very considerable risk for the last four years and we had survived more or less intact, so why risk it all on one more operation'.[14]

Andy Lassen had got his wish, he had seen a glimpse of 'big war', and it had cost him his life, and those of three of his men. 'Thus we come to the old equation,' reflected Ian Smith. 'Was the sacrifice of such an outstanding officer and men, and my men were the pick of the bunch, worth it for such a vague objective?... No doubt it all seemed worth it at the time and Andy was certainly on the Gung Ho half of the mess.'[15]

Andy Lassen was the last man from the Special Boat Squadron to die in action during the war. Once across Lake Comacchio, the British Eighth Army drove north, overcoming dogged German resistance until, on 29 April, they reached Venice. General Clark's Fifth Army made similar spectacular progress, transporting five divisions across the River Po by the end of the month. On 28 April Benito Mussolini was executed by Italian partisans near Lake Como, his body and that of his mistress strung up for all to see. On the same day a high-ranking German officer arrived at the HQ of Field Marshal Harold Alexander, Supreme Allied Commander in the Mediterranean, to discuss terms for a surrender.

The SBS meanwhile remained hundreds of miles south at their base in Zara. L Squadron had gone on leave, and Milner–Barry spent the last days of April sightseeing in the islands of Rab and Pag. In Rab, on the evening of 30 April, he watched with amusement as the partisans ushered in May Day with bonfires and drink. Then they began shooting off their weapons, wounding a sailor and a female partisan in the ensuing bedlam.

Milner-Barry arrived back in Monopoli on 2 May, the day that German forces in Italy officially laid down their arms. Within hours of the surrender rumours began sweeping the SBS base. David Sutherland confided to Milner-Barry and his other officers 'that there was a possibility that the whole unit might be required to drop in Austria'. What did they think of the idea? Milner-Barry told Sutherland 'at this stage, none of the troops are very keen'.

Sutherland agreed and the next day he and Milner-Barry concocted a letter to Brigadier Davy, commander of Land Forces Adriatic, advising against such an operation.[16]

The letter was rendered irrelevant by events elsewhere. On 7 May Milner-Barry wrote in his diary, 'The war's over tomorrow and we celebrate officially. But began today, and after dinner I found myself lured into the men's canteen and made to sing a song.' To the lusty cheers of the men Milner-Barry gave a pitiful rendition of *Oh Mabel, Darling Mabel*. Informed that his presence was now required in the sergeants' mess, Milner-Barry beat a hasty retreat to the officers' mess.[17]

On 8 May the war in Europe ended, and the celebrations began in earnest for the SBS. 'A riot of gaiety,' wrote Milner-Barry in his diary. 'We organised a funfair

The SBS party celebrate VE Day in suitably raucous fashion by burning a 'guy' in the form of Hitler. L–R: Trooper Donachie, US medic Porter Jarrell, Greek soldier Dmitri Baffilos, Martin Corby, Hank Hancock and Mick D'Arcy. (Imperial War Museum, HU 71366)

'*Was the sacrifice of such an outstanding officer and men, and my men were the pick of the bunch, worth it for such a vague objective?... No doubt it all seemed worth it at the time.*'
Ian Smith

for the troop with unsuitable officers dressed up as ballet girls, a wine bar, [Ken] Fox telling fortunes, Stud [Stellin] showing them how to flog kit, etc.'[18] There was also a greasy pole to climb with old mattresses underneath to cushion the fall of the increasingly inebriated.

Doug Wright recalled that they 'filled a water cart with wine and drank for a week'.[19] Captain Ian Smith remembered that at one stage the men coated a pig in lard and had a race to see who could catch the unfortunate animal. Sutherland eventually reined in his men late in the evening after they began firing flares into the night sky. 'I mounted on a pedestal wearing a top hat,' Milner-Barry wrote in his diary, 'which I had somehow acquired, and managed to make myself heard by shouting at the top of my voice, and succeeded in quelling the near riot.'[20]

The next day hangovers precluded most conversation. What chat there was centred on home, and how quickly the men might see it. Some of the soldiers' dreams were realised more quickly than others. Ian Smith, now a captain, 'couldn't believe his luck' when he received orders to report to the War Office in London. Catching a plane from Rome to Marseilles, Smith was back in Croydon just days after he had been chasing an Italian pig covered in lard.

Dick Holmes was also on his way home. By May 1945 he had spent four and a half years abroad, qualifying him for automatic home leave. Holmes returned to a London almost unrecognisable from the one he had last seen in December 1940. Everything appeared different, or destroyed. And where were the colours? He felt like a foreigner in his own land as he boarded a bus to his parents.

I said to the conductress, 'I'll have a tuppence ha'penny please.'

'What?' she said.

'Tuppence ha'penny, please.'

She asked where I was going.

'Stratford,' I told her.

'You've been away a long time.'

'Yeah, four and a half years.'

She smiled and said, 'You can have the fare for free.'

CHAPTER 18

THE END OF THE ODYSSEY

Walter Milner-Barry spent a few days in late May sightseeing in Rome. When he returned to the SBS base at Monopoli he discovered that Stewart Macbeth had called for volunteers to go to South East Asia Command. Two hundred men had come forward. The news was a surprise to Milner-Barry who, having slept on it, wrote to David Sutherland the next morning, 30 May, offering to go with the squadron to the Far East. Later in the day Milner-Barry 'lectured to the troops about the General Election [polling day was on 5 July] ... emphasising that they all had a duty to vote for one side or the other'.[1]

Sutherland received Milner-Barry's letter in London where he had been summoned by David Stirling upon his return from Colditz prisoner of war camp. After more than two years in captivity the founder of the SAS was eager to make up for lost time and a plan had been hatched for a combined unit of SAS and SBS troops to conduct a guerrilla campaign against Japanese forces in Manchuria. Stirling asked Sutherland if he would like to lead a 60-strong SBS squadron to the Far East. Sutherland replied that it would be an honour and he flew back to Italy in July.

From the 200 volunteers Sutherland selected 60 men, a process that left the rejected with 'glum faces'. Doug Wright was one of the 60, even though he

OPPOSITE
Albert Layzell and the rest of L Squadron were able to enjoy the sights of Rome once the Armistice had been signed. (Courtesy of Ian Layzell)

confessed that the idea of deployment in the Far East was not appealing. 'I wasn't looking forward to that, knowing what the Japs were like.'[2]

To honour those who would not be going to the Far East, a valedictory dinner was held under canvas in which the soldiers dined on crab bisque and peach melba and applauded an address by their commanding officer. Sutherland read a letter recently sent to him by Field Marshal Alexander in which he had written: 'The reputation you have made for yourselves in your successful operations in the Mediterranean, the Aegean Islands and the Adriatic coast will never be surpassed, and I would wish you all good luck and God speed wherever you may go.'[3]

Sutherland and his 60 men flew out of Italy on 6 August. By the time they reached London the first atomic bomb had been dropped by the Americans on Hiroshima. Nagasaki received a second bomb on 9 August and six days later World War II was officially over.

Within two months the Special Air Service, the Special Boat Squadron and the Long Range Desert Group had been disbanded. The SAS paraded for the last time on 8 October before men who had lived and fought alongside one another for four years went their separate ways. Four days later, on 12 October, the commander of the erstwhile SAS Brigade, Brigadier Michael Calvert, sent the 12 most senior officers of the three defunct units a memo entitled 'Future of SAS Troops'. Among the men to receive the memo were George Jellicoe and David Sutherland. Calvert had been instructed by the War Office to 'investigate all the operations of the Special Air Service with a view to giving recommendations for the future of SAS in the next war and its composition in the peace-time army'.[4]

It was Calvert's fervent belief that Britain must retain its special forces but that this would only happen if the War Office was made aware of their importance, in peacetime as well as when the country was at war. 'We all have the future of SAS at heart,' Calvert wrote in the memo, 'not merely because we wish to see its particular survival as a unit but because we have believed in the principles of its method of operations.' Therefore he urged all the 12 recipients of the memo to co-operate fully with Major-General Rowell, the Director of Tactical Investigation (DTI), when their views were canvassed. In particular Calvert wanted the men to have answers to the following concerns of the War Office: 'SAS is not adaptable to all countries', 'Volunteer units skim the regular units of their best officers and men', 'Expense per man is greater than any other formation and is not worthwhile', and 'Any normal battalion could do the same job'.[5]

Calvert ended his memo with a plea: 'We can no longer say that people do not understand if we do not take this chance to get our views put before an impartial tribunal whose task it is to review them in the light of general policy.'[6]

> *'The reputation you have made for yourselves in your successful operations in the Mediterranean, the Aegean Islands and the Adriatic coast will never be surpassed, and I would wish you all good luck and God speed wherever you may go.'*

Field Marshal Alexander

The verdict of the impartial tribunal came as no surprise to Calvert nor to any other recipient of his memo – there was no place for a special forces unit in post-war Britain. Politicians wished to look forward to decades of peace, to rebuilding the world, and that world would have no room for a force of guerrilla fighters. With Winston Churchill no longer Prime Minister (replaced by Labour's Clement Attlee) the special forces had lost a close ally.

It had been Churchill who had defended the SBS a year earlier during a sharp exchange in the House of Commons with Simon Wingfield-Digby. 'Is it true, Mr Prime Minister,' the Conservative Member of Parliament for West Dorset, had enquired, 'that there is a body of men out in the Aegean Islands, fighting under the Union flag, that are nothing short of being a band of murderous, renegade cut-throats?' To which Churchill replied: 'If you do not take your seat and keep quiet I will send you out to join them.'[7] The downfall of Churchill emboldened Wingfield-Digby and his ilk, men and women untutored in combat who naively believed that wars could still be chivalrous; gradually the SBS, like Bomber Command, discovered that in the new Europe few people wanted to talk about their part in freeing the continent from the tyranny of fascism.

L Squadron, SBS, taking part in what Emerton described on the back of the photo as a parade to mark the end of the war in Europe. (Courtesy of David Henry)

In December 1945 the parents of the biggest 'cut-throat' of them all, Andy Lassen, were presented with their son's posthumous Victoria Cross by King George VI at Buckingham Palace. Having first described his actions at Lake Comacchio, the citation ended by stating that: 'The high sense of devotion to duty and the esteem in which he was held by the men he led, added to his own magnificent courage, enabled Major Lassen to carry out all the tasks he had been given with complete success.'[8]

In 1986 an army-training centre in Scotland was named after Anders Lassen. George Jellicoe and David Sutherland were at its inauguration, two old men wearied by age reunited to honour a comrade and remember their youth. Sutherland gave the address, conjuring up an image for the audience of a brilliant soldier, 'tall, fair with striking good looks'. He described some of Lassen's exploits, sketched a brief outline of his character and finished by saying: 'I believe he was happy and fulfilled in the SBS. I also feel that he died as he would have wished … speaking for Lord Jellicoe as well as for myself, we were proud to serve with Anders and count it as one of the most rewarding experiences of our lives.'[9] Lassen's reputation had grown with the memory; he was an exceptional special forces soldier but not the paragon that Sutherland imagined.

Sutherland lived on for 20 more years, dying in 2006 at the age of 85 having worked in MI5 and served as deputy commander of the SAS from 1967 to 1972. George Jellicoe died a year after Sutherland, at age 88, after a colourful political career. In his obituary, the *Daily Telegraph* said Jellicoe had 'a ready intelligence, but masked it with schoolboyish levity and a disarming frankness about his own weaknesses'.[10] All of the men interviewed for this book held Jellicoe in the highest regard as a soldier and as a man.

Milner-Barry was 41 when he returned to England in the summer of 1945, a lost soul who felt out of place in peacetime and middle age. He dabbled in politics for a while, failed to win the nomination to become the Conservative candidate for Cambridge Town in the late 1940s, and then entered merchant banking. In 1958 he became a brother in the Venerable Order of the Hospital of Saint John, whose aim is to 'prevent and relieve sickness and injury, and to act to enhance the health and well-being of people anywhere in the world'.[11] Milner-Barry died at his Hampshire home in 1981 aged 77.

According to the son of Dion 'Stud' Stellin his father 'never really got over [Lassen's] death'. Stellin fought in the Malayan Emergency and later bought 12,000 acres to farm in a remote island off New Zealand because 'it reminded him so much of the Aegean Islands'.[12] He died from cancer in 1975 but Stellin's son continues to live on the island.

Ian Smith joined the family textile business after the war before moving to Ireland and starting a fish farm. He died in 2012. His great friend Ambrose McGonigal studied law after the war and was a High Court Judge at the height of the Troubles. Knighted in 1975, McGonigal was alleged to have carried a handgun under his robes because of the terrorist threat. He died of natural causes in 1979.

John Verney and John Lodwick both enjoyed successful literary careers after the war, with the latter drawing comparison with Evelyn Waugh for the power of his writing. Lodwick was at the height of his powers when he was killed in a car crash in 1959 aged 53. John Verney's artistic talents stretched to more than just writing and in his 1993 obituary *The Independent* newspaper described him as 'a writer, painter and illustrator … master of the ludicrous, inventor of the "Dodo-Pad".'[13]

Sean O'Reilly became a doorman at one of the big London hotels after the wars; Cyril Feebery became an antiques dealer; Duggie Pomford opened the Golden Gloves boxing club in Liverpool in 1949, still a thriving enterprise and recently described by the Amateur Boxing Association of England as a 'boxing institution'. In 1954 Pomford was awarded a medal by the Royal Humane Society for rescuing a man from the Liverpool docks. He died in 1969 aged 49, the result, his family believe, of ill-health brought on by the malaria he first contracted during the war.

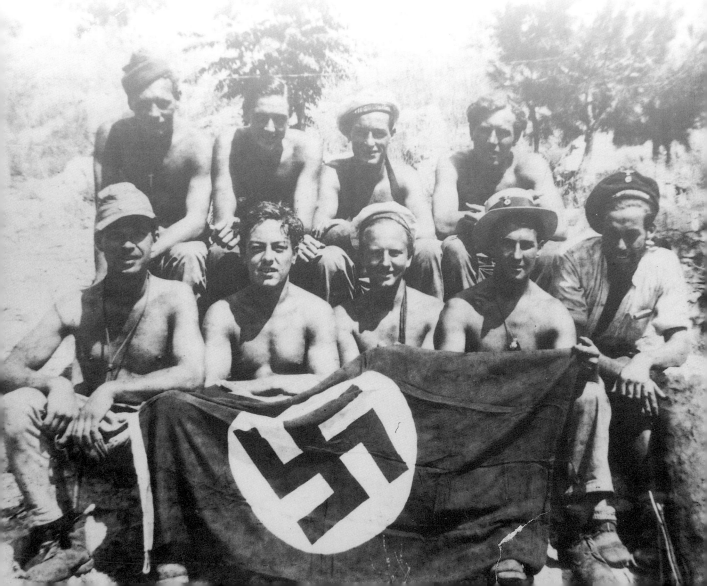

M Squadron with the spoils of war at Castelrosso, July 1944: top row: Ray Iggledon, John Johnson, Henry Smith and Albert May. Bottom row: Jim Horsfield, Ben Gunn, Jimmy Lees, Bill Mayall and Tommy Tucker. (Courtesy of the SBS Archive)

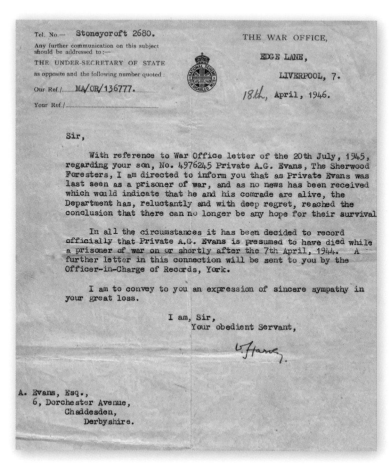

Tel. No.— Stoneycroft 2680.

Any further communication on this subject should be addressed to:—

THE UNDER-SECRETARY OF STATE as opposite and the following number quoted :

Our Ref./ MA/OR/136777.

Your Ref./

THE WAR OFFICE,

EDGE LANE,

LIVERPOOL, 7.

18th, April, 1946.

Sir,

With reference to War Office letter of the 20th July, 1945, regarding your son, No. 4976245 Private A.G. Evans, The Sherwood Foresters, I am directed to inform you that as Private Evans was last seen as a prisoner of war, and as no news has been received which would indicate that he and his comrade are alive, the Department has, reluctantly and with deep regret, reached the conclusion that there can no longer be any hope for their survival

In all the circumstances it has been decided to record officially that Private A.G. Evans is presumed to have died while a prisoner of war on or shortly after the 7th April, 1944. A further letter in this connection will be sent to you by the Officer-in-Charge of Records, York.

I am to convey to you an expression of sincere sympathy in your great loss.

I am, Sir,
Your obedient Servant,

A. Evans, Esq.,
6, Dorchester Avenue,
Chaddesden,
Derbyshire.

Only in April 1946, two years after their deaths and following the end of the war, did the War Office acknowledge the men of the Alimnia Patrol were dead. (Courtesy of the Evans family)

Porter Jarrell spent 44 years working for the International Organization for Migration, a humanitarian concern he helped found and which he illuminated with his 'compassion and principle'.[14] Many years after the war Jarrell appeared unannounced at an SBS reunion in London and as he walked through the door at the Duke of York's Barracks in London a voice exclaimed: 'Good God, it's the fucking Yank!'[15] He died in 2001.

Sid Dowland returned to the Grenadier Guards and eventually left the army in 1958 aged 40 with the rank of colour sergeant. The rest of his working life was spent working for an electronics firm in Surrey, where he died in 2002.

Keith Killby, the conscientious objector, returned to the family meat business in Spitalfields. In 1989 he established the San Marino Trust, a registered charity that awards bursaries to young Italians to come to England to improve their English skills. It was Killby's way of paying back Italy for the help its people gave escaped British POWs in the winter of 1943. At the time of writing Killby, in his 97th year, is still actively involved in the Trust.

Ken Smith remained in the Royal Marines before returning to his native Portsmouth where he still lives. Reg Osborn, veteran of the Levant Schooner Flotilla, is also still alive, living in London where he spent his working life as a press photographer.

Doug Wright played out the last act of his adventurous life in the Royal Hospital Chelsea, still cutting an imposing figure in the scarlet tunic worn by the pensioners. For a while he had tried civvy street, working as a farm manager in Cheshire, but the pull of the army was too strong and he re-enlisted in the 1950s. Wright was finally discharged in 1970 and spent the next 20 years in a variety of jobs – crane driver, butcher and prison warder – before entering the Hospital in 1998. He died ten years later aged 88.

Dick Holmes was determined to make up for the time lost to the war. He decided against returning to work as a window fitter, and became a teacher of physical education. He also married and then, in the early 1960s, he and his wife emigrated to Ontario where they continue to live. Both now in their 90s they go bowling with friends twice a week. Holmes is the last survivor of that band of men who were transferred from the SAS to the SBS at the end of 1942. He reflected:

I found my niche in the SBS. I enjoyed it, I was good at it, and it was the war I wanted to be fighting. There was no bullshit, no saluting … and best of all, you were among like-minded fellows who also hated spit and polish.

We didn't do anything that affected the war in any great way. We blew up bridges, destroyed airfields, shot up a few Germans. Niggling things that inconvenienced the enemy. But I think we slowed them down in the Aegean and we also tied up quite a few thousand of their troops when they would have been better deployed in Russia or France, and we were doing that with only a few dozen men of our own. So we felt we were doing something necessary.[16]

The 91-year-old Dick Holmes describes the 21-year-old Dick Holmes as an 'arrogant bastard' but then in his view the same applied to everyone who volunteered for the SAS in North Africa.

We were in action a hell of a lot and I told myself I was fighting men who hadn't done the training I had. They hadn't jumped out of aeroplanes or marched for miles on end. In my mind I was better than them and that gave me – and I think the rest of the boys – a tremendous advantage when we went on a scheme. We were superior not only physically but psychologically.

The SBS and the SAS had to be strong psychologically for in the last year of the war they knew of Hitler's Commando Order, instructing all captured British commandos to be executed. 'We operated under a death sentence and you can imagine the tension that decree introduced,' reflected Holmes.

––––––––––

In the summer of 1944 Walter Milner-Barry returned to England and paid a courtesy call to the wife of Bill Blyth, who had recently learned that her husband was in a German prisoner of war camp. For the families of Leo Rice, George Evans, Ray Jones and George Miller there was no such news to pass on to missing relatives. Nor too for the worried relations of Ronald Carpenter and Allan Tuckey.

Nothing had been heard from any of them since their capture in April 1944.

The mother of Allan Tuckey began writing letters in a desperate bid to discover the fate of her son. First she wrote to the War Office and then she contacted the Special Boat Squadron. They forwarded a letter from her to Bill Blyth's wife, who in turn posted it to her husband in Germany. Blyth received the letter on 8 January 1945 in Oflag 79 near Brunswick, the POW camp to which he had been transferred from Stalag 7A.

Blyth replied on the same day, describing their capture and how he and Tuckey had been separated from the rest of the men upon arriving in Rhodes. He stressed to Mrs Clark that her son had been 'in the best of health when I last saw him and was being well treated by the Germans'. Blyth concluded the letter by saying he was at a loss to know why Mrs Tuckey had received no communication from her son. 'The only conclusion that I can arrive at is that he might have attempted to escape or was taken to the Greek mainland by sea and met some accident en route.'[17]

Evans' mother, seen here with a young George, wrote repeatedly to the War Office who suggested he had probably 'met with some accident' while a prisoner. (Courtesy of the Evans family)

There was, of course, a third conclusion Blyth might have mentioned had he not known that his letter would be read by the Germans before being despatched to England via the International Red Cross. Curiously, however, even upon his release from captivity Blyth never raised the possibility that the men had been executed. In September 1945, in response to yet another letter from Tuckey's mother, the War Office replied that the six British prisoners 'may have been lost trying to escape [from Rhodes] as we have evidence that a few did try to swim to the [Greek] mainland'.[18]

When John Lodwick published *The Filibusters* in 1947 he described how Blyth had been 'well treated ... within a week of his capture he was playing hockey in an Oflag'. This information could only have come from Blyth himself. As for the fate of the missing men, wrote Lodwick, '... we never knew, and it seems now that we shall never know. The war is over but they remain listed as "missing".'[19]

One can only speculate why Blyth told Lodwick he was playing hockey a week after his capture, when in reality he was being tortured by Dr Mueller-Faure. Perhaps he was ashamed at having talked, despite the fact that he betrayed no one nor revealed to his inquisitors anything that could have comprised his comrades still operating in the Gulf of Kos. Blyth must have suspected that the rest of the men had been subjected to a similar brutal interrogation, but if he did then he kept these concerns to himself. Maybe Blyth wanted to save the families of the missing men from pain or perhaps by denying any torture had taken place this brave man was trying to alleviate his own misplaced sense of guilt.

The families of the missing men continued their campaign to discover the truth but in April 1946 the parents of George Evans received a letter from the War Office,

The fate of George Evans and the rest of the Alimnia Patrol remained a mystery for nearly 50 years. (Courtesy of the Evans family)

stating 'as no news has been received which would indicate he and his comrades are alive … there can no longer be any hope for their survival'. The letter, certainly sent to all the relatives, concluded by saying: 'It has been decided to record officially that Private A.G. Evans is presumed to have died while a prisoner of war, on or shortly after 7th April 1944.'[20]

The matter was now considered closed. Bill Blyth emigrated to South Africa – though he and David Sutherland met each year at Royal Ascot – and the mother of Allan Tuckey grew old and died. So did Blyth, reportedly in the early 1980s, the same decade when the fate of the Alimnia Patrol was finally laid bare, 'in a strange way', as Sutherland wrote later.[21]

For many years rumours had stalked Kurt Waldheim as the Austrian rose through the world of international diplomacy, rumours that intimated he had something to hide from the war years. Waldheim had always dismissed the whisperings as idle gossip spread by his political enemies. Yes, he had served in the war, but 'in a reconnaissance unit, and I served on horseback in its cavalry element'. Furthermore he had been 'wounded on the eastern front and, being incapacitated for further service on the front, resumed my law

10 DOWNING STREET
LONDON SW1A 2AA

THE PRIME MINISTER   9 March 1988

Dear Greg,

    Thank you for your letter of 22 February. I am
conscious of the great debt we all owe to the heroism of
servicemen like Mr. Evans, and can well understand why he is
held in such regard in Derby.

    As you know, the Ministry of Defence, in conjunction
with other interested Departments, is conducting a review of
the results of the investigation which it carried out in 1986
into the fate of captured British servicemen and the
involvement, if any, of the then Lieutenant Waldheim, in the
light of the Report of the Independent International
Commission of Historians. The review team will re-examine
all aspects relating to the fate of these men and a report
will be published once this process has been completed.

    I hope this outline will be of use to you to pass on to
your constituents and that if any of them, including any
members of Mr. Evans' family, has any information to give
which might be relevant to the review, they will submit it to
Ian Stewart in the Ministry of Defence.

Yours ever

Margaret

Greg Knight, Esq, M.P.

Once the fate of the Alimnia Patrol had been established in the 1980s, the then Prime Minister Margaret Thatcher wrote to the MP of the Evans family to express her gratitude for his 'heroism'. (Author's Collection)

studies at Vienna university where I graduated in 1944'.[22]

After his 'honourable' war Waldheim joined the Austrian Foreign Ministry, and in 1972 he was elected secretary general to the United Nations, a position he held until 1982. It was when he ran for the presidency of Austria in 1986 that Waldheim's political foes launched their attack, exposing his trail of untruths.

Waldheim's forte in the war had been intelligence, not reconnaissance, and as a first lieutenant he had served as an intelligence officer in Army Group E, based in Salonika.

Investigative journalists from around the world leaped on the revelation, and within months the full extent of Waldheim's deception had been uncovered. 'Kurt Waldheim did not, in fact, order, incite or personally commit what is commonly called a war crime,' wrote Robert Edwin Herzstein, a historian who played a pivotal role in bringing Waldheim to account, 'but this nonguilt must not be confused with innocence. The fact that Waldheim played a significant role in military units that unquestionably committed war crimes makes him at the very least morally complicit in those crimes.'[23]

Among the reams of German Intelligence documents painstakingly examined by historians and journalists were a handful relating to the capture of LS24 in Alimnia Bay. Waldheim was on leave at the time, and in this particular war crime he played no part, but his fellow intelligence officers were complicit in events outlined in a series of chilling reports and cables.

George Evans, Leo Rice, George Miller, Ray Jones, Allan Tuckey and Ronald Carpenter had not drowned attempting to escape from Rhodes, nor had they met with some other 'accident'; they had been tortured and executed. The only information missing from the files was the circumstance of their deaths. 'It's pretty certain that George and the others with him were executed close to the HQ of the Intelligence Branch Army Group E at the town of Arsakli, near Salonika,' said Holly Kendrick, the niece of George Evans.[24]

Kendrick, whose mother mourned her big brother for the rest of her life, believes the men were murdered shortly after Lieutenant-Colonel Von Harling ordered them to be handed to the SD for 'special treatment'. They were probably taken from their cells early in the morning, marched up into the hills 'with the lovely view above the town', and shot.[25]

Blyth lived because he fell into the hands of a decent man, Colonel Otto Burger, the commandant of Stalag 7A. Twice he was ordered to hand Blyth over to the local SD unit and twice he refused. He knew what they would do to the Englishman. Eventually it seems the Germans forgot about Captain Blyth; it was probably Burger who arranged his transfer to another POW camp, to further cover the tracks of a man the Nazis wanted dead.

The revelations failed to end Waldheim's political career. Indeed they were credited with whipping up a nationalist backlash in Austria with many voters seeing parallels between his ambiguous wartime career and their own. In 1986 Waldheim was elected president of Austria; the same year the British Prime Minister, Margaret Thatcher, ordered an inquiry into the extent of Waldheim's involvement in the execution of the Alimnia Patrol. The Ministry of Defence report concluded that Waldheim would have 'been aware of their interrogation but there is no evidence that he was involved in the fruitless interrogation in Salonika, either personally or by advising on treatment'.[26]

The report stated that Tuckey and the four SBS soldiers were probably executed soon after 27 April while Carpenter was shot in the first week of June. 'It is very much regretted,' concluded the Ministry of Defence report, 'that in spite of extensive research during this review it has not proved possible to obtain any definite evidence as to the final fate of the missing men'.

In May 1991, three years before Waldheim was awarded a papal knighthood by Pope John Paul II, a memorial service was held for the Alimnia Patrol in St Paul's Anglican Church in Athens. Among the congregation were relatives of Allan Tuckey, Ray Jones and George Evans. The Greece Minister of Defence was present, so too the British Ambassador to Greece. George Jellicoe read the first lesson, and then David Sutherland gave the address, 47 years after he had watched LS24 sail out of the Yedi Atala. 'Their courage and endurance under interrogation was incredible,' Sutherland told the congregation. 'They came through their appalling ordeal in triumph... I am proud to have served with them.'[27]

GLOSSARY

88mm	a German anti-tank and anti-aircraft gun
Brandenburg Regiment	German special forces
Bren gun	Czech-made light machine gun with a range of 2,000 yards
caique	Greek fishing boat used by the SBS
Carabinieri	Italian military police
DZ	drop zone for paratroopers and supplies
EAM	National Liberation Front; a left-wing political movement in Greece composed predominantly of communists
EDES	National Republican Greek League; a non-communist Greek resistance group
ELAS	Greek People's Liberation Army; the military arm of the EAM
Feldgendarmerie	German military police
folboat	collapsible canoe
Force 133	the Balkans wing of the SOE
Führer	German for leader; the title given to Adolf Hitler
Gestapo	Geheime Staatspolizei; the secret police force of Nazi Germany
GHQ	General Headquarters
L Detachment	the initial name given to the special force founded by David Stirling that later became the Special Air Service regiment
Layforce	the commando force (consisting of five 'troops') that was raised in 1940 and sent to the Middle East in 1941 under the command of Robert Laycock
LCA	Landing Craft Assault; 40-foot long vessel capable of carrying 35 men
LFA	Land Forces Adriatic
LRDG	Long Range Desert Group
LSF	Levant Schooner Flotilla
NCO	non commissioned officer

OCTU	Officer Cadets Training Unit
OR	other ranks
petrol bowser	petrol tanker
POW	prisoner of war
RFHQ	Raiding Forces Headquarters
RAF	Royal Air Force
RAMC	Royal Army Medical Corps
RTU	Returned to Unit
SAS	Special Air Service
SBS	Special Boat Squadron
SD	Sicherheitsdienst, the intelligence service of the SS
SOE	Special Operations Executive
Sonderbehandlung	'special treatment'; the Nazi euphemism for the execution of captured Allied commandos
SRS	Special Raiding Squadron; formed in 1943 from 1 SAS
SS	Schutzstaffel; the paramilitary force of Nazi Germany
Stuka	the nickname of the Luftwaffe Junkers 87 dive-bomber
TJFF	Transjordan Frontier Force
Tommy gun	Thompson submachine gun
Ustashi	Croatian Pro-Nazi militia
Vickers K	Rapid firing machine gun designed for aircraft and later used by the SAS
wadi	a dry river bed in the desert that contains water only when it rains heavily
W/T	wireless telegraphy

NOTES

Introduction

1. Letter from General McCreery to General Harold Alexander, September 1942. PRO WO 201/732
2. David Stirling Memo, 1946, SAS Archives
3. SAS war diary, 14 February 1943, National Archives WO218/98
4. Pleydell papers, privately held
5. Sutherland, David, *He Who Dares* (Leo Cooper, 1998), p.98

Chapter 1

1. Letter from Sutherland to Lodwick 1945, SAS Archives
2. Ibid.
3. Ibid.
4. Sutherland, *He Who Dares* (Leo Cooper, 1998), p.97
5. David Sutherland scrapbook, SAS Archives
6. Sutherland, *He Who Dares*, p.40
7. All quotes from Dick Holmes in this chapter are taken from an author interview, 2012
8. Author interview with Pomford family, 2012
9. All quotes from Sid Dowland in this chapter are taken from an author interview, 2002
10. Author interview with Doug Wright, 2002
11. Author interview with Keith Killby, 2002
12. Ibid.

Chapter 2

1. SBS war diary, 7 April 1943, National Archives WO218/98
2. Sutherland, David, *He Who Dares* (Leo Cooper, 1998), p.99
3. David Sutherland scrapbook, SAS Archives
4. *Mars and Minerva*, journal of the SAS Association, April 1992
5. Milner-Barry papers, Imperial War Museum, catalogue number 16758
6. Ibid.

7. Sutherland, *He Who Dares*, p.100

8. Ibid.

9. Milner-Barry papers, Imperial War Museum

10. All quotes from Dick Holmes in this chapter are taken from an author interview, 2012

11. Milner-Barry papers, Imperial War Museum

12. SBS war diary, 16 April 1943, National Archives WO218/98

13. Milner-Barry papers, Imperial War Museum

14. David Sutherland scrapbook

15. SBS war diary

16. Grant-Taylor, Leonard, *Close Quarter Battle*, quoted in Martin, D, *The Iron Hand of War*, available at http://www.cqbservices.com/?page_id=11

17. SBS war diary

18. Verney, John, *Going to the Wars* (Collins, 1955), p.24

19. Ibid.

20. SBS war diary

21. SBS training programme for week beginning 3 May 1943, SBS war diary

22. Author interview with Sid Dowland, 2002

23. Milner-Barry papers, Imperial War Museum

24. SBS war diary

25. Milner-Barry papers, Imperial War Museum

26. Ibid.

27. SBS war diary

28. Ibid.

29. Ibid.

30. Ibid.

Chapter 3

1. SBS war diary, National Archives WO218/98

2. Verney, John, *Going to the Wars* (Collins, 1955), p.139

3. Ibid.

4. Hughes, Quentin *Who Cares Who Wins* (Charico, 1998), p.56

5. All quotes from Keith Killby in this chapter are taken from an author interview, 2002

6. Verney, *Going to the Wars*, p.145

7. Ibid.

8. Hoe, Alan, *David Stirling* (Warner, 1994), p.146

9. Mission report by Sergeant Pat Scully, SBS war diary

10. Author interview with Doug Wright, 2002
11. Feebery, Cyril, *Guardsman & Commando* (Pen & Sword, 2008), p.94
12. SBS war diary
13. Ibid.
14. Ibid.
15. Dorney, Richard, *An Active Service: The Story of a Soldier's Life in the Grenadier Guards and SAS, 1935–1958* (Helion and Company, 2009), p.113
16. Ibid.
17. Feebery, *Guardsman & Commando*, p.101
18. Verney, *Going to the Wars*, p.178
19. SBS war diary
20. Author interview with Richard Dorney, 2002

Chapter 4

1. Milner-Barry papers, Imperial War Museum, catalogue number 16758
2. Ibid.
3. David Sutherland scrapbook, SAS Archives
4. Ibid.
5. Ibid.
6. All quotes from Dick Holmes in this chapter are taken from an author interview, 2012
7. Author interview with Jeff Du Vivier, 2003
8. David Sutherland scrapbook, SAS Archives
9. Ibid.
10. Ibid.
11. Sutherland, David, *He Who Dares* (Leo Cooper, 1998), p.108
12. David Sutherland scrapbook, SAS Archives
13. Sutherland, *He Who Dares*, p.109
14. Ibid.
15. *Egyptian Mail*, 6 July 1943
16. Sutherland, *He Who Dares*, p.111

Chapter 5

1. Milner-Barry papers, Imperial War Museum, catalogue number 16758
2. David Sutherland scrapbook, SAS Archives
3. Dick Holmes' papers
4. Langley, Mike, *Anders Lassen* (New English, 1988) p.140
5. All quotes from Dick Holmes in this chapter are taken from an author

interview, 2012

6. David Sutherland scrapbook, SAS Archives
7. Sutherland, David, *He Who Dares* (Leo Cooper, 1998), p.112
8. Milner-Barry papers, Imperial War Museum
9. Ibid.
10. Ibid.
11. Ibid.
12. Smith, Peter and Edwin Walker, *War in the Aegean* (Stackpole, 2008), p.34
13. David Sutherland scrapbook, SAS Archives
14. Jellicoe, Imperial War Museum sound archive, catalogue number 26767
15. Ibid.
16. Ibid.
17. Milner-Barry papers, Imperial War Museum
18. Ibid.
19. Ibid.
20. Jellicoe, Imperial War Museum sound archive
21. David Sutherland scrapbook, SAS Archives

Chapter 6

1. All quotes from Dick Holmes in this chapter are taken from an author interview, 2012
2. David Sutherland scrapbook, SAS Archives
3. Smith, Peter and Edwin Walker, *War in the Aegean* (Stackpole, 2008), p.41
4. David Sutherland scrapbook, SAS Archives
5. Milner-Barry papers, Imperial War Museum, catalogue number 16758
6. David Sutherland scrapbook, SAS Archives
7. Unattributed quotations in the following paragraphs are all from Milner-Barry papers, Imperial War Museum
8. http://durhamlightinfantry.webs.com

Chapter 7

1. Lodwick, John, *The Filibusters* (Methuen, 1947), p.82
2. http://samilitaryhistory.org/vol012dp.html
3. Langley, Mike, *Anders Lassen* (New English, 1988), p.143
4. Smith, Peter and Edwin Walker, *War in the Aegean* (Stackpole, 2008), p.146
5. Langley, *Anders Lassen*, p.176
6. Ibid.
7. National Archives WO373/14

8. Harder, Thomas, *Anders Lassen's War* (Informations Forlag, 2010), p.74
9. http://samilitaryhistory.org/vol012dp.html
10. Ibid.
11. Smith and Walker, *War in the Aegean*, pp.45–46
12. Ibid.
13. Sutherland, David, *He Who Dares* (Leo Cooper, 1998), p.117
14. Ibid.
15. All quotes from Doug Wright in this chapter are taken from an author interview, 2002
16. All quotes from Dick Holmes in this chapter are taken from an author interview, 2012
17. Smith and Walker, *War in the Aegean*, p.200
18. Ibid.
19. David Sutherland scrapbook, SAS Archives
20. Ibid.
21. Ibid
22. Ibid.
23. Ibid.
24. Ibid.
25. Ibid.
26. Ibid.
27. Ibid.
28. Smith and Walker, *War in the Aegean*, p.226
29. David Sutherland scrapbook, SAS Archives
30. Ibid.
31. Ibid.
32. Smith and Walker, *War in the Aegean*, p.267

Chapter 8

1. Lodwick, John, *The Filibusters* (Methuen, 1947), p.100
2. Milner-Barry papers, Imperial War Museum, catalogue number 16758
3. Ibid.
4. All quotations from Ken Smith in this chapter are taken from his interview, Imperial War Museum sound archive, catalogue number 18490
5. Milner-Barry papers, Imperial War Museum
6. Ibid.
7. All quotations from Dick Holmes in this chapter are taken from an author interview, 2012

8. Lodwick, *The Filibusters*, p.127
9. Donald Grant, in *Look* magazine, from the papers of Dick Holmes
10. Ibid.
11. Sutherland, David, *He Who Dares* (Leo Cooper, 1998), p.130

Chapter 9

1. Smith, Peter and Edwin Walker, *War in the Aegean* (Stackpole, 2008), p.259
2. Lodwick, John, *The Filibusters* (Methuen, 1947), p.132
3. Author interview with Dick Holmes, 2012
4. Seligman, Adrian, *War in the Islands: Undercover Operations in the Aegean, 1942–44* (Sutton, 1996)
5. Milner-Barry papers, Imperial War Museum, catalogue number 16758
6. Ibid.
7. Ibid.
8. Citation for Corporal Asbery's Military Medal

Chapter 10

1. Milner-Barry papers, Imperial War Museum, catalogue number 16758
2. All quotations from Dick Holmes in this chapter are taken from an author interview, 2012
3. Milner-Barry papers, Imperial War Museum
4. Ibid.
5. Ibid.
6. Ibid.
7. All quotation from Reg Osborn in this chapter are taken from an author interview, 2012
8. Milner-Barry papers, Imperial War Museum
9. Ibid.
10. Ibid.
11. Diary held by Wiener Library, London, Document 646, Waldheim papers

Chapter 11

1. Diary held by Wiener Library, London, Document 646, Waldheim papers
2. Evans Family papers
3. Ibid.
4. Ibid.
5. Author interview with Dick Holmes, 2012
6. Diary held by Wiener Library, London

7. Ibid.
8. Ibid.
9. Evans Family papers
10. Diary held by Wiener Library, London
11. Interview given to *Sunday Tasmanian*, 6 March 1988
12. German Interrogation report N0.308, Waldheim Papers, Wiener Library
13. Ibid.
14. Ibid.
15. Ibid.
16. Ibid.
17. Ibid.
18. Ibid.
19. Ibid.
20. Ibid.
21. Ibid.
22. Ibid.
23. Ibid.

Chapter 12

1. Sutherland, David, *He Who Dares* (Leo Cooper, 1998), p.137
2. All quotations from Dick Holmes in this chapter are taken from an author interview, 2012
3. All quotations from Doug Wright in this chapter are taken from an author interview, 2002
4. David Sutherland scrapbook, SAS Archives
5. Langley, Mike, *Anders Lassen* (New English, 1988), p.157
6. Ibid.
7. Ibid.
8. Ibid.
9. Ibid.
10. David Sutherland scrapbook, SAS Archives
11. Ibid.
12. Ibid
13. Ibid.
14. National Archives WO373/46
15. David Sutherland scrapbook, SAS Archives
16. Dick Holmes papers

Chapter 13

1. Lodwick, John, *The Filibusters* (Methuen, 1947), p.147
2. Ibid.
3. Ken Smith interview, Imperial War Museum sound archive, catalogue number 18490
4. Ibid.
5. Ibid.
6. David Sutherland scrapbook, SAS Archives
7. Ken Smith interview, Imperial War Museum sound archive
8. Lodwick, *The Filibusters*, p.154
9. Ken Smith interview, Imperial War Museum sound archive
10. David Sutherland scrapbook, SAS Archives
11. Ibid.
12. Author interview with Dick Holmes, 2012

Chapter 14

1. All quotations from Doug Wright in this chapter are taken from an author interview, 2002
2. All quotations from Dick Holmes in this chapter are taken from an author interview, 2012
3. Goni, Uki, *The Read Odessa: Smuggling the Nazis to Perón's Argentina* (Granta, 2002), p.202
4. David Sutherland scrapbook, SAS Archives
5. Major I.C.D. Smith MC, Imperial War Museum, catalogue number 15632
6. Ibid.
7. Lodwick, John, *The Filibusters* (Methuen, 1947), p.176
8. R.J.P. Eden papers, Imperial War Museum, catalogue number 13339
9. Ibid.
10. David Sutherland scrapbook, SAS Archives
11. Ibid.
12. Ibid.
13. Ibid.

Chapter 15

1. National Archives WO373/14
2. Milner-Barry papers, Imperial War Museum, catalogue number 16758
3. *The Lowell Sun*, 6 October 1944
4. Lodwick, John, *The Filibusters* (Methuen, 1947), p.188

5. Milner-Barry papers, Imperial War Museum
6. Ibid.
7. *Mars and Minerva*, April 1994
8. Milner-Barry papers, Imperial War Museum
9. Ibid.
10. *Mars and Minerva*, June 2000
11. Ibid.
12. All quotations from Doug Wright in this chapter are taken from an author interview, 2002
13. *Parsis News*, Texas, 2 November 1944
14. Ibid.
15. Mortimer, Gavin, *The Daring Dozen* (Osprey, 2011), p.27

Chapter 16

1. Milner-Barry papers, Imperial War Museum, catalogue number 16758
2. Major I.C.D. Smith MC, Imperial War Museum, catalogue number 15632
3. David Sutherland scrapbook, SAS Archives
4. Milner-Barry papers, Imperial War Museum
5. Ibid.
6. David Sutherland scrapbook, SAS Archives
7. All quotations from Dick Holmes in this chapter are taken from an author interview, 2012
8. SAS Archives
9. Ibid.
10. Ibid.
11. Ibid.
12. All the Ken Smith quotations in this chapter are from the Ken Smith interview, Imperial War Museum sound archive, catalogue number 18490
13. SAS Archives
14. Ibid.
15. Ibid.
16. Ibid.
17. Ibid.
18. National Archives WO373/59
19. Ibid.
20. SAS Archives
21. Ibid.
22. Milner-Barry papers, Imperial War Museum

23. All quotations from Doug Wright in this chapter are taken from an author interview, 2002; all quotations from Dick Holmes in this chapter are taken from an author interview, 2012
24. Major I.C.D. Smith MC, Imperial War Museum
25. Ibid.
26. David Sutherland scrapbook, SAS Archives

Chapter 17

1. Lodwick, John, *The Filibusters* (Methuen, 1947), p.237
2. Major I.C.D. Smith MC, Imperial War Museum, catalogue number 15632
3. Lodwick, *The Filibusters*, p.233
4. Harder, Thomas, *Anders Lassen's War* (Informations Forlag, 2010), p.289
5. Author interview with Dick Holmes, 2012
6. All the Ken Smith quotations in this chapter are from the Ken Smith interview, Imperial War Museum sound archive, catalogue number 18490
7. Langley, Mike, *Anders Lassen* (New English, 1988), p.243
8. SAS Archives
9. Langley, *Anders Lassen*, p.244
10. Ibid.
11. Milner-Barry papers, Imperial War Museum, catalogue number 16758
12. Ibid.
13. Ibid.
14. Major I.C.D. Smith MC, Imperial War Museum
15. Ibid.
16. Milner-Barry papers, Imperial War Museum
17. Ibid.
18. Ibid.
19. Author interview with Doug Wright, 2002
20. Milner-Barry papers, Imperial War Museum

Chapter 18

1. Milner-Barry papers, Imperial War Museum, catalogue number 16758
2. Author interview with Doug Wright, 2002
3. David Sutherland scrapbook, SAS Archives
4. SAS Archives
5. Ibid.
6. Ibid.
7. Ibid.

8. National Archives WO373/47

9. *Mars and Minerva*, Spring 1987

10. *Daily Telegraph*, 26 February 2007

11. http://www.sja.ca/Saskatchewan/AboutUs/Worldwide/Pages/default.aspx

12. http://www.barriergold.co.nz/history.htm

13. *The Independent*, 4 February 1993

14. http://www.pugwash.org/publication/nl/nlv38n1/porter-jarrell.htm

15. Ibid.

16. All quotations from Dick Holmes in this chapter are taken from an author interview, 2012

17. National Archives WO361/1089

18. Ibid.

19. Lodwick, John, *The Filibusters* (Methuen, 1947), p.135

20. Evans family papers

21. Sutherland, David, *He Who Dares* (Leo Cooper, 1998), p.150

22. *New York Times*, 4 March 1986

23. *New York Times*, 14 June 2007

24. Author interview with Holly Kendrick, 2012

25. Ibid.

26. Metropolitan archives ACC/3121/E/04/1040

27. Sutherland, *He Who Dares*, p.152

BIBLIOGRAPHY

Books

Carver, Lord, *The Imperial War Museum Book of the War in Italy* (Pan Books, 2002)

Dorney, Richard, *An Active Service: The Story of a Soldier's Life in the Grenadier Guards and SAS, 1935–1958* (Helion and Company, 2009)

Feebery, Cyril, *Guardsman & Commando* (Pen & Sword, 2008)

French, Patrick, *Younghusband: The Last Great Imperial Adventure* (Penguin, 2011)

Harder, Thomas, *Anders Lassen's War* (Informations Forlag, 2010)

Hoe, Alan, *David Stirling* (Warner, 1994)

Hughes, Quentin, *Who Cares Who Wins* (Charico, 1998)

Koburger, Charles, *Wine-Dark, Blood Red Sea: Naval Warfare in the Aegean, 1941–1946* (Praeger, 1999)

Kurowski, Frank, *Jump into Hell: German Paratroopers in World War II* (Stackpole, 2004)

Langley, Mike, *Anders Lassen* (New English, 1988)

Lefevre, Eric, *Brandenburg Division* (Histoire & Collections, 2000)

Lloyd-Owen, David, *Providence Their Guide* (Harrap, 1980)

Lodwick, John, *The Filibusters* (Methuen, 1947)

Mortimer, Gavin, *Stirling's Men* (Weidenfeld & Nicolson, 2004)

Mortimer, Gavin, *The SAS in World War II: An Illustrated History* (Osprey, 2011)

Mortimer, Gavin, *The Daring Dozen* (Osprey, 2012)

Newby, Eric, *Love and War in the Apennines* (Hodder, 1971)

Pitt, Barrie, *Special Boat Squadron* (Century, 1983)

Public Record Office, *Special Forces in the Desert War* (PRO, 2001)

The Royal Hospital Chelsea, *Before They Fade* (The Royal Hospital Chelsea, 2002)

Seligman, Adrian, *War in the Islands: Undercover Operations in the Aegean, 1942–44* (Sutton, 1996)

Sharpe, Michael and Ian Westwell, *German Elite Forces* (Chartwell Books, 2007)

Smith, Peter and Edwin Walker, *War in the Aegean* (Stackpole, 2008)

Sutherland, David, *He Who Dares* (Leo Cooper, 1998)

Thompson, Julian, *War Behind Enemy Lines* (Pan, 1999)

Verney, John, *Going to the Wars* (Collins, 1955)

Unpublished memoirs

Robert Eden, untitled

The Diaries of Walter Milner-Barry

Walter Milner-Barry, *The Happy Hedonistic*

Ian Smith, *The Happy Amateur*

Magazines, newspapers and journals

Daily Express

Daily Telegraph

Egyptian Mail

The Independent

Look Magazine

Lowell Sun

Mars & Minerva

New York Times

Paris News

The Times

National Archives

WO 373/46

WO 373/14

WO 218/212

WO 379/16

WO 218/98

Imperial War Museum

George Jellicoe, sound archive, catalogue number 26767

Walter Milner-Barry, documents, catalogue number 16758

Reg Osborn, sound archive, catalogue number 20296

Major I.C.D. Smith MC, catalogue number 15632

Ken Smith, sound archive, catalogue number 18490

SAS Regimental Archives

David Sutherland Scrapbook

Mars and Minerva

Operational reports

Author interviews

Sid Dowland (2002)

Dick Holmes (2003 and 2012)

Keith Killby (2002)

Reg Osborn (2012)

Malcolm Pleydell (1998)

Jeff Du Vivier (2003)

Doug Wright (2002)

INDEX

References to illustrations are shown in **bold**.

Acropolis **4**, **191**
Adriatic islands 200–203, 219
Adriatic operations **199**, **201**, 201–202, 203–208
Aegean Islands 76–77, 88, 89–91, **91**, 110, 169, 177, 225
   German invasion 90–91, 110, 123–124
Aegean Sea **73**, 76–77, 89, 102, 124, 169
   map **10**
Albania **180**, 185
Albanian partisans **185**, 185
Alexander, FM Harold 81, 219, 224, 225
Alexandria 121
   64th General Hospital 94
Algiers 44
Alimnia 142, **143**, 145, 148, 149–150, **153**, 153
Alimnia Patrol 145–146, 147, **148**, 148–150, 157
   fate **228**, **231**, 231, **232**, 232–233
   members captured 149–154, **151**, 155, 157, 167
Alinda Bay **104**, 107, 108, 109
Allen, Cpl 202
Allott, Capt 16
Amorgos 162–163, 164–165
Anderson, Capt Morris 128–129, 130–131, 208
Anderson, Gen Kenneth 169
Andrew, Princess, of Greece 192
Ankara 128
Apostolos 40
Araxes 188
Arkhi 131
Arnold, Gen Allan 128
Asbery, Cpl William, MM 129–130, 131
Astypalaia (formerly Stampalia) 124, 129–131, 142
Athens **189**, 191, 192, 199
   Acropolis **4**, **191**
   St Paul's Anglican Church 233
Athlit SBS base **24**, 27–29, 32, 33, **36**, **37**, **39**, **49**, 73, 75, 76, 78, 114, 115–116, 117
atomic bombs 224
Azzib, Raiding Forces HQ 73, 80, 113, 114, **118**, 119, 141, 155, 157, 165
Azzib SRS base 33, 36

Baalbek, temple of Bacchus **34**
Badoglio, Gen Pietro 76, 78
Baffilos, Dmitri **220**
Baker, James 38
Balkan Air Force 207
Balkans theatre 89, 102, 119, 178–181, **180**, 182–183, 185, 187 *see also* Yugoslavia
Balsillie, Lt Keith **140**, 141, 159, 160, 167, 191
Bari 177, 200
Bartie (SBS member) **158**

Bay of Salamis **4**, **187**, 191
Beagley, Sgt 65, 66, 67
Beirut 18
   St Georges Hotel 18, **20**, 80
Belcher, Capt Thomas 103
Bimrose, Capt Charles, MC 100, 170, 188–189, 191, 217, 218, 219
Bishop, Tom 101
Blyth, Capt Hugh 'Bill' 108, 117, 135, 147–148
   Alimnia operation 142, **143**, 145, 149, 157
   post-war 231
   as POW 150–151, 154, 155, 167, 230–231, 233
   in Turkey 141
   wife 229, 230
Bodrum 127, 128
Bogarde, Dirk 17
Brinkworth, Capt Ian 47, 48, 50, 53
British Army *see also* SAS; SBS
   Anders Lassen training centre 226
   Army, Eighth 78, 219
   Coldstream Guards 22
   Durham Light Infantry, 1st Bn 87–88, 93, 94
   Grenadier Guards, 6th Bn 21–22
   King's Own Royal Regiment, 1st 106
   Land Forces Adriatic (LFA) 177, 187, 191, 200, 211
   Long Range Desert Group (LRDG) 88–89, 106, 109, 117, 177, 187, 188, 224
   Officer Cadets Training Unit (OCTU) 36, 38
   Parachute Bn, 11th 87, 113
   Parachute Brigade, 4th Independent 191, 193
   Royal Corps of Signals 95
   Royal East Kent Regiment (The Buffs) 106
   Royal Engineers 178, 180
   Royal Irish Fusiliers, 2nd 106
   Royal Tank Regiment 78
   Royal West Kent Regiment 88
   South East Asia Command 223–224
   Special Raiding Squadron (SRS) 27, 33, 36, 38, 78
   Special Service Brigade, 2nd 211
Brown, L/Cpl Bill 52–53
Brook, Harold 'Ginger' 36, **204**
'Bucket Force' 188
Burger, Col Otto 155, 233
Bury, Lt Bob 170, 195

Caesar 149
Cafferata, Raymond 78
caiques (Greek fishing boats) **43**, **48**, 100, 107, 125–126, 137, 139–140, **173**, **187**
   in German use 129–130, 148, 149, 171
Cairo 80 *see also* Middle East HQ
   Gezira Sporting Club 113
   Groppi's café 71, 73, 157
   Shepheard's Hotel 80, 113

Calchi 142, **143**, 145, 148, 149
Calvert, Brig Michael 224–225
Cameron, Sgt Jock 204, 205
Campbell, Lt-Cdr John 136
Campioni, Adm Inigo 80, 81, 82, 84, 85
Carmichael, L/Cpl James 191
Carpenter, Ronald 143, 145–146, 148–149, 151–152, 153, 155, 229–230, 232–233
Cass, Sgt 51
Castelorizzo 82, **83**, **84**, 84, 85, 123, 127
Castelrosso 78, 82, **83**, 84, 85, **227**
Casulli, Lt Stefan 135, 141, 142, **154**, 159, 160, 167
Cedars, Lebanon **133**, 133, **134**, **135**
Christmas Party, 1943 **118**, 119
Churchill, Randolph 46–47
Churchill, Winston 74, 76, 79, 102, 110, 127–128, 153, 187, 225
Clark, Lt David 131
Clark, Lt-Gen Mark 211, 214, 219
Clarke, Capt Kingsley 'Nobby' **79**, 121, 141, 162, 163, **164**, 164, 165, 201
Close Quarter Battle 35
Clynes, Capt Charles 173, 174
Cochran, Lt John 48, 49, 50, 51
'Cockleshell Heroes' 172–173
Comacchio operations 211–212, **212**, **213**, 213–218, **217**, **218**, 219
Conby, Cpl Martin 'Gyppo' **27**, 56, 121, **158**, **218**
Conlon, Lt 201, 205
Corby, Martin **220**
Corinth 191
Courtney, Roger 15–16
Cree, Jock **28**, **79**, **158**
Cretans 62, 67, 68, **69**, 70 *see also* Janni
Crete 77, 125, 200
Crete operation (1943) **55**, 55–59, **57**, **60**, 60–68, **62**, **63**, **65**, **66**, **67**, **69**, 70–71, 73–74, **74**
   members captured 50–52, 53
   motor launch crew 70
Crouch, Tpr Freddy **79**, **81**, **83**, 162, 163, **212**, 212, 214, 215, 216, 219
Croxton, Lt-Cdr 107
Cunski 202
Cyclades Islands 76–77, 89, 123, 125, 141, 157, 158, 162
Cyprus exercise 39–40

D'Arcy, Mick 56, **158**, **220**
Daily Telegraph 226
Das Signal 123
Davy, Brig George 177, 207, 220
decorations **69**, 73–74, **90**, 101–102, 120, 121, 131, 147, 165, 206, 208, **215**, 218, 225
Dobrski, Count Julian ('Major Dolbey') 80, 81–82
Dodecanese Islands 76–77, 88, 89–90, 125, 127, 149, 157–158, 171 *see also* Castelorizzo; Kos; Leros; Rhodes
   German invasion 97, 99–100, **100**, 102, 123
   plans for invasion 78–80
'Dolbey, Major' (Count Julian Dobrski) 80, 81–82
Donachie, Tpr **220**
Dönitz, Grand Adm Karl 89
Dora 149

Dowland, Cpl Sid 21–22, 23, 39, 46, 49, 51–52, 53
   post-war 228
Duggan, Marine John **17**, 17, **20**, 58
Duggin, Lt Allan 46, 49, 52
Dunkirk evacuation (1940) 21–22

EAM fighters, Greek **192**, **193**, 199
Eden, Anthony 110
Eden, Robert 182–183
EDES (Royal National Republican Greek League) **192**, 199
Egyptian Mail 71
ELAS (Greek People's Liberation Army) 170, 195, 197
Elliott, Denholm 17
Emerton, Jack **196**, **225**
equipment 39–40
   berets **11**
   boots 119
   Davis submarine escape 38
   'folboats' (folding canoes) 15
   insignia **16**, 155
   jacket, hooded **93**, 167
Evans, Pte A George, MM **146**, 146–147, **148**, 152, **228**, 229–230, **230**, **231**, 231, 232–233
   mother **230**, 231
Evans, RQMS **78**

Famagusta 40
Fanetza, Col 82, 84, 85
Far East operations proposed 223–224
Feebery, Sgt Maj Cyril 20, 24, 29, 46, 49, 52
   post-war 227
female partisans **185**
Fenn, Tpr **204**
Ferris, Flt Lt Robert 'Hank', MC 98, 100–101, 102
Field Return (April 1943) **31**
Filibusters, The (Methuen, 1947) 15, 27–28, 124, 162, 230
fishing boats, Greek *see* caiques
Flavell, Cpl **126**
floats, Goatley 213
Florina 193–194
Folboat Section (later Special Boat Section) 15–16
Fox, Lt Kenneth 174–175, 221
'Foxforce' 187
French soldiers 40–41
Fritz 149

Gallagher, Lt Brian 202–204, 208
Gander, L. Marshland 107–108, 109
Gargano Peninsula 177
Geddes, Pte 93–94
German forces 77–78, **97**
   Afrika Korps 77
   Army Group E, High Command 152
   Army Group E, Interrogation and Counter-Intelligence branch 151, 152, 153–154, 233
   Brandenburg Division 90, **104**, **105**, 107–108, 109
      Jäger-Regiment 110
      Küstenjäger-Abteilung, 1st 148
   invasions
      Aegean Islands 90–91, 110, 123–124, 169
      Dodecanese Islands 97, 99–100, **100**, 102, 123

Kos 90–95, 97, 98, 102
  Leros **103**, 103, **104**, **105**, 106–110
  paratroopers **104**, **105**, 107–108, 109
  retreat from Balkans 187
  surrender 220
  Turkoman Division, 162nd 215, **217**
German Luftwaffe 58, 59, 60, 61, 175
  Aegean operations 90, 99, 100, 101, 102
    Leros **103**, 103, **104**, **105**, 106, 107, 108, 109,
      110–111
German Navy 145, 172, 173
Germans, captured (Heinz and Ulrich) **67**, 68, 70, 71,
  73
Gestapo 178
Gill, Pte 51
Glaze, Sgt-Maj Gus 'Nelly' 23
Going to the Wars (Collins, 1955) 53
Goldie, Tpr **204**
Grant, Donald 119–120, 141, 142, 167
Grant-Taylor, Lt Leonard Hector 34–35
Greaves, Cpl Sydney, MM 41, 56, 59, 60, 61–62, 65,
  71, 73, 74, 101
Greece **4**, 77, **97**, **116**, 185, 187, 188–189
  advance through 189, **190**, 191–195, **196**, 197,
    199–200
Greek collaborators 188, 191
Greek EAM fighters **192**, **193**, 199
Greek fishing boats *see* caiques
Greek League, Royalist National Republican (EDES)
  192, 199
Greek People's Liberation Army (ELAS) 170, 195, 197
Greek Sacred Squadron 108, 110, 164, **170**, 172, 173,
  174, 175, **177**, 187
Greeks 170, 175, 185
Green, Pte Fred 215
Gruda railway bridge raid 178–181
Gulf of Gökova 127
Gunn, Ben **227**

Halkiti, Moskamberis 150, 153, 157
Hancock, L/Cpl Rodney 'Hank' **50**, **95**, 99, 106, **126**,
  138, **158**, **165**, **220**
  Comacchio raid 214, **218**
  Lussino mission 202, **203**
Harden, Lt Dick **124**, 131
Harling, Lt-Col von 155, 233
Harrison, 'Tig' **158**
Hawkes, Sgt Ernest 103, 117
He Who Dares 75
'Hedgehog, The' **76**
Heidenstam, Lt Oscar 38
Henderson, Sgt B B 'Patsy' 32, **50**, **56**, 56, 58, **158**, **218**
Henshaw, Capt James 179, 195, 208–209
Heraklion **97**, 200
Herzstein, Robert Edwin 232
Hill, Cpl 'Windows' 192
Hiroshima 224
Hitler, Adolf 77, 89–90, 127
  Commando Order 152, 229
Holmes, L/Cpl Dick 'Jeff', MM **28**, 34, 35, 71, 75, **76**,
  77, **81**, 84, 88, **113**, **115**, 119, 133, 135, **137**, 142,
  147, 157, **159**, 175, 204, 213
  in Adriatic 208, 209

  in Alexandria 121
  awarded Military Medal 73–74, 120
  in Balkans 178, 179, 180–181
  on Crete 56, 57–58, **59**, 62, 63–64, 65, 66, 67, 68,
    69, 70, 120
  in Dodecanese Islands 106, 107, 110–111, 117, 119,
    163
  with Levant Schooner Flotilla 136, **165**, 167
  on Nisiro 162, 163–164
  Ossero bridge raid 207–297
  'piracy' operations 125, 130
  post-war 229
  recruitment and training 21, 22, 23–24, 29, 33, 36,
    38
  returns home from war 221
  in Yugoslavia 201, 202–204
Holt, Capt Desmond 108
Horsfield, Jim **227**
Hospital of Saint John, Venerable Order of 226
Howells, Pte Ellis 183
Hughes, Jack 160
Hughes, Lt Jimmy 44
Hughes, Stan 215, 216
Hughes, Marine Wally 16

Iggledon, Ray **227**
Imbert-Terry, Edward 52–53
Imperial Airways 133
Independent, The 227
Indian Field Company, 9th 87–88
Indian Infantry Division, 4th 200
insignia **16**, 155
International Organization for Migration 228
Ionides, Capt Hugo 80
Ios 157, 162
Italian armistice 78, 79, 80, 82
Italian forces **87**, **89**
Italo–Turkish war (1911–12) 77
Italy 177, 200, **209**, 211–212, 213–221, 223, 224
  after Mussolini overthrown 76, 78
  canoe raid on coast (1941) 16
  invasion of (1943) 76, 78, 79–80

Janni (Cretan guide) 57, 58, 62–63, 64
Jarrell, Porter 'Joe', GM 101–102, 107, **158**, 212–213,
  220
  post-war 228
Jellicoe, Col Lord George 18, 41, 89, 117, 121, 134,
  142, 181, 199, 224
  on Castelorizzo 84–85
  in Greece 188, 189, 191–192, 193
  and Italian invasion 76, 78, 79–80
  on Leros 107, 108–109, 110, 117
  and Operation *Hawthorn* 44, 45, 47, 53
  and 'piracy' operations 124, 127
  post-war 226, 233
  recruitment and training 25, 27, 28, 29, 32, 33, 34,
    36, 75, 113–114, 162
  Rhodes operation 81–82
Jenkins, Sgt William George 'Bill' **15**, **22**
Jerusalem, King David Hotel 29
Johnson, John **227**
Johnstone (signalman) 51

Jones, Pte Ray, MM 41, **50**, 56, 59, 60, 61–62, 73, 74, **90**, 120, 147, **148**
  fate of **151**, 152, 229–230, 232–233
Jones-Parry, Lt 205, 206
Jude the Obscure 94
Junkers Ju52 **104**, 107, 108, 109
Junkers Ju87 Stuka 58, 59, 60, 61, 99, 100, 101, 102, **103**, 103, 106, 110–111
Junkers Ju88 58, 60

Kabrit SAS base 18, 20, 23–24, 25
Kahane, Karl **75**, **78**
Kalymnos 88, 89, 91, 102, 107, 171–172
  Raiding Forces HQ 88
Kastelli airfield, Sicily 55, 56, 58–59, 60–61, 73, 74
Kendrick, Holly 233
Kershaw, Sgt Dave 21
Kesterton, Sgt 80, 81
Keyes, Admiral of the Fleet Lord 15
Killby, Keith 25, 44, 46, 47, 48, 49, 50, 51
  post-war 228
Kingston, Sgt Frank 160, 167
Kitchingman, Marine Tommy 204, 206, **207**, 207
Kleemann, Gen Ulrich 81, 100, 124, 148
Kos **21**, 77, 85, 87–88, **88**, 90, 113
  Antimachia airfield 87, 90, 92, 94
  German invasion of 90–95, 97, 98, 102
Kos Town 87, 92
Kosbab, Jim, MM 21, 22, 23, 39, 44, 46
Kozani 193
Kronsbein, Maj Curt 150
Kühne, Hptm Martin 108
Kythira 187–188

Lake Comacchio 211–212, **212**, **213**, 213–218, **217**, **218**, 219
Lakki (Porto Lago) 102–103, 172, 173
Lamonby, Lt Kenneth 34, **41**, **47**, 55, **59**, 71, 73, 75
  on Crete 56, 57, 58, 64, **65**, 68, 70, 71
Lang, Obgefr Adolf 158
Langton, Tommy 18, 20, 25, 32, 43, 75
Lapraik, Capt Ian, MC 75, 80, **88**, 97–98, **100**, 100, 101, 102, 169, 172, 173, 175, 187
Lassen, Maj Anders 'Andy', VC MC★★ 29, **69**, 71, 73, 74–75, **103**, 117, 121, **135**, **154**, 165, **166**, 187, 200, **211**, 212–213, 226
  army-training centre named 226
  in Balkans 178, 179, 180
  on Crete 56, 57, 58, 59, 60–62, **65**, 68, 70
  death 216, **217**, 217, 219, 226
  in Dodecanese Islands 99, 100, 107, 110, 111
  Dog Tom 212
  gravestone **215**
  in Greece 194–195, 197
  Italian operations 212, 213, 214–215, 216
  Santorini raid 158, 159, 160
  VC awarded **215**, 225
Latakia exercise 39, 40–41, 56
Laverick, Grainger **44**, **158**
Layforce 18, 77
Lecomber, Pte 'Lofty' 208, 209
Lees, Capt Jimmy 116, 141, 170, 171, 172, 185, 200, 202, 205, 206, 207, **227**

Lees, Col Sir John 116
Lees, Lady Madeline 116–117, 207
Leros 77, 85, 89, 102–103, 106–107, 117, 119–120, 124, 148, 172, 173
  Alinda Bay **104**, 107, 108, 109
  German forces invade **103**, 103, **104**, **105**, 106–110
Lewes, Jock 59
Lewis, Cpl 33
Linder, Pte **27**
Lisgaris, Michele 142, 151, 155
Lisso 131
Liverpool, Golden Gloves boxing club 227
Lochner, Oblt 154
Lodwick, Capt John 15, 16, 17, 27–28, 116, 119, 121, 135, 136, 142, **158**, 169–170, 171, 172, 212, 230–231
  on Mykonos 160, 161–162
  and 'piracy' operations 124, 127
  post-war 226–227
Look magazine 119–120
Louis, Joe 177
LS9 (command vessel) 136, 141, 143
LS24 (converted sponge fishing boat) 142–143, 145, 146, 147, 148–149, 150, 232, 233
Lucas, Lt Allan 202, **204**
Lussino 200, 202, 204, 205, 213
  Villa Punta raid **204**, 204–207, **207**, 208, 213
Lynch, Parachutist **158**, 161

Macauly, 'Mac' **137**, **159**, **164**
Macbeth, Stewart 169–170, 171, 173, 174, 200, 216, 223
McClelland (SBS member) **137**
McDougall, Sgt 206
McGonigal, Capt Ambrose, MC★ 182, 183, 199, 202, 204, 205, 206, 207, 208, 209
  post-war 226
McKendrick, L/Cpl Robert 100
McKerracher, Sgt Duncan 51
Maclean, Fitzroy 32, 33–34, 55, 75, 100
McLeod, Lt Aled 195
malaria 44, 46, 48, 49, 51, 52
Malona 148
Malorie (SBS member) **158**
Mariani, Don Francesco 216
Marshall, Des **178**
Mascheroa, Adm 85
Mavrikis, Jason 194–195
May, Albert **227**
Mayall, Bill 171–172, 207, **227**
Mayne, Maj Paddy **12**, 27, 33, 36, 38, 78
Mepacrine 44
Messerschmitt aircraft 175
Middle East HQ 47, 71, 78, 79, 80, 85, 124, 125
Middle East Ski School **133**, 133, **134**, **135**
Middle East training depot 25
Miller, Sgt George, MM 40, 147, 150, 152, **153**, 153, 229–230, 232–233
Milner-Barry, Capt Walter 'Papa' **21**, 29, 55, 73, 76, 79–80, 85, 88, 89, 117, 121, 128, 133, 134–136, 141, 199, 207, 229
  aunt Annie 29

and Castelorizzo 82, 84
  in Greece 188, 189, 191–192, 194
  in Italy 200, 217, 218, 219, 220–221, 223
  on Kos during German invasion 91, 92–93, 94, 95
  post-war 226
  recruitment and training 32–33, **33**, 34, 39, 40, 78, 94, 113, 114, 115
Ministry of Defence 233
Mitford, Capt Bruce 131
Monte St Angelo SBS base 177, 200, **209**
Montevicchio 51
Morris, Pte Dick 40, 41, 136, 199
Morrison, William 100
Mosquito, HMS (coastal forces base) 143
Mueller-Faure, Dr 154–155, 157, 231
Murray, Pte James 49, 51
Mussolini, Benito 76, 77, 219
Myers, Brig Eddie 117, 119
Mykonos 157, 160–162

Nagasaki 224
Napier, Cpl **27**
Naxos 165, 167
Neresine Harbour 202, **203**
New Zealand regiment 36
Next of Kin, The (film) 43
Nicholson, Sgt Les 'Jack', MM 40, **45**, **50**, **53**, 71, 73, 74, 107, 160
  Crete operation 56, 59, 60, 61–62, 65
nicknames 121
Nisiro 163–164
Nixon, L/Cpl 129, 130
Noriega, Frank 46, 52
North African campaign 77–78

Oflag 79 POW camp 230
Olib 200, 201
operations
  Anglo (Rhodes raid) 16–17
  Bronx (training exercise) 39–41, 56
  Hawthorn (Sardinia airfields mission) 44, 45–46, 47, 48–53
    members captured 50–52, 53
  Overlord (invasion of France) 102, 124
  Polar Bear (German invasion of Kos) 90–95, 97, 98
O'Reilly, Sgt Sean 20, **27**, **51**, 99, 121, **158**, 160, 214, 215, 217, **218**, 219
  post-war 227
Osborn, Reg 137, 139–140, 141
  post-war 228
Ossero 202, 203–204, 207–209, 213
Otto 149

Palestine, Ramat David, British Parachute School **18**, 25
Palestine sports programme 36, 38
Parachute School, British **18**, 25
Paros 165
Partridge, Tpr **204**
Patmos 88
Patras 188–189
'patrols' 32
  B Patrol 55, 56, 57–58, 62–64, 67, 68, 70

C Patrol 55, 56, 57, 58–59, 60–62, 67, 68, 70
D Patrol 55, **56**, 56, 62, 64
E Patrol 214
J Patrol 208
K Patrol 208, 209
P Patrol 208
Q Patrol **204**, 205–206
Y Patrol 214–215, 216, 219
Z Patrol 208
Patterson, Maj Ian 113–114, 116, 127, 129, 131, 136, 141, **187**, 188, 189, 191, 192, 199
Pelagos 170–171
Peza fuel dump, Crete 62, 63–64, **69**, 73–74
Philippeville (now Skikda) 43, 44, 47
Piraeus 191
Piscopi 124, 131, 167
Poliza, Sonderführer Helmut 151, 152, 153
Pollock, Cpl **218**
Pomford, Duggie, MM★ 20, **24**, 29, **33**, **50**, **77**, 88, 111, **113**, **133**, **137**, 177, 185
  on Casteorizzo **83**
  in Cyclades Islands 162, **164**, 165
  and 'piracy' operations **79**, **173**
  post-war 227
  recruitment and training **23**, **44**, 177
'Pompforce' 193
Port Deremen 127, **128**, 141–142, 136, 152
Porto Lago (Lakki) 102–103, 172, 173
post-war lives of members 226–229, 231
Prendergast, Lt-Col Guy 88, 91

Rab 200, 219
Raiding Forces HQ 73, 80, 88, 113, 114, **118**, 119, 141, 155, 157, 165
Ramat David, British Parachute School **18**, 25
Ramsayer, Lt-Cdr Leslie 174–175
Randell, Tpr **218**
Reeves, Billy 159, 162
Rhodes 76, 77, 78, 85, 87, 88–89, 124, **137**, 150–151, 157, 169, 230
  operation (1943) 80–82
  plans for invasion 78–79, 80
  raid (1942) 16–17, **20**
Rhodes Town, Demokratias Street 150–151
Rice, Pte Leo 'Digger' 41, **50**, 142, **145**, 147, 152, 229–230, 232–233
Rigopoulous, Rigas 142
Roberts, Cpl Edward 212, 215, 216, 219
Robinson, Sgt 40, 41
Rome **223**
Rommel, Erwin 77
Roosevelt, Franklin 102
Rowe, Lt Ronald **56**, 56, 62, 64, 66, 67
Rowell, Maj-Gen 224
Royal Air Force 127, 140
  No.74 Squadron 98
  personnel 92, 93, 98, 99
  Regiment 87, 94, 193
Royal Marines 114–116, 134
  Boom Patrol Detachment 172–173
  Commandos, No.2 and No.9 214
Royal Navy 127, 207
  Levant Schooner Flotilla (LSF) **80**, 125–127, **126**,

128, **130**, 131, 134, 136–137, **138**, **139**, 139–140, **141**, 141, 142–143, 145–146, 148–149, 150, 152, 157, **166**, 167, **169**, 172, **173**, **174**

Salmon, Sgt 119
Salonika 151–154, 155, 194, 195, 197
Samakh SBS base, Jordan Valley 117, 127, 133, 134
Samos **87**, 88, **89**, 106, 107, 110–111, 124
San Marino Trust 228
Sanders, Alan 162, 163, 164
Santorini (Thira) 157, 158–160
Saoufar 78
Saphos 167
Sapshead, Pte Eddy 56, 57–58, **59**, 64
Sardinia airfields operation 44, 45–46, 47, 48–53
  members captured 50–52, 53
SAS (Special Air Service) 133, 154–155, 224
  D Squadron 21, 25
  L Detachment **11**, 16, 17
  L Squadron **24**
  organizational diagram **13**
  origins 17, 20
  recruitment 21, 22, **25**, 25
  Regiment, 1st 148
  Regiment, 2nd 44
Sassari 51, 52, 53
SBS (Special Boat Section/Squadron)
  absorbed into SAS 17, 20
  disbanded 224
  missing men **228**, 229–231, **230**, **231**, **232**, 232–233
  in 1941 **17**
  origin of Section 15–16
  origin of Squadron 27–28
  qualities needed for 36
  recruitment 25, 29
  strength after formation of Squadron (1943) 29, **31**
Scarpanto 124, 142
Schiller, Lt 163, 164
Schoet, Signaller Viv **59**
Schofield, Flt Sgt Charlie, MM 99
Schofield (signalman) 51
Scott, L/Sgt John 52–53
Scully, Sgt Pat 48, 50, 51, 52, 53, 114, 117
SD (Sicherheitsdienst – SS intelligence service) 152, 153, 155, 233
Seligman, Lt-Cdr Adrian 125, 126, 136–137
sergeant, SBS **194**
Shackelton, Cpl 51
Sharp, Pte **59**
Shirley, Judy **118**, 119
Shohot, Viv 88
Sicily 44–45, 78
Simi 84, **88**, 97, 98–102, 124, 131, 173
  raid (1944) 172, 173–175, **177**
Simi Town 99, **100**, 100, 173
Skikda (formerly Philippeville) 43, 44, 47
Smith, Henry **227**
Smith, Capt Ian, MC★ 182, 200, 208, 209, 212, 219, 220, 221
  post-war 226
Smith, Cpl Ken 114, 115, 116, 171–172, 173, 174, 213, 214, 217–218

Adriatic operations 204, 205, 206, 207
  post-war 228
SOE (Special Operations Executive) 125, 182–183
  Force 133: 145, 148
Solomon, Martin 194
South African Air Force 87
Sparrow, Aylmer 38
Special Air Service *see* SAS
Special Boat Section/Squadron *see* SBS
Special Operations Executive *see* SOE
Special Raiding Squadron (SRS) 27, 33, 36, 38, 78
Sporades Islands 76–77, 123, 125, **161**, 170
squadrons
  L Squadron **30**, 32, 39, 43, 44, 45–46, 47, 48–52, 53, 75, 113, 114, 116, 127, 128, 129–130, 155, **180**, **181**, 199, 219, **225**
    in Greece **187**, 188, **189**, 189, **190**, 191, 192, **193**, 193–194, **196**, 199–200
    in Italy **223**
    members captured 50–52, 53
  M Squadron **30**, 32, 33, 55, 75, 76, 82, 84, 97, 98, 99–101, **100**, 102, 155, **157**, **161**, **166**, 169, 170, 171–172, 175, 187, 211
    in Aegean Islands **227**
    in Greece 195, 197
    Italian operations 212, 213–219
    Simi raid 172, 173–174, 175
  S Squadron **30**, 32, 33, 34, 39–40, 55, 75, 76, 80, 82, 84, 85, 87, 110–111, 133–134, **134**, 135, 136, **138**, 139, **141**, 141, 142, 147, 149, 155, 162, **163**, 163–165, 167, 181, 200
    Adriatic operations 201
    B patrol 55, 56, 57–58, 62–64, 67, 68, 70
    C patrol 55, 56, 57, 58–59, 60–62, 67, 68, 70
    captured on Alimnia recce 149–151, **151**, 152–154, 155, 157, 167
    D patrol 55, **56**, 56, 62, 64
    on Leros 102–103, 106, 107, 108, 109, 110
Stalag 7A POW camp 154, 155, 233
Stampalia (now Astypalaia) 124, 129–131, 142
Stellin, Dion 'Stud' 75, 185, 214, 221
  post-war 226
  son 226
Stephenson, Les 214, 216
Stirling, David **9**, 16, 17, 18, **19**, **25**, 25, 47, 147–148, 223
Straud, Oblt 151, 153–154
submarine escape equipment, Davis 38
Suez Canal 77
Sutherland, Maj David 'Dinky', MC★ 15, **16**, 17, **20**, 27, 29, 32, 33, **34**, 58, 73, 75, 76, 78, 84, 87, 121, 134, 141, 149, 211, 212
  Adriatic operations 201, 202, 209
  assumes control of SBS 199
  Balkans operations 182, 183, 185
  in Beirut 18
  Christmas, 1944 200
  Crete operation 55–57, **60**, 62, 64–65, **65**, 66, 67, 68, 70, 71, 73
  in Cyclades operations 157, 158, 159, 162, 167
  Dodecanese operations 102, 106, 107, 109, 110
  Far East operations proposed 223, 224
  in Italy 220, 221

on Kalymons 88, 89, 90–91
on Leros 103, 106, 107
at Port Dereman 142, **143**
post-war 226, 231, 233
recruitment and training 16, 18, 28, 35
wife **16**
Syrian exercise 39, 40–41

Takiarkis **126**, **130**, 136, **138**, **139**
Tempanyro, Louis 47, 48, 50, 53
Tewfik 127, **128**, **130**, 136, 141, 142, 157, **165**
Thatcher, Margaret **232**, 233
They Who Dare (film) 17
Thomas, Pte Bill 21, 51
Thomas, Leonard 46, 49, 51
Thomason, Lt Donald, MC 204, 205, 206, 208
Thomson, Capt John 49, 51
Tilney, Brig Robert 106, 109, 110
Tod, Brig Ronnie 187, 211, 213, 214, 218
Trafford, Roy 'Sammy' 121, 159, 160
training 18, 25, 32–33, **33**, 34, 35, 38, **39**, 39–41, **43**, **46**, 78, 116, 119
    Levant Schooner Flotilla 126
    Palestine sports programme 36, 38
    programme (1943) **30**
    shooting 34, 35
    ski **133**, 133, **134**, **135**
    submarine 43
Triandaphillou, Demetrios 142
Tripolitis, Davelis 150, 153, 157
Tsouroutis, Nikita 150, 153, 157
Tucker, Tommy **227**
Tuckey, Sub-Lt Allan 142, 143, 148, 149, 150–151, 153–154, 229–230, 232–233
    mother 230, 231
Turbine 172, 173
Turkey 77, 79, 111, **123**, 127–128, **136**, 136, 141–142, **166**
Turks 127, 128, **131**
Turnbull, Brig Douglas 73, 76, 80, 84, 85, 88, 89, **118**, 119, 172, 173, 174, 175, 177
Turnbull, Lt 214

Unie 202, **204**
uniform *see* equipment
United States Army: Fifth Army 219
Ustashi fascists 178, 179, 180

Vathi 143, 171, 172
VE Day celebrations **220**, 220–221
Velesariou, Nikolaos 142, 151
Verney, Capt John 32, 36–37, 43, 44, 45, 46, 52–53
    post-war 226, 227
Viebrock, Sgt Helmut 150–151

Vittorio Emanuele, King 76
Volos 194

Waite, Sgt Ronald 215, **218**
Waldheim, Kurt 231–232, 233
Walshaw, Cpl George 108, 117
Wandrey, Oblt Max 110
War Office 224, **228**, 230, 231
Warlimont, Gen Walter 155
Watler, Pte Ronald 92, 95
Watson, L/Cpl **21**, **44**, 93–94
weapons 146
    anti-tank gun, Oerlikon 20mm 125, 145
    bomb, Lewes 59–60, 61, 63
    bomb, Mills 61
    cannon, Breda 20mm 97, 99
    machine guns, Browning .50 125
    machine guns, Vickers .303 125, 145
    pistol, Colt 45: 35
    pistol, Lancaster 145–146
    pistol, Smith & Wesson .38: 35, 111
Whitehead, L/Cpl Billy 56
Whiteside, Billy **76**
Whittle, Sgt 101
Wilson, Gen Henry 'Jumbo' 73–74, 79
Wilson, Lt 'Tug' 16
Wilson, Sgt 129
Wilson (signaller) 48, 50
Wingfield-Digby, Simon 225
Wolfson, Cdr Vladimir 128
Workman, Chris 'Jumper' 21, 44, 46
World War II ends 224
Wright, Sgt Doug 'Roger', MM **29**, 49, 75, 84, 121, **137**, 177, 188, 207
    Adriatic operations 208, 209
    in Balkans 178, 179, 180, 181
    in Cyclades Islands 162, 164, 165, 167
    in Dodecanese Islands 103, 106, 107, 111, 157–158
    Far East operations proposed 223–224
    in Greece 195, 197
    in Italy 221
    and 'piracy' operations **79**
    post-war 228
    recruitment and training 21, 22, 23, 39

Yedi Atala SBS base 142, 143, 233
Young, Commander **69**, 70
Younghusband, Sir Francis 117
Yugoslav partisans 178, 179, 180, 182
Yugoslavia 178–181, 182–183, 185, **201**, 201–202, 203–208

Zara 201, 204, 208, 209, 219